THE "HOW TO"
GRANTS MANUAL

Part of the American Council on Education Series on Higher Education

Susan Slesinger, Executive Editor

Other titles in the series:

THE "HOW TO" GRANTS MANUAL
Successful Grantseeking Techniques for Obtaining Public and Private Grants

Seventh Edition

David G. Bauer

Published in partnership with the

AMERICAN COUNCIL ON EDUCATION
Leadership and Advocacy

ROWMAN & LITTLEFIELD PUBLISHERS, INC.
Lanham • Boulder • New York • Toronto • Plymouth, UK

Published in partnership with the American Council on Education

Published by Rowman & Littlefield Publishers, Inc.
A wholly owned subsidiary of The Rowman & Littlefield Publishing Group, Inc.
4501 Forbes Boulevard, Suite 200, Lanham, Maryland 20706
http://www.rowmanlittlefield.com

Estover Road, Plymouth PL6 7PY, United Kingdom

British Library Cataloguing in Publication Information Available

Library of Congress Cataloging-in-Publication Data
Bauer, David G.
  The "how to" grants manual : successful grantseeking techniques for obtaining public
and private grants / by David G. Bauer. — 7th ed.
    p. cm. — (ACE American Council on Education series on higher education)
  Includes index.
  ISBN 978-1-4422-0418-8 (cloth : alk. paper) — ISBN 978-1-4422-0420-1 (electronic)
  1. Fund raising. 2. Grants-in-aid. 3. Nonprofit organizations. I. Title.
  HG177.B38 2011
  658.15'224—dc22   2010045581

♾™ The paper used in this publication meets the minimum requirements of American
National Standard for Information Sciences—Permanence of Paper for Printed Library
Materials, ANSI/NISO Z39.48-1992.

Printed in the United States of America

Contents

Part 2: Public/Government Funding Opportunities

Part 3: Private/Foundation Funding Opportunities

Part 4: Private/Corporate Funding Opportunities

Exhibits, Figures, and Tables

Note that all exhibits are found online at
www.rowmanlittlefield.com/ISBN/1442204184

Exhibits

Figures

Tables

Introduction

THE CHANGE AND THE RATE OF CHANGE in the grants marketplace are astounding. Twenty-five years ago when I created the first edition of The *"How To" Grants Manual* I could not even have predicted the changes associated with *publishing* the preceding editions. Moreover, two of my other books, *The Complete Grants Sourcebook for Higher Education* and *The Complete Grants Sourcebook for Nursing and Health*, have been replaced by databases. With this new edition, all exhibits are now offered online at www.rowmanlittlefield.com/ISBN/1442204184 in an interactive format.

The ease and speed in which we can search for grant opportunities has also changed. It has been greatly improved. In addition, access to government grant program information, the Office of Management and Budget (OMB) circulars, *Federal Register* postings, and federal contract opportunities (FedBizOpps) continues to expand. Furthermore, the online submittal of federal proposals (Grants.gov) has replaced the more traditional forms of submittal such as the United States Postal Service, Federal Express, United Parcel Service, and hand delivery.

The area of preproposal contact has also changed. Using the telephone and face-to-face exchanges to make contact with prospective grantors is being replaced by e-mail and other forms of technology. This change provides new challenges and opportunities to grantseekers who are trying to gather necessary insights into grantor agendas.

Fortunately for me, I am constantly apprised of the latest changes in grantseeking through my consulting. While I still perform grants seminars, I am now also spending more and more time conducting one-on-one hourly consultations with staff and faculty members from various institutions. The purpose of these meetings is to help these individuals develop and implement grants strategies aimed at improving their grants success and moving them toward their personal career goals. These consultations have grown into twelve- to twenty-four-month fellowship programs at colleges and universities throughout the United States.

As this diverse group of grants fellows has run into new challenges resulting from the rapidly changing grants marketplace and the stresses of meeting a variety of professional responsibilities, I have been able to adapt my grants system accordingly. For example, my work with the fellows has proven to me and to them that developing and following a structured process is the key to grants success. Hence, this seventh edition of *The "How To" Grants Manual* includes more time management techniques to help grantseekers use their time more productively. In fact the biggest factor that makes this edition different from the others is the added emphasis on techniques to help the grantseeker be more proactive, begin the grantseeking process earlier, and determine the best grants strategy from the onset.

Besides changes related to grantseeking, there have also been dramatic changes in the funding that supports the private and public grants marketplaces. These changes have been so dramatic that they created a scenario I have never encountered before in my forty years of grants experience.

Over the past ten years foundations have lost 50 percent of the value of their grant-supporting stock portfolios. Because of this, foundation grants decreased sharply. Then in late 2009 and early 2010 foundations experienced a boost in their grant-supporting portfolios and private grants support began to increase. However, it still has not reached the 2005 peak level.

While these changes were going on in the private grants marketplace, the economy experienced the recession, bank and corporate bailouts, and unemployment rates unheard of since the Great Depression. These events resulted in increased government granting through President Obama's and Congress's passage of the stimulus program. Subsequently, grants success rates increased as many federal programs added extra deadlines and special awards. This book looks at how these changes impact current grantseeking strategies and what new changes may necessitate future strategy adjustments.

In the last edition I warned the reader about the deceitful grant schemes that had begun to spread over the Internet. In the past year I have been retained by prosecuting attorneys at the Federal Trade Commission to provide expert testimony in their efforts to shut down these fraudulent websites. In providing the documentation for prosecuting these cases I was provided with an identity and a credit card that allowed me to enter the member sections of these websites and access the services they offered. It was an experience that troubled me immensely because these schemes discredit the real grants process that I have spent almost my entire professional career using and defending.

The most disheartening aspect of my Federal Trade Commission experience was the ease in which these criminals preyed on individuals who believe there are federal grants available to

- pay off mortgage and credit card debt, and
- provide free money to expand small businesses.

Unfortunately, the actions of these criminals have an impact on those who seek to access these funds for legitimate purposes. For example, I was instructed by these fraudulent websites to submit a one-size-fits-all proposal to numerous foundations and government programs that have never, and probably will never, fund paying off a mortgage or credit card debt. Besides that, if I had sent the suggested mass-produced proposal to everyone and anyone (rather than a tailored proposal to someone in particular), I would have contributed to a bad situation. Grantors are already more overwhelmed and understaffed than ever before, making it harder for them to provide the attention that each proposal needs.

While there have been a multitude of changes in the grants marketplace and in many aspects of grantseeking, one of the same pitfalls still exists that predetermines grants success rates. While we have had politicians on both sides promise that they will not continue to circumvent the honest, peer-review system by earmarking federal grants for their predetermined constituents, earmarks still account for huge amounts in some programs. For example, the Fund for Improvement of Postsecondary Education (FIPSE) has federal budget cycles where nearly all of their competitive grants have been earmarked. Hopefully these earmarks will be eliminated in the near future. Meanwhile, grantseekers must employ a system that takes into consideration how earmarking and other factors affect their likelihood of success before dedicating all of the effort a finished proposal requires.

Among all of these changes and considerations, the basic tenets of developing a winning proposal remain relatively stable. Developing a quality proposal still entails

- initiating the grantseeking process early to avoid the deadly mistake of submitting hastily prepared proposals at the last minute,
- researching each prospective grantor,
- obtaining proposal review criteria, and
- using all of the procured information to create and tailor a quality, compelling proposal that meets the grantor's agenda.

Therefore, this edition follows the same "how to" format as the other editions. Like the previous editions this book includes worksheets to help seasoned as well as novice grantseekers become grant winners. As noted earlier, these exhibits are available for download at www.rowmanlittlefield.com/ ISBN/1442204184.

As you read this book you will understand why I never tell my seminar participants or fellows good luck. Luck has very little to do with successful grantseeking. The real keys are organization and the implementation of a well-planned grants strategy.

Part 1

GETTING READY TO SEEK GRANT SUPPORT FOR YOUR ORGANIZATION

1

The Keys to Grants Success

Being Proactive and Focusing on the Grantor

Following a proactive grants system and staying focused on one's grant-seeking goals sounds simple. However, time constraints can make the process difficult. Whether grantseeking is your full-time job or a part-time pursuit you probably have a hard time accomplishing everything you need to in the time you have available.

If you are a teacher or a faculty member, you are trying to integrate grantseeking with teaching, advising, doing research, publishing, and attending department and committee meetings. If you are a nonprofit manager, you are trying to integrate grantseeking with board meetings, staff meetings, and other multitasking duties. And if you are a nonprofit staff member or volunteer, finding the time to allocate to grantseeking might seem impossible. Therein lies the dilemma we all must face. What can we accomplish today and what can we put off until tomorrow?

When faced with a task that comes with a future deadline many people choose to put the task off until tomorrow or as long as possible. Unfortunately, grantseeking is one of those tasks usually perceived as deadline driven. Let's face it. The fact that proposals must be submitted by a certain date is the absolute bane of the grantseeker's existence. The meetings we have, the students we need to advise, and the classes we must teach today cannot be put off. But our grantseeking can be put off until some time in the future, closer to the deadline. (Or at least we think it can.)

Lack of time isn't the only thing that keeps prospective grantseekers from accomplishing their goals. Many believe that the proactive steps needed to ensure grants success are difficult. Some even feel that they require them to act outside of their comfort zones. This became apparent to me in my consulting. In my grantseeking fellows program I require the participants to develop a contract that lists the grantseeking steps they will carry out over the next ninety days. Every ninety days they must meet with me and report on their success. What I have discovered is that they frequently do not like to make the various forms of preproposal contact with their prospective grantors that I suggest. They will go to great lengths to avoid making face-to-face, telephone, and even e-mail contact with funders—especially federal program officers. They will wait until right before I am back on campus to complete as many of the tasks as possible on their contracts. Unfortunately, while this procrastination may be normal and even understandable, in the long run it will sabotage their grant success.

This book provides a systematic approach filled with proactive steps to help you cope with the time issues and other hurdles that accompany grantseeking. The system has been implemented at large and small nonprofit organizations throughout the United States including hundreds of schools and universities and is applicable whether one grant proposal is produced per year or twenty. The proposal development sequence you choose to implement from this book is designed to foster grants success immediately and be the basis for your grantseeking well into the future. I am certain of the success of this system and know for a fact that its use yields an overall grants success rate of well over 50 percent and has a proven and documented success rate of more than 80 percent for several of my clients.

There are hundreds of billions of dollars that will be granted this year. In fact, these funds must be awarded or grantors will either lose the money or, in the case of foundations, be penalized by the Internal Revenue Service if 5 percent of their assets are not awarded each year. The question is, are you motivated *enough* to learn and practice the relatively simple, proactive steps outlined in this book to successfully access these funds? My background in psychology reminds me that all behavior is motivated. Even last-minute, reactive grantseeking is evidence of grantee motivation. What you need to do is ask yourself if you are sufficiently inspired to put into practice the proactive steps that will increase your grant success and ensure that the time you invest in grantseeking is well spent. Some of my seminar sponsors have mistakenly praised me for motivating their faculty and staff to get interested in pursuing grants. The truth is that I cannot motivate anyone. Only you can motivate yourself. The question is whether you are ready to make a concerted effort to apply a proactive, timely approach to grantseeking.

Before your dancing digits hit the keyboard or you put pen to paper, spend a little time asking yourself the following questions and reviewing the corresponding principles that are integral to a proactive, successful grants system.

First, how do the grant funds you are seeking fit with your predetermined goals and those of your institution/organization?

Second, what does the prospective grantor want and how does this correlate with what you want?

Third, what problem will these grant funds solve or impact?

Obviously, we have our work cut out for us. So let's start with the first principle.

Principle 1: All proposals you create should take your organization or institution toward its predetermined goals. To refresh yourself with these goals, review your organization's or institution's mission statement and identify its stated purpose and objectives. To be more specific, apply this concept to your particular division, department, program, or center rather than your entire organization or institution. One large foundation I encountered had a stated rule that they would entertain only one proposal per institution or nonprofit organization. In this case the university I was working with interpreted this to mean each college within the institution could send in one proposal. Therefore, they sent in eight proposals to the same foundation. The foundation returned all eight proposals and instructed the university to review its priorities and submit the one proposal that had the potential to move the institution toward its main concern. The foundation added that it was not its job to pick one of the eight because that action could actually move the university away from its mission.

Principle 2: The grantor is concerned about meeting its program's goals and objectives, not yours. Grantors do not care what you want. They are concerned with what they want. They fund projects for their reasons, not yours. Therefore, in order to create a compelling proposal that motivates the grantor to send you money you must follow a basic writing rule. Always write from the reader's point of view.

Principle 3: Grantors want to know that their grant will solve or impact a problem. They want to believe that their funding will hasten an action that was going to happen anyway but probably at a slower pace and over a prolonged period of time. They view their funding as a catalyst in an equation, and they want to be assured that the program or project initiated with their grant funds is the correct course of action to take for themselves (the grantor) as well as for the grantee. In fact, I have even expressed to a grantor that my organization was prepared to do the project even without the grantor's support but that it would take years to be able to put it in place. The grantor wants assurance that it is not just the opportunity to apply for their grant funds that motivates the prospective grantee. The grantor wants to feel confident that the grantee was headed in that direction anyway.

Grantors want to believe that your organization or institution is the right one to fund and that you will work to continue the project or research after their support ends. They want to feel they have made a gift that will keep on giving. By following principles 1, 2, and 3, you set up a logical framework for some type of continuation.

Whether you are starting your career, restarting your career, looking to achieve tenure at a university, moving ahead in your nonprofit field, or having fun assisting your favorite charity, reflect on your goals, time commitments, and motivation. Successful grants procurement will have a dramatic, powerful, positive impact on your career. Few skills that I have developed have propelled my career as a researcher and educator more than grantseeking.

This chapter is all about you. Take a few minutes now to review why you are seeking grant funds and to determine how your actions and their results will influence your career plan and the mission of your organization. By doing this, you will be much more eager about using the proactive, reality-based system for grant success outlined in this book.

Your consideration of a career-enhancing grants strategy does not begin with a specific grantor and a looming deadline. If you are reading this chapter with perspiration dripping from your forehead because of a rapidly approaching deadline, stop! My first suggestion is to forego the application and read on, since pursuing this grant will most likely result in rejection. You simply do not have enough time to take advantage of the proactive grants system suggested in this book. However, if this is impossible (because your supervisor, manager, or administrator is forcing you to apply, or for some other reason), skip the first eight chapters of this book and move on to those dedicated to proposal development. When your proposal is rejected, you can then read the first eight chapters to help you determine how best to approach a resubmittal.

The grants strategies in this book require you to use the same system each time you approach the grants marketplace for a research project or a program. The key to success is recognizing that you do not inherently know how to approach grantors or to write your proposals. The grants marketplace is based upon *change*. The very fact that grantors (be they federal, foundation, or corporate) solicit requests is based on their desire to fund *new* approaches, protocols, and solutions to problems.

This represents a planning dilemma. The strategy or approach that worked in the last proposal is not likely to work in the next one. It is in the past. Even the proactive grantseeking techniques we employed may need to be changed. To be successful we must constantly question the way we like or prefer to approach grantseeking and force ourselves to determine with each and every application or proposal if the field has changed and, therefore, whether our approach must change.

Grantseeking should be thought of as the successful negotiation of a maze. We must be open to looking at various avenues and hope that we do not ultimately choose the wrong one, or a dead end. You may find the book *Who Moved My Cheese?*[1] as helpful as I have in this respect. The book is short and easy to read, and while the lessons are universal, they are particularly insightful with respect to negotiating the grants maze. Just the names of the characters should entice you into reading it. The two main characters are mice named Sniff and Scurry. (How many grantseekers have you seen sniffing for the money and scurrying after it?) The book's other two characters are little people named Hem and Haw. They successfully navigate the maze and find the cheese (grant money) but refuse to believe that their previously successful strategies are not working to find new cheese (more grants). They try nonproductive strategies over and over again hoping for different results. The book's main tenet is that you must be ready to change again and again because the cheese (a metaphor for what you want) is always being moved.

I understand now why I sometimes fail at getting grantseekers to employ my suggested strategies. It is tough to manage one's time effectively and to act proactively when surrounded by constant change. However, this book will show you that by collecting grantor research before scurrying off to write a proposal, you will be able to uncover changes that have occurred and then be able to take these changes into account when developing your ever-evolving grants strategy.

The purpose of this chapter is to provide a compelling basis for moving you, the well-intentioned grantseeker, from submitting a last-minute, self-focused proposal to a proactive, planned approach based on the grantor's needs and wants. So far you have looked at how the grantor's needs and those of your organization complement each other. It is also appropriate to look at how grantseeking fits into your career plan and leads to the accomplishment of your professional and life goals.

Developing Your Career Grants Plan

In a few chapters you will be moving through the maze to grants success. Each successful grants quest leads to more knowledge, but also to more questions and additional grant opportunities. Success gathers momentum. But beware that if money is your only goal, you may be propelled down a pathway that leads to areas where you have little professional interest, or may not want to spend a lifetime pursuing. Being forewarned is being forearmed. Once you succeed, publish, and speak at conferences and so forth, your grants interests can take on a life of their own.

In a survey of my grants seminar participants, less than 2 percent reported that they left graduate school with a five-year career plan, and none had considered how grantseeking could fit into a career plan. Exhibit 1.1 helps you determine your personal vision of where you want to be in five years and what role grantseeking will play in that vision. I have found that this visioning process as outlined in Denis Waitley's classic book *The Psychology of Winning*[2] is one of the keys to success. He states that to *achieve* something you must first *conceive* it and then believe it. Your first step is to conceive your grants plan and then to believe in it. It is important that you alone create a definition of success, for both yourself and your career. If you are an academic, or a non-profit program manager, state your vision of success and define it. How much time will you devote to grants? to research? to teaching? to program management? to administration? Quantify each part of your vision.

Exhibit 1.1 helps you refine your vision by asking what resources you think you will need. For example, will you need special release time or time specifically allocated to your grant as opposed to your regular workload or schedule? If so, how much time will you need to achieve success? Do you require partial release time for your grant-funded project or full-time release time? Remember, you cannot perform your current workload plus your grant workload unless you want to risk working 200 percent of your time and violating the laws that define payment allowed under grants. For example, if you make $80,000 and are released 50 percent of your time to accomplish the tasks outlined in your project, you will need to get $40,000 in salary from your funded grant.

Continue to answer the questions regarding your five-year vision. What personnel will you require? project coordinators? lab assistants? work study students? graduate assistants, and so on? By estimating the cost of the components you need to fulfill your five-year plan you can come up with a total cost and then determine if any of the cost may be covered by your normal budget process. If so, subtract this amount from the total so that you can arrive at an estimate of the amount you must procure through grants.

When developing your vision it is important to include how you will disseminate the results of your work. Question 6 in exhibit 1.1 requires special attention. Will you publish the results of your work? If so, how many articles will you publish and in what journals? Will you create a website to make your findings available to others in your field? Will you present your findings at a meeting or conference? If so, which one? For your vision to provide you with guidance and direction you must outline specific tasks that are indicative of your accomplishment of success. In *The Psychology of Winning* the author insists that you give a number or a quantifier to everything on your five-year plan. You cannot merely say you will publish *several* articles. You must be explicit in terms of the number of articles and the time frame in which they will be published. For example, one article in twenty-four months, three articles in the next thirty-six months, and so on.

EXHIBIT 1.1
Your Personal Grants Plan

1. Vision
   - What is your vision of success in your field?
   - What part of that vision will you have achieved in five years?
   - What projects, programs, and research will you be performing?
   - How do these projects, programs, and research fit into your vision of success?
   - What part of these will be grant supported?

2. Released Time: What percent of your time each year will be devoted to these projects/programs/research as opposed to your current job responsibilities?

   Year 1 _____ Year 2 _____ Year 3 _____ Year 4 _____ Year 5 _____

   Based on the percent of time you will be devoting to projects/programs/research, what is the estimated cost of your grant related salary/wages including fringe benefits each year?

   Year 1 _____ Year 2 _____ Year 3 _____ Year 4 _____ Year 5 _____

3. What personnel will you need to help you perform the tasks you would like to accomplish each year of your vision and what is the estimated cost?

   Project Coordinator(s)
   Number: Year 1 ____ Year 2 ____ Year 3 ____ Year 4 ____ Year 5 ____
   Cost: Year 1 ____ Year 2 ____ Year 3 ____ Year 4 ____ Year 5 ____

   Laboratory Assistant(s)
   Number: Year 1 ____ Year 2 ____ Year 3 ____ Year 4 ____ Year 5 ____
   Cost: Year 1 ____ Year 2 ____ Year 3 ____ Year 4 ____ Year 5 ____

   Graduate Assistant(s)
   Number: Year 1 ____ Year 2 ____ Year 3 ____ Year 4 ____ Year 5 ____
   Cost: Year 1 ____ Year 2 ____ Year 3 ____ Year 4 ____ Year 5 ____

   Work Study Student(s)
   Number: Year 1 ____ Year 2 ____ Year 3 ____ Year 4 ____ Year 5 ____
   Cost: Year 1 ____ Year 2 ____ Year 3 ____ Year 4 ____ Year 5 ____

   Other (list):
   Number: Year 1 ____ Year 2 ____ Year 3 ____ Year 4 ____ Year 5 ____
   Cost: Year 1 ____ Year 2 ____ Year 3 ____ Year 4 ____ Year 5 ____

(*continued*)

EXHIBIT 1.1
(*Continued*)

4. What facilities will be required to house these individuals each year? In-house, off-campus, and so on. What do you estimate the required square footage to be each year?

Facility	Square Footage
Year 1: _____	_____
Year 2:_____	_____
Year 3: _____	_____
Year 4: _____	_____
Year 5: _____	_____

5. What new equipment (computers, software, machines, vehicles, etc.) will you and your staff need each to accomplish the projected tasks and what will the estimated cost be?

New Equipment	Estimated Cost
Year 1: _____	_____
Year 2:_____	_____
Year 3: _____	_____
Year 4: _____	_____
Year 5: _____	_____

6. Will you submit each year

   Articles for publication? If yes, how many and in what journals?

	#	Journal
Year 1:	_____	_____
Year 2:	_____	_____
Year 3:	_____	_____
Year 4:	_____	_____
Year 5:	_____	_____

   Books or chapters for publication? If yes, how many and under what titles?

	#	Title
Year 1:	_____	_____
Year 2:	_____	_____
Year 3:	_____	_____
Year 4:	_____	_____
Year 5:	_____	_____

EXHIBIT 1.1
(*Continued*)

Presentations at conferences/meetings? If yes, how many and at what conferences/meetings?

	#	Conference/Meeting
Year 1:	_____	_____
Year 2:	_____	_____
Year 3:	_____	_____
Year 4:	_____	_____
Year 5:	_____	_____

7. Based on salary/wages, personnel, and equipment, what is the total amount of resources needed each year? Of this total how much each year will be needed from your organization/institution? How much will be needed in grants each year?

	Total	From Organization/ Institution	From Grants
Year 1:	_____	_____	_____
Year 2:	_____	_____	_____
Year 3:	_____	_____	_____
Year 4:	_____	_____	_____
Year 5:	_____	_____	_____

This visioning process is critical in that it will help you develop benchmarks to keep your five-year plan in focus as you start out toward your first-year goals. Your plan will provide you with a guide for success as defined by you, and it should be reviewed, updated, and changed on a yearly basis.

Exhibit 1.2 will help you break your five-year plan into a one-year plan and assist you in determining the immediate resources you will need. First, review your five-year plan and write down what initial steps are critical to begin movement toward your vision. What smaller steps must you take now to begin the process? What components will require grant funding? Second, determine who might be able to help you achieve the initial steps. Consider organizing a small group of individuals who are interested in your project or research area and have had experience working with you. Potential group members could include individuals from your undergraduate, graduate, and postgraduate work. Consider advisors, mentors, and colleagues as potential project consultants, coinvestigators, or consortium partners.

EXHIBIT 1.2
Setting Your Goals and Enlisting Support

---

1. What steps can you take in the next twelve months to move you toward your five-year vision?
   (These steps could include procuring smaller start-up or initiation grants, needs assessment grants, grants to develop preliminary data, or grants for a minimal amount of essential equipment or software.)

2. What resources do you need to help you initiate these first steps?
   (These resources should include a list of potential advisors, mentors, colleagues, and so forth with whom you can brainstorm your topic, enlist support, and/or develop a consortia approach.)

3. Whom will you contact and when?

Who	When
_____	_____
_____	_____
_____	_____
_____	_____

Developing a Proactive System

Once you have your five-year grants plan written, you are ready to begin the process of developing the grant support needed to make your plan a reality. Many well-intentioned grantseekers begin the process by creating a proposal and searching for a grantor, or they learn of grants with a rapidly approaching deadline and try to get a proposal completed quickly. However, this is called reactive grantseeking and results in high rates of rejection (90 to 100 percent).

By contrast, in proactive grantseeking you spend time researching a prospective grantor before writing and submitting a proposal. As a proactive grantseeker you will uncover information that will help you increase your chances of acceptance by

- determining what the grantor is really looking for (the grantor's hidden agenda),
- predicting your likelihood of success before investing additional time, and
- tailoring your proposal to the funding source's needs.

The difference between reactive and proactive grantseekers is *when* and *how* they invest their time and how these variables influence their success rate. Proactive grantseekers put in small amounts of time *throughout* the grantseeking process. The reactive grantseeker invests a lot of time just prior to the deadline. This approach often results in last-minute, general proposals that are designed to fit almost any possible grantor's guidelines, lack specificity, and are not targeted or tailored to the needs of the grantor. In addition, they are usually easily recognizable because of a preponderance of statements beginning with "We want," "We need," and "We propose to do" and contain little reference to why the grantor would want to fund the proposal.

Unfortunately, this self-focus has been aided by the use of computers for researching grantors. In many cases, overzealous and self-focused grantseekers will secure printouts of all the grantors who have funded projects even remotely related to theirs and then send the same proposal to every grantor on the list. What these grantseekers overlook is that this shotgun approach results in high rates of rejection and negative positioning with funding sources.

Whenever your proposals (or those of your nonprofit organization) result in failure, you risk positioning your organization in a negative manner. Of course, grantseeking will always result in a certain percentage of rejection. That is bound to happen. But how much rejection can you, the grantseeker, and your organization afford before the very appearance of your name on a proposal elicits a negative reaction from grantors? What is the success rate you need to achieve to avoid negative positioning? Anything less than a 50 percent success rate results in negative positioning. An 80 or 90 percent failure rate could not possibly create a positive image for your organization with the grantor's staff or reviewers.

Embracing a proactive approach to grantseeking means starting the process early. This enables the grantseeker to employ quality assurance techniques to increase his or her chances of success and avoid negative positioning. A proactive grantseeker has enough time to conduct a quality circle exercise or mock review of his or her proposal before submittal, using the same review system that is to be used by the grantor. This technique helps to ensure that the submitted proposal represents the grantseeker's best effort. By starting early and finishing your proposal three to four weeks before the grantor's deadline, you will be able to have your proposal read and scored by friendly role-players who can pick up any errors before your proposal is submitted for its real review. While chapters 14 and 23 provide details on how to use a grants quality circle to improve a proposal, the simple fact is that you will not have enough time to use this invaluable technique unless you become a proactive grantseeker!

Exhibit 1.3 shows what kinds of reviewer comments are likely to be received when proactive grantseeking is abandoned. Quickly put together, last-minute submissions often contain spelling, grammar, and punctuation errors, especially when they are submitted electronically since grantor websites do not provide tools such as spelling and grammar check. You can be sure the

EXHIBIT 1.3
Sample Reviewer's Comments

APPLICATION NUMBER

Technology Innovation Challenge Grant Program
Individual Technical Review Form—Tier 1

SUMMARY ASSESSMENT

Please summarize your overall thoughts about the application in light of your
previous comments on "significance" and "feasibility," and mention any
important points on which the application is unclear so that these points can be
raised with the applicant.

The conversational style was welcome and easy reading. For once there was an
absence of educational "buzz words." However, watch out for too much informal style
(e.g., the phrase "parents don't have a clue").

Don't forget to identify acronyms: GSAMS was identified only in a letterhead in the
appendix.

It is extremely important to proofread your application. There were no less than
nineteen grammar and punctuation errors. If simple details like these are not corrected
as a matter of professionalism, can one reasonably be expected to properly manage
several million dollars?

OVERALL GRADE: <u>B</u>
A = high, B = medium, C = low

---

staff and the reviewers will remember poor-quality submissions like this, but
for all the wrong reasons!

I quickly learned that the best strategy for winning grants was to tailor each
and every proposal to the perspective of the potential grantor. After a reactive
grantseeking failure, I remembered a theory I learned as a psychology major
and I applied it to grantseeking. Forty years later, I can unequivocally say that
this theory has helped me develop millions of dollars in successful projects
and research for nonprofit organizations. I share this theory with you to help
you approach grantseeking from the grantor's perspective and to provide you
with the basis for developing a tailored proposal to each grantor.

Festinger's Theory of Cognitive Dissonance

Dr. Leon Festinger developed the theory of cognitive dissonance[3] while
performing research on cognitive development and the assimilation of new

information. In summary, Festinger found that preconceived ideas and constructs have a filtering effect on newly presented information. If the new information does not support preexisting concepts, students react negatively to learning and to assimilating the new data. Festinger labeled this resistance to new information as "dissonance." According to his theory, individuals do not view new data with an open mind, and that which does not match their preexisting constructs creates static or dissonance. In essence, we want to maintain homeostasis, and we tend to see and hear that which reinforces our existing beliefs and omit that which does not.

In my first attempt to write a proposal, I remembered Festinger's work and wanted to be sure my proposal would be "seen" by the reviewers. In fact, I concluded that to truly be read and understood, I needed to know more about the way the grantor viewed the world. The first grants seminar I attended dedicated hours on how to write clearly. And while I believe that writing clearly is very important, I was more intrigued by the idea of creating consonance rather than dissonance. At that point I remembered my high school English teacher's mantra—write from the point of view of the reader. That is when I realized how important it was that I understood how my prospective grantor saw the world and the way in which his or her grant funding impacted and changed it. That is also when I realized how important it was for me to do my grantor homework.

Values-Based Grantseeking

By expanding Festinger's theory, I developed the values glasses theory and the concepts of values-based grantseeking. A common mistake of grantseekers is to write their proposals based on their own values. They assume that their prospective grantors have similar values to themselves and that they will read their proposals from their (the grantseekers') point of view. This is a mistake. Using a proposal to try to change the values of a grantor or to show that the funding source's granting pattern is unenlightened is another mistake that usually results in dissonance and rejection. Some grantseekers also make the mistake of using their own vocabulary in proposals, forgetting that grantors will read and react to proposals based upon their (the grantors') vocabulary.

Figure 1.1 illustrates the grantseeker's predicament. As a proactive, values-based grantseeker he or she must strive to get the facts through the lenses (filters) of the grantor over to the brain of the grantor who controls the hand, arm, and money (check) the grantseeker wants.

The ensuing chapters are all based on uncovering the information you need to understand the values of the grantor so that your proposal can

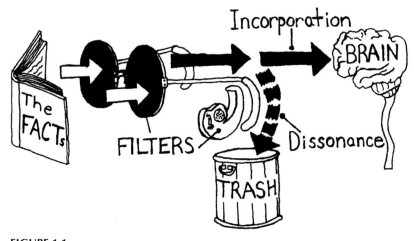

FIGURE 1.1
Values-Based Grantseeking

be written and presented in such a way that it reinforces your prospective grantor's values. Values-based grantseeking entails uncovering information about the grantor that will help you develop an appreciation and understanding of the grantor's values glasses. Once you have this information, you can use it as a guide to your approach, helping you select the right needs data and vocabulary to include in your proposal and ensuring that you present a compelling case for funding.

Successful grantseekers avoid jeopardizing their chances at being funded by remaining sensitive to the values of the grantor. They do not pander to the grantor, or wrap a wolf in sheep's clothing, but their approach to proposal preparation does reflect their knowledge of the grantor and, ultimately, respect for the grantor's values.

If you follow this theory through, it will be obvious to your prospective grantor that you know what the grantor values and that rejecting your proposal would be a repudiation of his or her (the grantor's) own values. In fact, not funding you would be unpleasant, create internal static, and produce dissonance!

This theory does not apply just to private funding sources (foundations and corporations). Proposals to federal and state grantors are read by staff and peer reviewers who are also likely to give the best scores to proposals tailored to their beliefs. In fact, reviewers selected by government bureaucrats are likely to be professionals who have perspectives and values similar to those of the government bureaucrats.

To be truly successful, your proactive grants system should be based on a triple win—meeting the needs of the grantor, your organization, and you (the proposal developer). You need not invest more time in the process than the reactive grantseeker; you just need to invest your time earlier and more wisely. Instead of a seventy-two-hour, last-minute, Herculean proposal effort, invest ten hours per month for seven months. This will give you plenty of time to research the grantor, make preproposal contact, and construct a tailored proposal—all without the stress of a last-minute effort!

Now that you know some of the advantages of proactive grantseeking, you have come to your first major grantseeking crossroads. Yogi Berra once said, "When you come to a fork in the road, take it,"[4] and you will. I have always preferred having a plan and have told all my students that if you do not have a plan, any road will get you there. The only problem is you will not know when you are there. I hope you understand the necessity of having a plan and are ready to move into the next phase of successful grantseeking. The projects, programs, and research you propose are important to you, your career, your organization, and the fields you will impact.

If there is one lesson that grantseeking has taught me in the millions of dollars of grant-funded projects I have completed in my forty-year career, it is that you can make a living doing a lot of things, but what is truly important is making a living while making a difference. If the strategies outlined in the following chapters help you move toward achieving and living your vision, then I have reached my goal in writing this book.

Notes

1. Spencer Johnson, *Who Moved My Cheese?* (New York: G.P. Putnam's Sons, 2002).

2. Denis Waitley, *The Psychology of Winning* (New York: Berkley Books, 1984).

3. Leon Festinger, *A Theory of Cognitive Dissonance* (Stanford, CA: Stanford University Press, 1962).

4. Yogi Berra, *The Yogi Book* (New York: Workman Publishing, 1999), 48.

2

Searching the Literature to Document Your Project's Statement of Need

Creating an Urgent and Compelling Case

WHENEVER I AM AFFORDED the chance to interact with government or private grant personnel, I ask, "What are the most common mistakes that grantseekers make in their proposals?" It turns out that the most common mistake is not following instructions. The second most common mistake is not developing a clear and credible statement of the need to be addressed or the problem they are proposing to solve.

In their zeal and enthusiasm to get money and to get started, proposal writers often present their project methods or protocols before establishing the *need* for any solution. While this rush to action is understandable—grantseekers are, after all, action-oriented "doers"—this jump to the solution assumes that both you and the grantor know the importance of addressing the need/problem. By making this assumption, you forfeit your opportunity to

- demonstrate your command of the latest research in the field,
- reinforce your credibility as an expert in the field, and
- show confidence in a thorough knowledge of the need/problem that will reinforce an exemplary solution.

Take a moment now to focus on the need/problem that your project seeks to impact. Develop a three- or four-sentence description that describes the need/problem that your proposal (and the grantor's money) will address. Review your need/problem statement to be sure that it *does not* contain or present a solution. That proposal component will come later. Start with the problem, not your solution.

To ensure that your need/problem description is clear and concise, present it to a colleague whose level of expertise is similar to that of your prospective grantor (its reviewers, board members, or staff members). If your test elicits a response that indicates that he or she sees the problem, you are on the right track. Too much jargon or the use of vocabulary that requires an advanced understanding is not good. Trying to be too complex to impress your reader will introduce confusion. Remember, even the National Science Foundation cautions you to write for a scientifically literate lay reader.

Many grantseekers make a fatal error when attempting to provide evidence of the need or the problem by documenting the *means* to an end, rather than the end. For example, a prospective grantee who desires a building might try to show evidence of need by providing architecture plans and the documentation of a leaky roof and the presence of asbestos in the existing building. These are not reasons enough for a grantor to fund a building. What the grantseeker should document is the difference between what can be done in the existing facility and what more a new facility would enable the organization to do. In other words, the grantseeker should let the prospective grantor know how a new building would facilitate increased research, programs, and services, or better solve the problems of the organization's clients. The building (or lack of it) is not the problem. It is the means to an end, and the end is what needs to be documented.

Researchers are faced with a similar dilemma. The need is not the research protocol they propose to carry out but rather the benefits of their research and the problems it will be used to solve. Even pure bench research must seek to close a gap of knowledge in the field. The documentation of the need must include a cohesive explanation of how current research has driven the researcher to ask additional questions, seek to test other relationships, and advance the field so that new and even more poignant questions can be asked and answered in the future.

After you are satisfied with the quality and appropriateness of your description of the need/problem, place it under question 1 on the Needs Assessment Worksheet (exhibit 2.1).

Documenting the Need/Problem

The way to demonstrate that the need/problem *really* exists, and is not just your opinion, is to collect and organize a search of the most relevant literature in the field. This literature search is a *must* for every type of grant, be it research, demonstration, or project. How do you know that there is a need? How do you know this is a problem? What has been explored to date?

EXHIBIT 2.1
Needs Assessment Worksheet

1. What is the problem?

2. What data do we have to document the problem? (What exists now?)

3. What information do we need to create a compelling and accurate assessment of the problem?

4. What information do we have to provide a clear picture of the desired state of affairs that should or could exist? (What ought to be in the future?)

5. What will happen in the field if the problem is not addressed in a timely manner? (The urgency and motivation)

Who has done work on solving the problem, and what has their work left unanswered?

At this point you should collect all the information you can on the need/problem. This includes information on past attempts that have failed to solve the problem, and successful attempts that have reduced or affected the problem somewhat, and moved the field ahead to its current position. Use the Internet in your search. Using your favorite search engine, put in the descriptor terms associated with your problem area. To reduce the number of hits, look at what journals or other publications have reported on the problem. Journals are one of the best sources for reviewed and, hence, credible research. Make note of any references to how the research was supported (government funding source, private grantor, etc.). This information may prove valuable to you later when you begin to research the grants marketplace. Collect international, national, regional, and local data. This way you will be prepared to make the case for the problem irrespective of your potential grantor's geographic focus. Enter several of your most significant examples of data that document the problem under question 2 on the Needs Assessment Worksheet (exhibit 2.1).

As you consider the literature and studies that exist you will begin to make observations about the data you wish you had to make a more thorough case. List the information you need to create a more gripping and accurate assessment of the problem under question 3 in exhibit 2.1. If your completion of exhibit 2.1 demonstrates that you are weak in the area of needs documentation, or if it becomes difficult to locate studies, literature, or data to document the problem you seek funds to solve, you may find that you need to attract a small foundation or corporate needs assessment grant to help you. For example, if data or studies exist on a *national* level only, you may decide to prepare a proposal to develop knowledge on a *regional* or *local* problem. Yes, it may be possible to locate a local or regional grantor that will value the fact that its modest investment may help you document the problem where it "lives" and ultimately make it possible for you to attract larger grants from other funding sources for conducting your project. A needs assessment grant also can help to position you as the resident expert in your field and provide you with valuable insights into the problem. It may also provide you with an improved tool to use in the measurement of the need or later in evaluation. See chapter 20 for information on how to locate potential private funding sources for small needs assessment grants.

Creating a Gap between What Exists Now in the Field and What Could or Should Be

Being selected as a grant recipient is based upon several variables, many of which will be addressed in this book. The most important variable is how well you provide a clear and documented statement of the problem. Grantors are motivated by a desire to alter or impact a problem. Their motivation is enhanced when proposal developers reinforce the importance of their (the grantors') commitment for change. Grantseekers can do this by creating a discernable gap between what exists now (based on their search of the literature) and what could or should be.

As you search the literature, be on the lookout for statements or quotes from influential granting officials, corporate executives, foundation directors, or field experts concerning the importance or relevance of solving or reducing the problem. These types of statements or quotes can serve as documentation of the gap between what we know now and what would, could, should, or ought to be. What or who can you quote that documents the value of knowing, proving, or reducing the problem and what ought to be in the future? Record information you gather on the desired state of affairs on the Needs Assessment Worksheet (exhibit 2.1, question 4).

The first edition of this book over twenty years ago warned the proposal writer to avoid suggesting the *value* of the results of his or her proposal. At that time, this was seen as researcher bias and suggested that the researcher had previous knowledge of the results of the research, and thus the outcomes of testing his or her hypothesis. Much has changed since then as corporations and government agencies have moved from viewing research as a way of expanding knowledge to viewing it for application possibilities and what it can be worth. Even basic researchers must document how their research will move the field forward, save time and money, and expand knowledge that another scientist will use to apply to unique solutions. The focus has changed to the potential application of the advances your work will bring to the field.

In addition, all proposal developers, including researchers, need to identify the possible impact of not addressing the problem *immediately*. It is imperative that they provide grantors with a futuristic reference to why the problem needs to be addressed *now*. Since your proposal will be evaluated against hundreds of others, and grantors will often have to address multiple gaps in one field, your needs documentation must be compelling. What will continue to happen that is counterproductive in your field, or cannot happen, if this question is not answered? How is time and money wasted if we do not "know"? Use exhibit 2.1, question 5, to record your thoughts on this question.

Types of Needs Assessment

The two basic grants marketplaces—public (federal, state, and local government agencies) and private (foundations and corporations)—rely on very different forms of needs assessment. However, at this point in the grants process you may not know for certain which marketplace you are pursuing, or which specific grantor or grant program you will be approaching. Therefore, you will need to review this section on needs assessment to select the documentation best suited to win your grant *after* you have completed the process of developing solutions, redefining your project, and conducting a thorough search and analysis of possible grantors. When you are ready, use the Statistically Based Needs Documentation Table (table 2.1) and the Needs Assessment Table (table 2.2) to help you decide which approach to adopt.

Since you do not know at this point which type of grantor you will be pursuing, you might be wise to search for and record needs documentation data that you might normally overlook because it is not scientifically valid. (Remember, many grantseekers who assume they will be approaching only federal grant sources discover that they could benefit from a small needs assessment grant from a local foundation or corporate grantor to strengthen their larger federal proposal.)

Most researchers and innovative program and project developers seeking government (federal and state) grants and sizable grants from larger

TABLE 2.1
Statistically Based Needs Documentation Table

Method	Positives	Negatives
Statistical Analysis—Most funders like to see a few well-chosen statistics. With this approach you use existing data to develop a statistical picture of the needs population: • Census data/records • Govt. studies/report • Other reports and research articles	• Abundance of studies and data • Little cost to access data • Allows for flexibility in drawing and developing conclusions • Analysis of data is catalytic in producing more projects and proposals as staff "sees" the need	• Can be very time consuming • Bias of staff shows up in studies quoted • Belief on funder's part that anything can be proven with statistics • If original data have questionable validity, your extrapolation will be inaccurate
Survey—Very commonly used approach to gathering data on the needs population. This approach is useful even when the survey is carried out with volunteers and has limited statistical validity. Accurate surveys may entail control groups, random samples, computers, and statistical analysis. However, acknowledging that the results of your survey cannot be extrapolated beyond the sample group will prove more than adequate in most situations.	• High credibility with funders • Excellent flexibility in design of survey to get at problem areas and document exactly what you want to document • Demonstrates local need • Provides proof of your concern for the problem well in advance of proposal preparation • Small sample sizes and identified needs population provide for an inexpensive means of assessment	• Takes time to conduct survey properly • Small sample sizes and nonrandom samples make it impossible to extrapolate to the entire needs population
Studies—Citing of relevant research in the field/area of need. Common approach to document the gap between what is and what ought to be for research &model projects. The search should focus on literature that resulted from a controlled study or use of a scientific approach.	• Citing studies demonstrates the proposal developer's thoroughness and expertise in the area and command of the subject data • Studies provide an unbiased approach to documentation of need	• Unless properly organized, the literature search may seem disjointed and overwhelming to the reader • Time consuming

TABLE 2.2
Needs Assessment Table

Method	Positives	Negatives
Key Informant—Solicit information from individuals whose testimony or description of what exists for the client population or state of affairs is credible because of their experience and/or expertise. This includes elected officials, agency heads, police chiefs, delinquency case workers, parole officers, and so on. Funders may value their opinions and insights.	• Easy to design • Costs very little • You control input by what you ask and whom • Excellent way to position your organization with important people (shows you're working on common problems/ concerns)	• Most funding sources recognize that you have selected and included comments from those individuals sympathetic to your cause, and that you may be leaving out parts of the population who feel differently
Community Forum— Host or sponsor public meetings. You publicize the opportunity to present views of the populace and invite key individuals to speak.	• Easy to arrange • Costs very little • Increases your visibility in the community • Promotes active involvement of the populace • Funder may like the grassroots image it creates	• Site of forum has profound effect on amount and type of representation • You can lose control of the group and have a small vocal minority slant that turns the meeting into a forum for complaints
Case Studies—An excellent way to assist the funder in appreciating what representative members of the client population are up against. Select individuals from the needs population or client group, and provide an analytical, realistic description of their problem/situation, need for services, and so on.	• Easy to arrange • Costs very little • Increases sensitivity to the client's "real world" • Very moving and motivating	• Your selection of a "typical" client may be biased and represent a minority of cases • You must describe one "real" person, not a composite of several; the anonymity of the person must be ensured

foundations will search for and record information derived from the three sources outlined in the Statistically Based Needs Documentation Table (table 2.1)—statistical analysis, survey, and studies. These types of grantors have educated and professional staffs, use a peer-review process that is based on their knowledge of the major contributors in the field and their work, and prefer needs statements based on facts and studies. Use the information outlined in table 2.1 to categorize and evaluate the data you have collected. Are there problems with the data or the approach? Are there gaps or conflicting results?

Researchers should be wary of becoming so impassioned in the documentation of their project that they run the risk of being perceived as arrogant or disrespectful of their fellow scientists. Imagine you are writing a proposal for a research project, and you have decided to document the need by citing relevant research in the field. Besides making sure that your references document both the urgency of the problem and your command of the current knowledge in the field, be certain not to include statements about the citations that minimize the work of other researchers, or make them appear ignorant because they did not understand the importance of reducing or eliminating the problem the way that you do. Remember that the researchers quoted in your citations, or one of their graduate students, doctoral students, or friends, may be on your prospective grantor's review committee. Keep sight of the fact that the last thing you want to do is cause dissonance in the reviewers.

Be aware also that you could cause dissonance by citing references, researchers, or data that the reviewers do not favor. While the reviewers' reactions to specific information are not totally in your control, the more you know about the values and background of the reviewers and decision makers, the better able you will be to avoid this problem.

Most foundations and corporations do not have professional staff. Nor do they use outside reviewers or formal scoring systems to evaluate proposals. They are generally interested in seeing a few references concerning the current research in the field, but they are more concerned with the local or regional impact of the proposed work. In fact, the use of a statistically driven needs assessment may prove counterproductive in helping these types of grantors *visualize* the need. Corporate and foundation grantors usually respond well to case studies or examples of the human side of the need. Review the Needs Assessment Table (table 2.2) for some ideas on how you might collect some less statistically based but motivating data. While the strategies outlined in table 2.2 do not hold up well under scientific review, they do help at getting the grantor to *see* the problem.

After reviewing exhibit 2.1 and tables 2.1 and 2.2 you may be thinking of what additional needs assessment tools might be required to make a compelling case to the grantor, or how you can combine the different techniques to make the greatest impact. I have seen a federal review group react very positively to the placement of a case study in a very statistically and scientifically based proposal. The fact that the project initiators took the time to interview clients put a very real human side to their proposal. Whatever the case may be, by having a variety of needs assessment techniques at your disposal, you will enhance your ability to tailor your proposal to your specific grantor.

After you, the grantseeker, document a need, ask yourself the following question: Would you dedicate your own money to closing this gap between what we know now and what we could know or do? Many grantseekers say no to this question, but they are happy to take someone else's money. Compelling and motivating proposals come from grantseekers who truly believe that their project is critical to closing the gap and would use their own money if they had it.

Many proposals contain very innovative and creative solutions that could result in a great impact in its field. But because the proposal developer has failed to document the gap and problem accurately and definitively, the grantor is left doubting whether the grantee will be able to prove that a change has occurred. The current grants marketplace emphasizes accountability. Government and private grantors want you to demonstrate that the gap/problem will be reduced. Only by a thorough search of what has been done and how it has been measured and documented can you prove to the grantor that you know the problem thoroughly and will be accountable for measuring the impact they (the grantor) can take credit for.

3

Using Time Management to Integrate a Proactive Grants System into Your Career

FROM THE PREVIOUS CHAPTERS you have already figured out that a reactive, last-minute, hastily prepared proposal is a formula for rejection and a waste of valuable time. The remaining chapters of this book focus on the techniques and proactive steps to grants success. I know that they have provided my grants career with over a 50 percent success rate. In my recent consulting as a grants coach I have witnessed over 80 percent success rates. One of my fellows turned a failure rate of 0 for 8 proposals to 7 out of 8 funded for a total of $900,000 over an eighteen-month period. He credits his success to the proactive steps outlined in the sixth edition of this book. I credit him for adapting his grantseeking into an efficient time management system. He did this adapting and integrating while maintaining the demanding roles of faculty member, researcher, parent, spouse, and dedicated church member.

What I have learned from my grants coaching is that managing one's time is extremely difficult and that changing the way it is allocated is even harder. Faculty member, nonprofit manager, or staff person, your everyday duties and personal obligations force you to distribute your time to those tasks that are the "do it now" type like reports, budgets, meetings, and the student that requires immediate attention. Since your potential grant might have a deadline that is six or eight months away it is no wonder that you push the proactive steps to grants success off until next week or even next month. Most of you barely have time to read this book, let alone implement the suggested steps.

I sometimes feel bad that as a grants coach the proactive steps I promote can be viewed in the same vein as your six-month dental checkup and cleaning. The appointment every six months is a good oral hygiene practice but you simply have more pressing needs. This is why you get a phone call or e-mail to remind you of your dental appointment. The benefits of routine oral checkups and cleanings are in the future just as the benefits of implementing a proactive grants system are.

In most cases, proposal developers are expected or encouraged to perform grantseeking activities in addition to their normal job responsibilities and in their *spare* time. In the college and university setting, grantseeking is done after preparing course work, teaching, advising, and participating in committee assignments. Seldom are faculty members or staff given release time to write their proposals. The goal, they are told, is to work extra hard to prepare a proposal and get it funded. Then they can get release time from their normal duties to carry it out. While carrying it out, the successful grantseeker is expected to find the time to create yet another proposal. There is precious little time left for anything else—like having a life!

Rarely are there personnel at nonprofit organizations, including colleges and universities, whose main job responsibility is to write grants for other staff members or faculty. While there are some job descriptions that include proposal preparation as a job responsibility, these are usually jobs in state or regional government agencies, where federal grant moneys are passed through to local grantseekers. And the fact of the matter is that even individuals hired solely as grant writers often do not have enough time to fulfill their duties. In addition, the hired grant writer rarely has the expertise needed to create a funded proposal. A hired grant writer can help in the process but in the long run, only the content expert can create a winning proposal.

Many grantseekers are overwhelmed by the *total* amount of work involved in proposal preparation. Because of this, they procrastinate and avoid approaching proposal development until it is too late to do an adequate job. Yet they still do it, because they are driven, creative, and value the contributions they may have the possibility of making in their fields.

Over the past forty years I have researched and experimented with many time management efficiency systems. My interest was to see which techniques could be successfully applied to this proactive grantseeker's dilemma. My background in psychology, and particularly in the field of personal motivation, has provided me with a unique framework to consider why people engage in the proposal creation process and why proactive grantseeking is embraced by some grantseekers and not by others.

Nonprofit managers and university administrators frequently remark that my seminars and materials have motivated their staff or faculty to get involved in grantseeking. I remind them that I cannot motivate anyone and that all human behavior is motivated by the individual. What has always been difficult for me is to observe the wasted time grantseekers spend on a reactive grants process that ultimately ends in rejection. But I am reminded that what I am dealing with is a reward process that is similar to delayed gratification. Complete the proactive steps now and in six months you will be ready and able to prepare the grant-winning proposal and a year from now you will be spending the grantor's money to make your grants plan a reality. Now that is deferred gratification!

The following time management strategies are working very well for my grants fellows. The purpose of this new edition of this book is to provide you with the latest and most useful strategies. One mistake I have made in previous editions is a failure to include those older strategies that are working. In this edition I am including tried and proven methods while suggesting ways to use technology to improve them. With this concept in mind, I consider the older time management techniques as well as the latest, more technology-driven ones. I suggest you review all of them and then put into practice a combination of those that you think will work best for you on your road to grants success.

Alan Lakein, an early leader in time management, suggests in his book *How to Get Control of Your Time and Life*[1] that when you face a large, complex task that cannot be accomplished in a short time span, you divide it into smaller, less overwhelming parts. In his book, a mouse is faced with its dream—a huge piece of cheese. However, the mouse must move this large, heavy chunk of cheese. Instead of putting off the task because it feels overwhelmed, the mouse decides to turn the solid block of cheese into Swiss cheese by eating small pieces at a time. Basically, the mouse divides the chore into manageable parts so the final task of carrying the cheese away is less onerous (see figure 3.1).

Lakein's example of a mouse confronted by the job of carrying away a huge piece of cheese is analogous to a grantseeker presented with the prospect of creating a grant proposal. While preparing and getting your proposal funded may seem like an overwhelming, crushing task, you can eat holes through the process and break it into smaller, controllable parts by strategically employing a number of logical steps (the scope) in a particular order (the sequence). The secret is not to dwell on the whole proposal preparation process. By accomplishing the smaller steps that lead up to the desired end, you can maintain a sense of control or as I often refer to it, a sense of order in the universe.

I have applied Lakein's concept to grantseeking and developed what I call a Swiss cheese book (referred to professionally as the proposal development workbook). The Swiss cheese book consists of a set of tabs placed in a three-ring binder dedicated to a problem that you, the proposal developer, have selected to seek grants to impact. I have divided the task of developing a proposal into steps, with each corresponding to one tab in the Swiss cheese book. The worksheets, letters, e-mails, forms, and tables in each chapter have

FIGURE 3.1
The Swiss Cheese Concept

been designed to be completed and placed behind the corresponding tabbed sections. Please note that all of these materials can also be found in an interactive version on the publisher's website by going to www.rowmanlittlefield .com, entering *The "How To" Grants Manual* in the advanced search field and clicking on "exhibits." It is easy to construct a proposal development workbook. First make the tabbed sections by purchasing an inexpensive set of tabbed index dividers that comes with precut, blank tab inserts and type the appropriate title on each tab. Or you may print out the Swiss cheese tab titles listed in exhibit 3.1 and insert each of them into the precut tabs. Then print the exhibits from this book, complete them, and file the three-hole punched copies behind the appropriate tabbed sections in your three-ring binder.

As a case in point, if you came across a research study particularly relevant to your problem, you could make a copy of the article and place it under the tab for "Introduction and Documenting Need." Or you could place a copy of just the article's summary or abstract under the tab, but include with it a complete article citation and a reference to where you have the whole article filed. The Swiss cheese book system will also work for filing and retaining possible solutions, advisory committee notes, grantor research, preproposal contact results, and so forth.

EXHIBIT 3.1
Proposal Development Workbook (Swiss Cheese Book) Tab Titles

Introduction and Documenting Need	Submission and Follow-Up Public/ Gov't Proposals	Researching Private/ Corporate Grantors
Developing Solutions and Redefining Ideas	Researching Private/ Foundation Grantors	Contacting Private/ Corporate Grantors
Credibility and Partners	Contacting Private/ Foundation Grantors	Creating Private/ Corporate Proposals
Researching Public/ Gov't Grantors	Creating Private/ Foundation Proposals	Submission and Follow-Up Private/ Corporate Proposals
Contacting Public/ Gov't Grantors	Submission and Follow-Up Private/ Foundation Proposals	
Creating Public/ Gov't Proposals		

Review the following list of suggested Swiss cheese tabs.

- Tab 1—Introduction and Documenting Need

  Chapter 1: The Keys to Grant Success: Being Proactive and Focusing on the Grantor

  Chapter 2: Searching the Literature to Document Your Project's Statement of Need: Creating an Urgent and Compelling Case

- Tab 2—Developing Solutions and Redefining Ideas

  Chapter 4: The Grant-Winning Approach: Expanding Your Possible Solutions

  Chapter 5: Developing Key Search Terms to Identify the Best Grantor(s): Redefining Your Project and Improving Your Research/Grants Profile to Get the Right Hits

- Tab 3—Credibility and Partners

  Chapter 6: Why Grant Funds to You and Your Organization: Capitalizing on Your Capabilities

  Chapter 7: Creating Grant-Winning Teams and Consortia: Involving volunteers through Advisory Committees and Advisory Groups

- Tab 4—Researching Public (Government) Grantors

  Chapter 10: Understanding the Government Grants Marketplace

  Chapter 11: Researching the Federal Government Marketplace

- Tab 5—Contacting Public (Government) Grantors

  Chapter 12: Contacting Government Grantors, Past Grantees, and Past Reviewers

- Tab 6—Creating Public (Government) Proposals

  Chapter 13: Planning the Successful Federal Proposal
  Chapter 14: Improving Your Federal Proposal: The Grants Quality Circle

- Tab 7—Submission and Follow-Up, Public (Government) Proposals

  Chapter 15: Submission: What to Do and What Not to Do
  Chapter 16: Federal Grant Requirements
  Chapter 17: Dealing with the Decision of Public Funding Sources
  Chapter 18: Follow-Up with Government Funding Sources

- Tab 8—Researching Private (Foundation) Grantors

  Chapter 19: Understanding the Private Foundation Marketplace
  Chapter 20: Researching Potential Private Foundation Grantors: How to Find the Foundation That Is Best Suited to Fund Your Project

- Tab 9—Contacting Private (Foundation) Grantors

  Chapter 21: Contacting a Private Foundation before Submission

- Tab 10—Creating Private (Foundation) Proposals

  Chapter 22: Applying for Private Foundation Funds: Letter of Inquiry and Letter Proposal

- Tab 11—Submission and Follow-Up, Private (Foundation) Proposals

  Chapter 23: Proposal Submission, the Decision, and Follow-Up: Private Foundation Funding Sources

- Tab 12—Researching Private (Corporate) Grantors

  Chapter 24: Understanding the Corporate Marketplace
  Chapter 25: Researching Potential Corporate Grantors: How to Find the Corporate Funding Source That Is Best Suited to Fund Your Project

- Tab 13—Contacting Private (Corporate) Grantors

  Chapter 26: Contacting a Corporate Grantor before Submission

- Tab 14—Creating Private (Corporate) Proposals

  Chapter 27: Applying for Corporate Funds

- Tab 15—Submission and Follow-Up, Private (Corporate) Proposals

  Chapter 28: Proposal Submission, the Decision, and Follow-Up: Corporate Grantors

You will find that the Swiss cheese concept and the creation of proposal development workbooks will provide you with an organized approach to proposal preparation and a more effective use of your time. In addition, this approach will help you improve your organization's image with funding sources by enabling you to present your project as well planned and thought out. Grantors are favorably impressed during preproposal contact with an organized grantseeker who can reference and substantiate the important points he or she may explore in an interview. They want to fund a project director or principal investigator who will be as organized in carrying out the proposal as he or she is in introducing and discussing it with them.

The same techniques employed in a hardcopy version of the Swiss cheese book could also be employed electronically. You could create a computer file for each of your proposal development tabs, scan pertinent information like relevant literature into your laptop, and place the information under the appropriate automated file. But please note that while some may prefer to do this, a computer CD may be difficult to use with a potential funding source during a visit. Therefore, a hardcopy may still be useful.

David Allen in his book *Getting Things Done: The Art of Stress-Free Productivity*[2] provides several useful strategies that my grants fellows have applied to proactive grantseeking. One basic tenet of his is that to-do lists do not work effectively when you try to apply them to proactive grantseeking. I agree with Allen in his observation that a project list is of minimal use because you cannot do a project. You can only do the action steps that the project requires.[3] The proactive grantseeking process does not translate well to a to-do list since you cannot do a grant proposal. You can only do the proactive steps required in creating a winning proposal.

Allen's book and his organizational system may work for you in rearranging all of your work and, indeed, your life. However, keep in mind that his focus is not on the nonprofit or a university workplace. It is on the corporate marketplace. I personally gravitated to the nonprofit world to avoid focusing totally on corporate productivity. While I enjoy an intellectual atmosphere too much to be as organized as David Allen, I still found several of his concepts useful at keeping track of the quest for proactive grants success.

One of Allen's techniques that can be adapted and easily applied to grantseeking is the development of a tickler file. David Allen suggests you label twelve manila folders with the months of the year and thirty-one daily files labeled 1 through 31 to represent the days of the month.[4] While Allen uses these files differently than you will, the purpose is the same. The purpose of the files is to keep you on task when projects take multiple steps and the integration of time to collect data, recontact collaborators, and so on. Basically, the tickler file system will help you keep the necessary proactive grants step in front of you at all times.

For example, you select the file folder for the current month and place the appropriate day file folder behind it. On March 1 you remove any tasks left undone in February's folder and reinsert them in March's thirty-one daily folders. The interactive exhibits that go with this book (which can be found at www.rowmanlittlefield.com/ISBN/1442204184) will help you determine the tasks to put in the files and collect the data needed for your winning grants approach.

If you were going to contact a colleague to discuss his or her role as an advisor to your proposal effort or possible interest as a collaborator, you put that action step in a folder. But wait, maybe you want to e-mail him or her a one-page concept paper first. Okay, then you must place that action step earlier in March. Pick a date (a folder) and place a note in it to write the concept paper and send it to your colleague in preparation to you contacting him or her. Then contact your colleague on the date selected for follow-up. The rest of this book comprises the actions you should take each month until the *deadline*. Once you determine the program and the deadline you back up from that date to the present and write your daily prescription for success—the proactive steps in the monthly folders that will ultimately be placed in the daily folders.

If you cannot complete all of the proactive steps before the deadline, recalibrate and look at the next deadline date. Many federal programs rely on two or more deadlines in their yearly grants cycle. Above all, be realistic. Can you get the necessary steps done in view of your time constraints, academic calendar, holidays, vacations, and those other things you *must* do?

Many of the critical proactive steps can be accomplished while at a professional meeting or conference if you practice advanced planning. Preproposal contact with a grantor at a conference is often achievable if it is set up months in advance. In other word, put a note in your March tickler file to contact the granting official to arrange a meeting at the September conference you both will be attending. What day will you phone, e-mail, and follow up with the granting official?

One of my grants fellows successfully integrated the proposal development workbook concept with David Allen's tickler file system. The necessary data is stored in the three-ring Swiss cheese binder but the tickler files keep him on track each month. Other fellows have successfully used other systems for making sure that the proactive grants steps are accomplished when they need to be. One uses Visio Microsoft 2007, while another uses Microsoft Office. Several have set up tickler files to automatically e-mail them on preselected dates to remind them to make appointments, write one-page concept papers, and so forth.

The necessity to incorporate whatever means you choose to keep you on track will be more evident as the rest of the steps in the proactive, winning grants system unfold. The need for a system to organize these tasks will become more obvious.

Why is it so difficult to allocate the time necessary to complete the grants steps? For one thing there are many unknowns. For example, setting up that discussion with your potential advisory committee member may take several e-mails or phone calls and therefore much more time than you had anticipated.

I challenge my fellows in the following way. I ask them if their grant acquisition and all it entails is worth one hour per week (fifty-two hours per year) to their field, their students, and their career. Of course they answer yes. Then I ask them to find the hour. It could even be two 30-minute periods per week. Some say they will use a lunch hour. Others choose to go to work one hour earlier one day per week. Some will carve the hour out of their at-home office time. The important thing is to force yourself to set it aside. Do whatever it takes—phone off, door locked, whatever. You are worth it and the results will astound you.

A lot can be accomplished in an hour. You can use the time to update your literature search or to develop a concept paper to discuss with a potential advisory committee member or collaborator. You can also use it to do one of the other proactive steps we have not yet discussed. Since we have just begun describing the proactive steps necessary in a successful grants system you will soon have many more steps to consider adding to your files and accomplishing in the hour you have set aside weekly.

The marketplace for time management aids is overwhelming. The key is to evaluate your individual situation and determine what will work best for you. You can employ a high-tech tool or something as simple and basic as a written calendar system like the one produced by the Planner Pad Company (www .plannerpad.com, (800) 315-7526). Irrespective of what you choose, your application of a time management technique to proactive grantseeking will pay off with huge career rewards.

At this point, I have encouraged you to develop a proactive grants system and to consider adapting a time management strategy to integrate the necessary steps into your monthly and, ultimately, daily to-do lists. You are now beginning to recognize the need for and the benefits of a twelve- to eighteen-month approach to each grantor and its deadline. Once you embrace this proactive grants system you will select multiple grantors (both public and private), each one requiring its own tailored plan. This may seem complex. However, remember that the grants process in itself is simple and it works.

FIGURE 3.2
Action Steps' Chart: Sample Five-Year Plan

You just repeat the process for each grantor and, since you may have more than one area of interest, for each of your distinct projects.

To avoid being overwhelmed and losing sight of your five-year goal, I suggest you consider using a simple computer program/software tool to help you envision the *whole* five-year process. You may already have a program that you use for outlining projects. Or you may have access to one that your organization has purchased the rights to use. For the purpose of organizing this book and for demonstrating how to keep your proactive grants system integrated into your five-year vision, I have chosen to use the *SmartDraw* software program (www.smartdraw.com, (800) 768-3729).

You can use a Gantt chart or a PERT (program evaluation review technique) chart software program. For simplicity's sake, and to keep your vision alive, *SmartDraw*'s basic PERT chart software works just fine. The key to this visualization is that there is a scope and sequence to the steps you take for each grant opportunity you pursue. Some steps or activities can be done simultaneously. Others can only be accomplished after a previous task is successfully completed.

Figure 3.2 provides a visual representation of what I refer to as an action steps' chart throughout the remainder of this book. This particular chart depicts a sample five-year plan. The start date is March 2011 and proposal #1 has a deadline of December 2011. The rest of the proactive grants system steps that must be placed on the 2011 chart follow in each of the remaining chapters. At this point, you need to place "Update Needs Assessment/Search of the Relevant Literature" in the field on your action steps' chart for this chapter. This planning/management concept will culminate in chapter 29, "Putting It All Together to Work for You." The question marks in the boxes represent the other steps that must be integrated into the plan to put a grant in submission in 2011.

Notes

1. Alan Lakein, *How to Get Control of Your Time and Life* (New York: American Library, 1974).
2. David Allen, *Getting Things Done: The Art of Stress-Free Productivity* (New York: Penguin Group, 2001).
3. Allen, *Getting Things Done*, 38.
4. Allen, *Getting Things Done*, 174.

4

The Grant-Winning Approach

Expanding Your Possible Solutions

FROM THE PRECEDING CHAPTERS you can already deduce that the grant-winning solution is not based on which approach *you* favor. It is based on the one that the grantor or the reviewer thinks is the best. Since *best* is a values-based term, the strategy suggested in this chapter is to review the problem and to develop at least two or three approaches that could be used to solve it without introducing your own biases or values. Since you have not identified all of your prospective grantors at this point and researched what they want, keep an open mind and generate a variety of solutions that could appeal to that unknown, but perfect grantor.

The purpose here is to create several possible alternative solutions or protocols that work to solve the identified problem. These alternatives will be used to uncover potential grantors and in discussions with grantors during preproposal contact. By developing several approaches you demonstrate that you are flexible and that you are willing to eventually settle on a solution that fits both you and the grantor. However, it is important to be clear that your final proposal will embrace only one approach. You will not be sending the prospective grantor three ways to solve the problem and asking it to pick one. Your final proposal will be very focused. But you are not there yet.

Using a scientific method would require that you review the literature first, develop solutions, and then evaluate them to identify the best choices. The truth is that most grantseekers display their own biases by deciding on an approach, intervention, or solution first and then identifying data that reinforce it. Essentially, their values glasses use selective discrimination to view only the data that validate their selected approach.

I urge you not to succumb to this very natural tendency because it may keep you from uncovering unique and sometimes novel grant-winning solutions. Try as best you can to be impartial and to explore at least several of the possible solutions. In my seminars I like to remind myself, as well as my participants, of Joyce Cary's (1888–1957) quote, "It is the tragedy of the world that no one knows what he doesn't know—and the less a man knows, the more sure he is that he knows everything."[1]

In addition to appearing open-minded, this approach will generate many possible solutions that can be used with grantors in preproposal discussions to elicit their feedback and to uncover the criteria they may be using to select their grant recipients. The grantseeker who approaches a potential grantor with only one solution to the problem not only demonstrates a myopic viewpoint, but also has little to fall back on if the grantor is not interested in that particular approach or indicates that that approach has already been tried with poor results. Your project/research is important enough that in these cases you will be sure to have several "backup" solutions, protocols, or approaches to present.

Also, it is crucial to recognize that granting agencies, their staffs, and their reviewers all have their own values glasses that they use to view and evaluate ideas and approaches. By having several solutions ready, you will have a much better chance of hitting the grantor's hot spot. To develop and present the approach that you believe will be the grant winner, you must uncover the variables that the grantor will consider in making its selections. Will it see the *best* approach as the one that

- is the most cost efficient?
- is the most reliable and valid?
- will have the greatest impact in the field?
- is likely to be applied in the field?

The strategies for gathering grantor research that are presented in chapters 11, 12, 20, 21, 25, and 26 will help you determine the variables considered by your prospective grantor. But at this point you need to come up with a variety of solutions and to develop a system you will eventually employ to evaluate them.

Brainstorming More Fundable Ideas

One of the most productive techniques for developing a wide variety of alternative solutions to problems is to organize a brainstorming session. Ask a small group of colleagues who have some related knowledge or interest in your problem area to join you in exploring unique and creative approaches to solving or reducing the problem. Whether this exercise is accomplished in a small face-to-face group setting, through a conference call, or over the Internet, inviting others to share in idea generation taps the collective genius of the group and builds support for your proposal. In fact, the brainstorming process can even promote the feeling that your project includes the input of others. This way colleagues and volunteers will be more willing and eager to work at night and on weekends in an effort to promote a proactive approach that exceeds the deadline. This initial group may even form the nucleus of a project team, advisory group, or consortia (more on this in chapter 7).

Care should be taken to explain the purpose of the brainstorming session to the group. At this point, you will just be exploring possible alternative solutions to the problem. However, many researchers are reluctant to share their ideas and creative solutions because they fear that they will be stolen by colleagues. In the majority of cases this fear is unwarranted. Most colleagues can be trusted and discussing proposal ideas and solutions with them will help eliminate the development of narrow, self-focused grant ideas. In addition, more and more grantors are interested in sponsoring consortium grants, and brainstorming ideas can provide an ideal way to foster the development of a consortium. Since you may be employing this technique as a vehicle to create partners and consortia, it is critical that you share ideas in a noncompetitive forum. However, if any concerns should arise related to the ownership of the ideas as intellectual property or as part of a noncompetitive agreement, they should be addressed immediately. Universities can provide intellectual property agreements, noncompetitive agreements, and patent/copyright forms and are usually willing to share these forms with nonprofit organizations.

Brainstorming is a simple technique for quickly generating a long list of creative ideas. To obtain maximum benefit from the process, provide your group participants with Rules to Successful Brainstorming (exhibit 4.1). While most individuals will say they know how to brainstorm, many frequently stop the creative brainstorming process too soon and start evaluating approaches before they should. Reviewing the rules in exhibit 4.1 will help avoid this.

Cost-Benefit Analysis

An important aspect of any fundable idea is its economic feasibility. Funding sources want to know that you have chosen methods that will produce the best results for the least amount of money. The following Cost-Benefit Analysis Worksheets (exhibits 4.2 and 4.3) will help you demonstrate fiscal

EXHIBIT 4.1
Rules to Successful Brainstorming

1. Break your participants into groups of five to eight.
2. Ask for a volunteer to act as a neutral group leader to facilitate the process (encouraging and prodding other members, checking the time, etc.). Appoint one if necessary.
3. Ask for a volunteer to act as a recorder. Appoint one if necessary.
4. Set a time limit. Ten minutes will be plenty.
5. State one question or research problem (e.g., reducing the number of high school dropouts, nutritional needs of pregnant adolescents, increasing awareness of wildlife preservation, the role of genes in obesity).
6. Ask the group members to generate and present as many possible solutions to the problem as they can within the time limit.
7. Encourage the group members to piggyback on each other's ideas (suggesting a new idea that adds to the one already given).
8. Record all answers, combining those that are similar. Actual electronic recording of the session is optimal if everyone agrees to it.
9. Avoid any evaluation or discussion of the ideas until the process is over. This rule is critical for productive brainstorming. The recorder can ask to have an idea repeated but should allow no comments, negative or positive, from others (e.g., "We can't do that!" "That's stupid!" or "I love your thinking!").

accountability. If your problem area involves solutions that will be part of a demonstration project or program, use exhibit 4.2 to help grantors compare and evaluate the approaches you present to them. If your problem is clearly related to a solution that would commonly be called a research protocol, then exhibit 4.3 will be more useful.

Take a few minutes to complete the exhibit you find most appropriate for your situation. Select two or three solutions that present different approaches. Some variables to consider are differing cost estimates and expected benefits, and the inclusion of consortia or large-scale solutions.

Instructions for Completing Exhibit 4.2

Column 1. Place brief descriptions of two or three approaches you are considering in column 1. For example, a project to feed senior citizens could range from a meals-on-wheels program, to group meals, to a food cooperative of the elderly. The approaches you present should meet the goals of the project from your brainstormed list of ideas.

Column 2. Record the estimated total cost of each idea and methodology in column 2. This figure can be taken from your Preproposal Summary and Approval Form (see exhibit 9.1 in chapter 9) and is intended to be an estimate

EXHIBIT 4.2
Cost-Benefit Analysis Worksheet for Projects/Programs

Summary of Idea and Methodology	Total Cost for Each Idea and Methodology	Total Number of Persons Served for Each Idea and Methodology	Total Cost per Person Served for Each Idea and Methodology	Positive Points of Each Idea and Methodology	Negative Points of Each Idea and Methodology

EXHIBIT 4.3
Cost-Benefit Analysis Worksheet for Research Protocols/Approaches

Summary of Research Protocol/ Approach	Total Cost for Each Research Protocol/Approach	Broad Impacts in Field for Each Research Protocol/ Approach	Variables That Present a Challenge for Each Research Protocol/Approach

of the cost of the approach, not a final budget. One way to ensure variety in the approaches and in the amount of funds required is to select the approach you favor and determine how you would have to alter it if you could have only one-half of the amount requested.

Column 3. Use column 3 to estimate the total number of people who will be affected by each approach. Remember to roll out the benefits over several years and, if applicable, over the life of the equipment to be used.

Column 4. Enter the estimated cost per person or client served for each approach. This is essential since funding sources are apprehensive about sponsoring projects that possess an unrealistic cost per individual served. Projects with a high cost per person are considered a waste of money by many funders because grantseekers may have great difficulty securing continued or follow-up funding for such projects.

Column 5. Summarize the positive points of each idea and methodology in this column. By having this information on hand, some funders may actually consider supporting a more costly approach because they can see how the outlined advantages outweigh the expense.

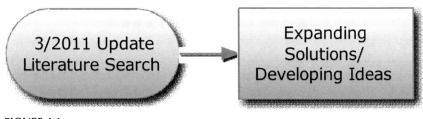

FIGURE 4.1
Action Steps' Chart: Expanding Solutions

Column 6. In this column, outline the disadvantages or drawbacks to each approach. This demonstrates your honesty, which will increase both your credibility with funders and their confidence in you. Funders know that each approach has pitfalls or variables that must be controlled, so be honest and point them out. While this may appear to be highlighting your Achilles' heel, you garner the grantor's confidence when you show that you will not forget the problems and will deal with them in your proposal.

Instructions for Completing Exhibit 4.3

Column 1. Place a brief synopsis of the protocol/approach you are suggesting to prove or disprove your research question.

Column 2. Estimate the total cost for each protocol/approach.

Column 3. For each protocol/approach listed, briefly state the broader impacts or significance to the field.

Column 4. In this column, list the limitations or extraneous variables that make each protocol/approach difficult. Be sure to include any variables that may restrict its usefulness or its possibility for extrapolation.

Use these worksheets each time you refine your project ideas or research protocols and bring completed Cost-Benefit Analysis Worksheets to preliminary meetings with funding officials. They will be impressed that you considered their financial interest while designing your project/research.

Executives of profit-making companies are very sensitive about maintaining cost efficiency in all of the investments they make. They carry over their corporate values glasses to their work with nonprofits. By taking costs into account when refining your project ideas or research protocols, you will win more grants. By brainstorming more approaches to solving problems you will not only appear to be open to considering more solutions, you will also initiate a process that can lead to uncovering more potential grantors.

Figure 4.1 illustrates the next step to place on your action steps' chart.

Note

1. www.brainyquote.com.

5

Developing Key Search Terms
to Identify the Best Grantor(s)

Redefining Your Project and Improving Your Research/Grants Profile to Get the Right Hits

---

THE SECRET TO TAPPING INTO the $500 billion in federal, foundation, and corporate grant funds is to find the right grantor for your research/project. And the first step to finding the right grantor is to determine the best key words or terms to use in your funding source database searches. Grants databases allow you to enter *key search terms* into their systems, which they then match to similar words in their database, and then to funding sources with interest in that area. The key search words contained in the databases are either selected by the grantors represented in the database or by the best efforts of data input personnel. A match between a key word and a grantor is frequently referred to as a "hit."

Online databases are improving every day. They are faster and contain more helpful information than ever to assist you in matching your proposal to the most appropriate grantor(s). But your success still relies on your development and use of the *right* key words for your search. Grantors and database managers look at the world through their own values glasses and unique lenses. The key words they select to describe the grantor's interests may be quite different than the key search terms you would use to define your research/project. That is why it is so important when developing key search terms to think about your project from a grantor's perspective and how others might describe it and its benefits. Unfortunately, the more zealous you are as a grantseeker, the harder it sometimes is to look at your project and its benefits with flexibility and an open mind. For example, when I was working with an organization assisting the blind, the grantseekers initially did not want to use the term *blind* as a search term. They felt it was an old and somewhat discriminatory term. I suggested using *visually impaired, visually challenged,* or *visually handicapped.* But they did not like any of these either. They preferred *people without sight.* However, when they used the phrase *people without sight* (with quotation marks around it) as their key search term, they did not get any hits. When they used *blind* and *visually impaired* they uncovered many granting opportunities. They decided that the use of these words was not so bad after all as long as it helped them find the money and the right grantor for their project. The moral of the story is to be wary of how your own values glasses and specialized jargon may keep you from recognizing and using the most productive key search words or terms.

Before you begin the process of determining your key words, review the literature in the field. What are the terms used in the literature, and what is their frequency of use? What are the terms commonly used in related news releases and presentations? Are there related terms that are consistently used throughout these sources? Are the terms changing and evolving? What terms from your literature search resulted in hits?

Many of the grants databases let you review the terms they use to categorize grants interests. Many of the grants databases discussed in this book use a thesaurus of key terms to help you develop a more productive list of search words. The secret is to use several terms and see which combination meets with what appears to be the most interested grantors. Also, take into consideration that most of the electronic databases allow you to place quotation marks around phrases to perform a more precise search. For example, if you search using *higher education* without quotation marks, the database's use of Boolean logic would search under *higher* and under *education* and then both *higher education* and *education higher.* But by placing quotation marks around the two-word phrase, it would search only for grantors whose interest area was *higher education.*

Redefining Your Research/Project to Develop More Key Search Terms

The more key words you can use to define your research/project and its benefits, the more grantors you may be able to uncover who could see how your research/project relates to their needs. By redefining your project you can develop more search terms and thus increase the likelihood of relating your project to new and different grantors. However, project redefinition calls for more flexibility than just identifying different terms. Redefinition requires that you look carefully at your project/research and ask how you could change it slightly to make it and its contributions valuable to other constituency groups, causes, or interest areas, thereby expanding the universe of your potential grantors.

For example, a project aimed at developing the writing skills of sixth-grade students was cleverly redefined to look at how the Internet could be used to increase reading and writing skills. In fact, the grantseeker (teacher) used the Internet to connect sixth graders to elderly individuals at a local senior center and residential facility who became their adopted grandparents and communicated with them via e-mail. Through e-mail the students strengthened their reading and writing skills and actually got writing tips from their adopted grandmothers and grandfathers. The high school computer club also got involved by training the students and the elderly on how to use e-mail to connect with one another, thereby making a community service project out of it. This example of redefinition moved the project from benefiting the sixth grade to a much larger world and allowed the grantseeker to expand her search words to include several relevant fields such as seniors and elderly. It also eventually led her to the key word that worked. Ultimately, the grantor selected was interested in techniques to slow the progression of Alzheimer's disease, and learning new skills to be able to use the Internet happened to be just one of these techniques!

Research grant ideas can also be redefined by extrapolating to other areas and fields. The focus of the research could be slightly changed, or others involved in similar projects with a slightly different approach could be invited to participate in a consortium grant. As with the generation of project grant ideas, you are limited only by your own level of creativeness. For example, if you use "*basic science*" in your field as your key search term, the National Science Foundation (NSF) will appear as a potential grantor. If in your quest to understand the basic science you could also impact a major health problem, you could use the potential extrapolation of your research to attract funding from the National Institutes of Health (NIH) as well. Both grantors could potentially fund you to set up your research to complete your protocol—but for two entirely different reasons. NIH might fund you because your research may create a new drug or procedure related to a specific disease. NSF might fund you because your research may demonstrate why and how molecules bond together to form a new and unique substance.

While the goal of this process is to uncover the less than obvious grantors, the process of redefinition is not intended to take you off track from your grants plan or to turn you into a grants mercenary who will do anything for money regardless of where it takes you or your organization. If you do not like the direction redefinition takes you, do not go there. But if redefinition allows you to locate even partial funding for a related project that keeps you, your career, and your grants plan operational, you may want to pursue it rather than be a purist with no funding.

To uncover your most operant terms complete the Redefinition/Key Search Terms Worksheet (exhibit 5.1). This worksheet should be used to help develop key search terms for identifying potential government funding sources, as well as foundation grantors. However, I suggest you use a different worksheet (exhibit 5.2) to help you develop corporate key search terms.

Searching for corporate grantors requires a special focus because of the unique way they (corporate grantors) view the grants process and its benefits. When searching for corporate grantors, you must take into consideration that corporations usually prefer to support where they "live" and like to fund projects that can be related to their profits, products, and workers. Use the Corporate Redefinition Worksheet (exhibit 5.2) to develop search terms associated with the following:

- hiring, retaining, educating, or training today's workforce as well as the future's,
- employee benefits and resulting corporate benefits, and
- positioning of the corporation as a concerned partner in the field and in your geographic area.

In addition, consider whether there is or could be a direct benefit between your project and increasing corporate profits through

- possible patents or new product development,
- product enhancement, redesign, or reengineering, and
- product position/sales.

Developing Your Research/Grants Profile

Many of the databases you encounter will encourage you to provide them with a profile consisting of your search terms so that a constant search for new potential grantors can be carried out automatically and sent to you by e-mail. This search component is available on several free, as well as subscription only, electronic funding databases. These databases will be discussed in greater detail in chapters 11, 20, and 25.

The success of all of these systems relies on your development of key words. The time to develop and redefine your project for the key words is when the need and the innovative solutions are fresh in your mind. After you have read this chapter and completed the accompanying exhibits you will increase your

EXHIBIT 5.1
Redefinition/Key Search Terms Worksheet

1. *Values*: What words would a grantor use to describe the value of their program to the field?

2. *Subject Area Terms*: Subject areas such as employment, environment, mental health, and child development are used as key search terms in many of the electronic grantor databases. List the subject areas that your project can be related to and/or impacts.

3. *Other Potentially Relevant Fields*: How could you change the focus of your project so that it could be potentially related to more subject areas/fields, and what would these areas/fields be?

4. *Constituency Groups*: Many government and private funding sources focus their grant priorities by the constituency groups they want to impact, such as children, at risk youth, elderly, economically disadvantaged, and so on. What constituency group(s) would a funding source have to care about to support your project?

5. *Project Location*: What is the geographic location for your project, and how could you redefine it to better appeal to a grantor's geographic perspective?

City/Community	County/Borough/Parish	State
Regional	National	International

6. *Type of Grant*: What type of grant support are you looking for, and how could you redefine your project to attract grantors interested in different types of support?

Model/Demonstration Project	Research Project	Needs Assessment Grant
Planning Grant	Training Grant	Discretionary
Unsolicited Proposal	Contract	Other

7. *Consortia Partners*: What potential partners/collaborators could you involve to assist in redefining your project and enhancing your funding perspective? What are the advantages of including them?

EXHIBIT 5.2
Corporate Redefinition Worksheet

1. How does your intended project/research relate to the concerns of corporate (for-profit) grantors? What are your shared values?

2. Does or can your project/research provide benefits to corporations in the areas of:
   - employee development/skill enhancement? If so, how?

   - employee benefits (including health, quality of life, low costs, or risks)? If so, how?

   - public relations (promotion of a concerned and responsible image in the community)? If so, how?

3. Can you redefine your project so that it increases corporate profits by:
   - promoting a lead to new product development (possible patents, etc.)? If so, explain.

   - enhancing current products through new applications, redesign, and so forth? If so, explain.

   - increasing sales through product positioning with clients, students, and so forth? If so, explain.

understanding of how you could conduct a database search for grantors that could be as specific as what grantor(s) funded projects related to these key search terms in the following zip codes!

To help you visualize the process thus far, you have done or are doing the following tasks.

1. You have clearly identified a problem—a need—a gap that must be closed.
2. You have identified colleagues that could potentially serve on your advisory group or act as coinvestigators, and you have come up with a plan to contact them.

FIGURE 5.1
Action Steps' Chart: Developing Search Terms

3. You are updating your search of relevant literature in your field as it relates to the identified problem.
4. You are developing ideas, methodologies, solutions, innovative protocols, projects, and research to increase knowledge and practices to impact the problem.
5. You are developing key terms to use in database searches to locate the most appropriate grantors.

A diagram of this effort to date might look like the one shown in figure 5.1. Each chapter will discuss another step in the proactive funding process. How will you work them into your plan and when?

6

Why Grant Funds to You and Your Organization

Capitalizing on Your Capabilities

WHY WOULD A FUNDING SOURCE select your organization and you, as the project director or principal investigator, to grant funds to? If your response is, "Because we thought up a fabulous project," you are not looking at your proposal from the grantor's perspective. Even if your approach to solving the problem is creative and dynamic, the grantor's ultimate decision is based on who it believes can best carry out the project. While grantors expect creativity and superior ideas, they make their final decision based on the grantee's ability to complete the project.

While the criteria used to evaluate federal applications vary from department to department, office to office, and program to program, most government grant applications will include review criteria that specifically address the capabilities of the project's key personnel and the extent to which the grantee's own resources can support the proposed project. For example, the Department of Education commonly refers to these selection criteria as "Quality of the Project Personnel" and "Adequacy of Resources." In terms of quality of the project personnel, the Department of Education wants to know the qualifications, including relevant training and experiences, of the project director/principal investigator and other key personnel. Often, they are also interested in knowing the extent to which the applicant encourages applications for employment from persons who are members of groups that have been traditionally underrepresented based on race, color, national origin, gender, age, or disability.

The National Science Foundation (NSF) evaluates these two variables under its general review criteria entitled "Intellectual Merit of the Proposed

Activity." Proposals to the NSF will be evaluated in part on how well qualified the proposer (individual or team) is to conduct the project, the quality of the proposer's prior work (when applicable), and if there is sufficient access to resources at the grantee's organization to support the project.

Many federal agencies and departments allocate points to each of the review criteria they select. Others rank them on a scale. While the scoring method used to evaluate the quality of key personnel and the adequacy of resources will vary with each program, you will be asked repeatedly to document why your organization's resources and you and your partners' skills and background make you the perfect choice to carry out the proposal. You will also be asked how you plan to address any areas of weakness.

While your proposed project/research is still in the idea stage and not fully fleshed out, it is appropriate to begin to think about the quality of your key staff and your institutional resources. As you think through personnel and resource requirements you can begin to identify those areas where you may come up short compared to your competition. By beginning to think about the following questions you will ultimately be better able to identify possible collaborators, coprincipal investigators, and consortia partners who will improve your funding chances. (Chapter 7 will specifically deal with developing teams and partners.) Although you are not expected to be able to fully address these issues at this stage in the process, taking a few minutes to think about them now will help you in the long run and prepare you for what you will need in the future.

- Do you have job descriptions that reflect the skills needed to carry out your proposed work effectively?
- Are the duties of personnel clearly defined?
- What relevant qualifications do the proposed personnel possess, especially the project director? (Focus on their experience and training in fields related to the objectives of the project, though other information may be considered.)
- Will proposed personnel need to be trained for the project?
- How much time will the proposed personnel actually devote to the project?
- To what extent do you encourage employment applications from and hire members of traditionally underrepresented groups?

When evaluating your adequacy of resources, determine if your facilities and equipment are adequate for your project purposes and what special sources of experience or expertise will be required.

The importance of this documentation is even more evident when you compete for government contracts. In this very competitive process of bidding on the completion of a well-defined deliverable, you must actually include a capability statement that documents your capacity, resources, and related experience in producing the desired end. Even if you are the lowest bidder for the contract, you can be passed over for a higher, but more capable, bidder.

In many instances, making a grantor's first cut means that you are now on a *short* list of potential grantees, which includes hundreds as opposed to thousands of applications. What can you do to enhance your proposal in such a way that it makes the final award list? Be ready with the facts about your capability and capacity to do an excellent job.

Fearful of appearing arrogant or boastful, many well-intended grantseekers are hesitant to enhance their proposals by emphasizing their unique qualifications. This is unfortunate. While you should not create falsehoods or downgrade your competition, you do need to analyze your institution's capabilities and the characteristics that differentiate you from the other applicants. Your prospective grantor needs to know that your proposal has a greater likelihood of success because of you and your collaborators' personal capabilities and your institution's distinct advantages. These advantages are not hypothetical but rather the actual resources involved in the successful completion of the activities and methods that your project or research will utilize.

Every funding source will want to know why you are its best choice for funding, and developing a list of your organization's special qualities or uniquenesses will go a long way toward convincing a grantor that yours is the right organization to fund.

When to Use Similarity as a Uniqueness

In model or demonstration grants, as opposed to research proposals, you may need to consider varying the uniqueness approach slightly. If one of the desired outcomes of the grant is to develop a model that can be applied to other client populations, organizations, institutions, or colleges, then you need to demonstrate your similarity to others in your field that face the same problem. You do not want to highlight the *unique* qualities of your institution because they limit extrapolation to similar groups and would weaken your case for the model's ability to be replicated. Instead, you want to identify the variables you share with others and focus on the uniquenesses that allow you and your organization/institution to develop, test, and produce materials that will be useful to those who will follow the results of your work or copy your model. For example, other groups may not have the ability to produce a training program and transmit it via satellites. However, they can still receive and use the training and then replicate the programs.

Uniqueness Exercise

Most foundations and corporations do not have as well a defined or documented review process as public funding sources. But they still have the same question in mind: "Why should we fund you and your organization to do this project?" Later, in parts 2, 3, and 4 of this book, you will learn where to include these important credibility builders (uniquenesses) in your proposal. But why wait to identify them until you are filling out your application? Consider developing a list you can use with many grant opportunities. Start now and be one step ahead of the game.

Use the following brainstorming exercise to develop a data bank of your organization's unique features. This exercise will add a little excitement and flavor to meetings and can be done with a variety of groups such as staff, volunteers, clients, board members, and grants advisory committee members. Keep the information you develop in your proposal development workbook, where it will be ready for use in proposals, endorsement letters, and preproposal contact. This material can also be placed on your organization's website and made available to others who might be able to use it in their proposal development.

Please note that you may encounter some initial reluctance to this exercise because some individuals think it promotes bragging. However, these same individuals probably believe that humility and occasional begging will move grantors to take pity on your organization and fund your proposals. They are wrong! From the grantor's point of view, the humble, woe-are-we approach does not highlight the reasons a prospective grantee should be funded and may actually do the opposite.

To combat this problem, remind all those participating in the exercise of its positive results. After the exercise, you will have a list of factors that make your organization a strong contender—a list from which you will be able to select those uniquenesses that may appeal to a particular funding source. Also, the exercise will refocus those participating in the activity on the positive attributes of your organization and away from the negative.

1. Distribute the Uniqueness Worksheet (see exhibit 6.1) to the group, remind the group of the rules for brainstorming (outlined in chapter 4), and set a time limit for brainstorming.
2. Record the group's answers to questions 1 and 2.
3. Ask the group to rank the order of the responses to the questions from a potential grantor's perspective with rank number 1 being the most positive uniqueness or qualification.

EXHIBIT 6.1
Uniqueness Worksheet

Federal and state proposal applications will require information on your
organization's ability to perform the tasks you outline in your proposal. Your
unique qualities or attributes are what enable you to perform these tasks. The
sections of government applications that require this information are sometimes
referred to as Adequacy of Institutional Resources and Quality of Project
Personnel.

On government applications these sections may be assigned a point value.
While these components may not be mandatory on foundation and corporate
proposals, the information they contain is equally important in convincing
private funding sources that your organization is the right grantee for them.

What makes your organization uniquely suited to carry out the work outlined in
your proposal, and provide the grantor with the assurance it will receive a job
well done?

1. *Adequacy of Institutional Resources*: Please list the positive qualities and
   uniquenesses that your organization/institution possesses that will ensure a
   grantor that you are the best place to do the job. When applicable, include
   factors such as:

   - relevance of purpose and mission
   - geographic location
   - relationship and availability to subject population
   - presence of animal laboratories
   - data analysis capabilities
   - _____
   - _____
   - _____
   - _____

2. *Quality of Project Personnel*: Please list the unique qualifications of your
   project personnel. Take into consideration factors such as:

   - years of related experience
   - number of publications and presentations
   - awards and special recognition
   - number and dollar amounts of grants and contracts successfully carried out
   - _____
   - _____
   - _____
   - _____

4. Have the group select the top three answers for both questions and combine them to develop a list of your organization's most positive uniquenesses/qualifications with respect to the adequacy of your institutional resources and the quality of your project personnel.

If your institution has a computer or decision lab, have the group meet there so you are in close proximity to the hardware and software necessary to provide instant rank ordering and frequency distributions.

Use the final list to select uniquenesses that will convince funders that their money will go further with you than with any other prospective grantee. For example, a particular funding source may be impressed with your total number of years of staff experience, central location of buildings, special equipment, and broad needs populations and geographic coverage.

Your uniquenesses list will also prove valuable in

- selecting consortia partners or additional team members who can fill personnel voids or improve your capabilities;
- recruiting and training staff, board members, and volunteers;
- developing case statements; and
- using other fund-raising techniques such as direct mail and wills and bequests.

Do not forget to include yourself, the proposal initiator, project director, or principal investigator, as a uniqueness. Your previous work, publications, collaborative efforts, awards, and recognition are important components of your organization's overall uniqueness.

One culminating activity is to have half of your group role-play a grantor and the other half role-play a prospective grantee. Review one of the problems or needs your organization is planning to address and your organization's proposed solution. Then have the individuals playing the grantor ask those playing the prospective grantee why the grantseeker's organization should be the one selected to implement the proposed solution. Have the grantee group start by saying, "Our organization is particularly suited to implement this solution because . . ."

Using Your Organization's Case/Mission Statement to Support Your Proposal

Your case or mission statement is another key ingredient in convincing the grantor that your organization should be selected for funding. When you submit your application for funding, your approach should be based on the following three important factors:

1. There is a compelling need for the project.
2. Your organization is uniquely suited to carry out the project.
3. The project supports your organization's stated purpose or mission and fits with what you are currently doing or planning to do.

The third factor is especially important. Your case/mission statement should demonstrate your organization's predetermined concern for the project area. If yours is a joint or consortia proposal, the mission or case statements of all the participating organizations should provide a documentable concern for the problem you will address. In short, this statement should give the funding source written documentation that the purpose of your organization (its reasons for existing), your project, and the grantor's values and concerns are a perfect match.

Using Your Existing Case/Mission Statement

Most nonprofit organizations have an existing case or mission statement. Educational organizations use it to provide the foundation for accreditation and in faculty and staff recruitment. While an institution's case/mission statement can provide the framework for a college, division, department, institute, or center, even the lowest level of the organization should be able to state its case for existence and inclusion in the future of the organization.

Grantors do not want their grant funding to influence what your organization becomes. Instead, they want you to tell them where your organization wants to go and how your proposal will help move it toward that goal.

If you have a case/mission statement, use it to convince the grantor of your purpose. If you do not have a case/mission statement, or if the one you have is no longer appropriate or too long, consider updating it, editing it to one concise page, or developing a new one tailored to the grants marketplace.

Elements of a Case/Mission Statement

Your case/mission statement should consist of how and why your organization got started, what your organization is doing today, and where your organization is going in the future.

How and Why Your Organization Got Started. Explain the original societal problems or needs that resulted in the formation of your organization. Most funding sources will find societal need today more important than the number of years your organization has been in existence. In fact, some funding sources actually have the greatest doubts about those nonprofit organizations that have been around the longest. These funders believe that such organizations generally are bureaucratic, have a tendency to lose sight of their mission, and have more so-called deadwood on their payrolls than younger nonprofit organizations.

What Your Organization Is Doing Today. Describe your organization's activities. What are its current priorities, programs, resources, and uniquenesses? Who are its clients? How has the passage of time affected its original mission and reason for being?

Where Your Organization Is Going in the Future. Because funding sources look at their support as an investment, they want to be sure they invest in organizations that will be around when their funding runs out. In other words, they want the organizations they invest in to have a five-year, ten-year, or even longer plan for operation. By demonstrating to funding sources that your organization has a long-range plan and the ability to secure future funding, you will show grantors that you are worthy of their funding and that the project they invest in will continue to benefit people for many years to come.

Use the Case/Mission Statement Worksheet (see exhibit 6.2) to determine what should be included in your case statement.

Remember, most potential grantors are more interested in how funding your proposal will move both of your organizations (theirs and yours) toward each of your missions. Funding sources consistently work to separate applicants who sought them out simply as a source of money from applicants who can demonstrate that the direction outlined in their proposal is predetermined and an important component of their organization's overall mission.

In a funded proposal to the BellSouth Foundation for over $250,000, the successful grantee told BellSouth that it was that organization's goal and priority to approach the very same problem that the BellSouth funding was designed to impact. In fact, the successful grantee told BellSouth it could show over five years' worth of meeting minutes and budget expenditures that demonstrated its commitment to dealing with the problem. The grantee also went so far as to suggest that it would be committed to the same course of action even without BellSouth's grant. Yes, the grantee told BellSouth that this course of action was so much a part of its goals, stated priorities, and mission that the organization would move ahead with the project anyway! Naturally the grantee also let BellSouth know the project would take ten years without

EXHIBIT 6.2
Case/Mission Statement Worksheet

This worksheet can be completed based on the broad definition of your organization, college, or university, or on a smaller sub unit such as your center, institute, school, department, or program.

1. *How and Why Your Organization Got Started:* _____
_____
_____

   Year: _____   Primary Movers/Founders: _____
   Original Mission: _____
   _____

2. *Today—Where Your Organization Is Now:* _____
   _____

   Changes from the Original Mission: _____
   _____

   Societal Need—Changes in Clients/Students: _____
   _____

   Current Priorities: _____
   _____

   Clients: _____
   Staff: _____
   Buildings: _____

3. *Future—Where Your Organization Will Be Five Years from Now:* _____
   _____

   Anticipated Changes in Mission: _____
   _____

   Anticipated Changes in Need: _____
   _____

   Resulting Changes in Facilities and Staff: _____
   _____

4. *Existing or New Opportunities That Will Be Present to Move Your Organization Toward Its Plans/Goals:* _____
   _____

BellSouth's money instead of three years with it. The BellSouth money would be the catalyst in the equation for change. It would hasten the result. BellSouth wanted to be a part of the project and funded it.

The importance of relating your proposal to your organization's mission cannot be overemphasized. Before soliciting a potential grantor, be sure to ask yourself whether you are going to the funder just because you heard it had money and you want some or because your proposal can serve the missions you both value.

Review the components of this chapter. You should have identified your strengths such as having the correct resources and personnel to complete the grant successfully. More importantly, your efforts thus far should have elucidated those areas where you may fall short and need to bolster your team.

Many grantseekers wait too long to determine their strengths and weaknesses and then do not have enough time to adjust their proposals accordingly. Do not be one of them.

Remember, knowing your uniquenesses and the elements of your case/mission statement will help you develop a successful proposal. In fact, this is one more proactive step the successful grantseeker will integrate into his or her grants plan. Will you add it to yours?

Figure 6.1 summarizes what your proactive system should look like at this point. When do you plan on brainstorming your capabilities and those of your organization and your consortia partners?

FIGURE 6.1
Action Steps' Chart: Identifying Your Capabilities

7

Creating Grant-Winning
Teams and Consortia

Involving Volunteers through Advisory
Committees and Advisory Groups

MUCH HAS CHANGED in the grants marketplace relative to the acceptance of proposals that call for consortia agreements between nonprofit organizations, for-profit companies, school districts, and institutions of higher education. When the first edition of this manual was written it was rare to find codirectors or coprincipal investigators. It was almost as if federal program officers thought a grant with two directors on a grant would be difficult to monitor and that it would be hard to hold codirectors accountable. Due to the complexities of research and model projects a new paradigm has been raised that values the advantages of sharing expertise, expensive equipment, multiple sites, recruitment of subjects, and the like. There are new funded projects with four and five principal investigators/project directors at sites in different states and even countries.

This change is generally positive and from the grantor's point of view works to ensure excellence, efficacy, and reduced costs. This trend makes your job harder. You must reach across organizations, disciplines, and experts in the field to create the most convincing team to get your grant awarded. But getting funded is just the start. Your consortia or team must work together effectively to implement the project you created. Through all the expectations, deliverables, expenditures, and problems, you are to keep your consortia/team together and still talking to each other over the span of a two- or three-year, or longer, project.

I was recently asked to investigate a failed attempt at a university to set up an interdisciplinary, innovative team that had expended over $1 million and did not produce one funded proposal. In fact, they did not produce any proposals. I met with the group and asked each member about his or her experience working in groups as a team member. (I could not even call this particular group a team. In fact, it was so dysfunctional that it should have been referred to as a committee.) Despite all of the advanced degrees they had, only a few had any instruction on how to be an effective team member, and the instruction was minimal. Follow-up work with major national and international nonprofit groups revealed the same results. Profit-making companies expend millions of dollars on team training while the nonprofit world spends very little. Nevertheless, grant proposal development and the formation of an effective team are critical to your grants success.

As I continued to conduct surveys on team building with my seminar participants, I began to reflect on how much of my success in grantseeking was really related to my ability to get groups to focus on the outcomes of our work and to develop respect for each other's contributions to our goals. Even with a major in psychology, a focus on motivation, advanced degrees in educational administration, and a school superintendent certification, I only had one formal course that even came close to providing team-building training—Psychology 402, Group Dynamics. I remember the class quite clearly. It was taught in a seminar hall with 150 students. There was no lab and we never met in any setting other than a large auditorium.

The success of a proposal and the completion of a project rely on the incorporation of a complex mixture of supporting partners and expertise. How this combined effort is created and maintained is fast becoming one of the most critical elements in attracting grant and contract support from government sources, as well as private foundations and corporations. In most cases the creation of these critically important relationships has been left to chance and luck. However, by employing the science of group dynamics and team interaction, you can move your grant-related groups away from relying on chance and toward increased efficiency and accountability.

The following suggestions for improving your grants success by increasing the effectiveness of your grant-related groups comes from my work and experience with grants professionals who have taken part in my effective grant team-building workshop. Participants of this workshop have been eager to improve how they function in groups and to work on developing more productive approaches to increase their group's effectiveness. I believe their positive responses to increasing personal and group effectiveness is a function of the difficulties they have encountered when attempting to work on proposal development with experts from interdisciplinary fields—something they are asked to do more and more frequently.

In today's grants marketplace, it is rare to find a project director or principal investigator who possesses *all* the expertise needed to complete a grant-funded project in any area, and research projects frequently depend on expertise in several disciplines that may have previously been thought to be unrelated. These interdisciplinary projects may now be completed by cooperating professionals who may think about and approach problems from radically different viewpoints. Even demonstration grants and model projects require community integration and support from partners who just a few years ago would not have been approached but now must provide board resolutions, letters of support and endorsement, matching contributions, or in-kind support.

Consider the following suggestions for evaluating and improving your own personal group skills and the team skills of your grant-related groups such as advisory committees, advocacy groups, proposal development teams, centers of excellence, multidisciplinary groups, consortia partners, and so on.

Recognizing the Roles That Make an Effective Team

There are many theories and much research on effective team formation and development in the corporate world. Applying successful techniques to the nonprofit world and colleges and universities has just begun. However, after helping several universities develop more effective grant-related volunteer groups and development teams, I believe the basic element to group success and team building is the role that individuals take in a group and how well the varying roles interact with one another to maximize strengths.

As you select the members for your grant-related groups or analyze the composition of your existing group or proposal development team, take into consideration the roles that must be assumed to ensure effective group functioning. While there are a variety of techniques and materials that can be used to assist team members in developing awareness of the roles involved in a productive team, one simple and easy-to-use system is the *Team Dimension Profile* by Inscape Publishing (order through David G. Bauer Associates, Inc.). This profile or survey helps individuals understand and value the contribution they make to successful innovation teams or groups by allowing them to determine their personal approach to thinking and behavior (conceptual, spontaneous, normative, or methodical) and their role on the team or group (creator, advancer, facilitator, refiner, or executor) without going into great detail. Basically, the process uses common sense.

Review the four basic approaches to thinking and behavior. Consider which one best describes the approach you use in the team innovation process and the approaches taken by those with whom you work. Keep in mind that many individuals use more than one approach and, in essence, develop their own unique team and task orientation.

- Conceptual Approach: The individual who takes a conceptual approach is the idea developer who likes to brainstorm alternatives, focus on the future, and develop new theories. These are the innovative, big idea generators. You need them on your team to ensure that the approach to the problem is fresh and new. However, having several of these types on your team can be problematic. While they can come up with multiple approaches when presented with a problem, they do not always think things through.

  In the aforementioned dysfunctional group that spent $1 million with nothing to show for it, three out of the seven team members had this orientation. When I asked why they had never written any of their solutions (grant ideas) down, they said, "Why bother? At our next meeting we will brainstorm even better ones."

- Spontaneous Approach: Those who take a spontaneous approach are freethinkers with little respect for traditions or rules. They move from one subject to another, focus on many things at once, and are sometimes impatient. Freethinkers are great at thinking outside of the box. They will come up with wildly creative projects. Three of my seven dysfunctional team members were high in this characteristic. As you might imagine, this turned out to be the formula for a group process disaster. Because the team essentially operated without any rules, members continually skipped meetings, which meant that the majority of each meeting was spent on updating the members who had missed the previous meeting.

- Normative Approach: The individuals who take this approach want to see consequences before acting, prefer the norm or the familiar, and rely on past experiences and expectations. They question all proposed plans and find holes in them before a reviewer or grantor does. Individuals with this perspective are critical thinkers. If a team is unbalanced and has numerous members with this orientation, proposed approaches can be overanalyzed and one may never be selected and put into a grant proposal because, in their view, it is not perfect yet.

- Methodical Approach: Those who take a methodical approach like order in the universe. They are rational, follow scientific methods and step-by-step processes, and prefer to focus on details that make everything fit together. Your team needs to have this perspective represented not only to get the proposal and budget completed, but also to keep everyone on task in carrying out the funded project.

The failed million-dollar team I mentioned actually had one of these types of individuals. This person ended up dropping out of the group. In reality, she was driven off because she slowed up the pace of the conceptual and spontaneous members by writing down their ideas.

These four approaches to innovation focus on how the individual approaches work together in a group and how the various combinations of these approaches affect the completion of the work inherent in successful group/team projects. (Research by Allen N. Fahden and Srinivasa Namakkal.[1]) Fahden and Namakkal's research resulted in their identification of five roles that must be present in a team or group to achieve project success—the creator, the advancer, the facilitator, the refiner, and the executor.

The theory is that in a well-functioning team all of the five roles are present and that the individual team members can hand tasks back and forth, utilizing the strengths that each role provides. Subgroups are developed when the team has more than one member who can function in each role and, therefore, can share tasks.

- Creator: Grant-winning solutions must be innovative and fresh and often require team members to think creatively. The creator does just that. This individual helps generate new and unusual concepts, ideas, and solutions to the problem and then passes them on to the advancer. Creators become bored discussing and explaining their new ideas (which to them are getting old) and can upset the group by coming up with newer and greater ideas before the team has completed working through the previous task. Creators will create grant proposal idea number 2 before number 1 is written. If not thoughtfully enjoined with the challenges and creativity of making idea number 1 work, they have a tendency to lose interest and skip group meetings.
- Advancer: In this role, the individual sees great ideas, solutions, or approaches and develops new ways to promote them. The advancer develops objectives and plans by the most direct and efficient means. On grants teams, advancers talk others through a new idea or concept, get the other team members on board, and keep them excited about the project. In addition, they are usually good at making preproposal contact with potential grantors.
- Facilitator: This is the group manager's role. This person monitors the proposal development process and work task distribution. This is a critical role for efficient proposal preparation and group productivity. When problems occur with the proposed protocol or solution, the facilitator hands tasks back to the responsible parties for their input and clarification.

- Refiner: This is the group's "devil's advocate." Refiners challenge, analyze, and follow a methodical process to detect process flaws or leaps in logic or process that creators sometimes make in brainstorming new approaches. They pass ideas and plans back to the facilitator to take to the creator and advancer.
- Executor: Executors are the workhorses of the group. They may not enjoy the more visible leadership roles. Their fun is in making the process an orderly and efficient one. Not only are they critical for developing the solution and proposal implementation plan, they are also essential in carrying out the proposal after it is funded. They pay attention to details and insist on quality.

On a successful team, the facilitator ensures that tasks are handed off from the creator to the advancer, from the advancer to the refiner, and from the refiner to the executor. You can probably see yourself in one or more of these roles and now understand why some of your group efforts have failed—one or more of the five team roles—creator, advancer, refiner, executor, or facilitator—were missing and no one recognized this or was willing to assume the missing role(s).

Poor team performance will result when there is an excess of team members assuming similar roles or coming from comparable orientations. A solid functioning group or team identifies the approaches and roles of its members, defines tasks, and hands them off from one role to another, allowing group members to focus on their strengths in the process. It also recognizes what roles are missing from the group. With awareness, the group can either add additional team members with the necessary orientation and skills, or the existing members can consciously take on the roles that are lacking and assume the subsequent tasks.

Higher education and nonprofit organizations are plagued by poorly functioning groups. From the dreaded committee assignments to proposal development teams, we have witnessed legendary failures.

The for-profit world has assumed the lead in developing highly successful teams at all levels, from the shop floor to top management. In his book *Teamwork Is an Individual Skill: Getting Your Work Done When Sharing Responsibility,*[2] Christopher Avery suggests that the first step to developing successful teams is to rid ourselves of the misconceptions we have about teamwork. One misconception we need to discard is that team members need to love each other. Believe it or not, we do not necessarily need to like each other's personality to operate successfully. What we need to do is appreciate each group member's specific approach and to understand how it helps to get the job done. The second misconception we must eliminate is that our own personalities and individual orientations are paramount. We should leave our personal needs and ego at the door of each group meeting. In actuality, being a team player does not mean you cannot be yourself or that you cannot expect something back from the group for your time. The key to group success is to be yourself, act normally but responsibly, and recognize and appreciate what each group member naturally brings to the table. This knowledge will help you develop teams comprising individuals with the mix of approaches and orientations necessary to achieve success.

The purpose of this chapter is not to make you a master guru of team building. Rather, it is to convince you of the importance of this concept in relationship to your grants quest. Hopefully you will begin to think about how you can use it and want to learn more about it. If you're interested, you might add to your to-do list a little reading in the area including the works of Patrick Lencioni, author of the *New York Times* best-seller *The Five Dysfunctions of a Team*[3] and *Overcoming the Five Dysfunctions of a Team—A Field Guide.*[4] (While I also enjoyed his book *Death by Meeting*[5] I will confine my comments to his team-related series.) In his books, Lencioni refers to five dysfunctions that affect teams. I have found that briefly discussing these concepts with my grant fellows seems to create the right atmosphere in team meetings and helps to avoid the blockages caused by personality problems.

Legal Guidance for Those Involved in Your Project/Research

While I do not want to raise your concern to a level of paranoia over individuals who may steal your ideas and projects, you must consider how to protect yourself and your collaborators from this type of problem. In order to keep your professional and personal relationships on a positive, trustworthy basis it is necessary to discuss the professional expectations and ethical standards you expect from each other.

Consortia partners, team members, and advisory group members should be briefed concerning your expectations related to the following:

- Conflicts of interest: Does working with your group conflict with their own research or grant-related projects or other groups in which they are an active member?
- Nondisclosure agreements: It is not uncommon to be asked to sign an agreement that assures the group (project initiators) that you will not inform other people or groups about the project, its protocols, or the ideas that are brainstormed and discussed.
- Noncompetition agreements: This upfront agreement acknowledges that all parties will work together and that one partner will not split from the

consortia/group and submit a proposal that competes with the team's proposal.

- Patent/copyright agreement: If the project in question could result in a product, approach, article, book, or theory it is recommended that the grounds for ownership and the sharing of any of these be spelled out in advance.

For readers who are part of a college or university, the vice president for research will usually have an Office of Intellectual Property that will supply forms, agreements, and guidance on how to approach your partners and retain the necessary records. In some instances this office will even apply for copyrights and patents for you. For those of you in a nonprofit organization, I suggest that you recruit an individual from higher education to be on your advisory committee and ask him or her to get any agreements/forms you may need from his or her university. Then you can tailor these agreements/forms to fit your needs.

Involving Volunteers

One of the most important resources in a successful grants effort is the involvement of volunteers. When grantors are faced with volunteers who believe so strongly in a project that they are willing to work to further it with no personal benefit, the credibility of your project and the lead applicant's organization is greatly enhanced.

Involving others to increase your potential to attract funding suggests that *who* you know may be more valuable that *what* you know and how you write your proposal. But a poorly developed idea and proposal will need much more than just friends and the suggestions presented here. If you have a great idea or proposal, however, you owe it to yourself and to your team to take advantage of every possible edge in your quest for funding. This includes involving individuals who can help ensure that your proposal receives the attention it deserves. One foundation director told me that approximately one-third of her foundation's grants went to the board members' favorite organizations and projects, one-third to the board members' friends' favorite projects, and the remaining one-third to the most skilled grantseekers.

While this may sound like politics, hold your condemnation just one more minute. The politics of grantseeking is a fascinating area that spells m-o-n-e-y for those who master the art. Do not be frightened or disgusted by the word *politics*. The politics of grantseeking is a very understandable process that enables individuals to become advocates for what they value and believe in.

Those people who know your organization and identify with your cause or mission deserve to know how they can be of service to you and the cause or field you represent. When asked to become advocates for your project, individuals are free to say no or that they are too busy, but you should not make this decision for them by assuming that they would not want to be involved. There is no harm in asking, and you will be surprised by how many individuals welcome your invitation.

Consider exploring the area of advocacy and how you can help others help you. The worksheets in this chapter will assist you in determining who your advocates are and how they can best serve you. You will probably discover that there are more supporters for your project than you realized.

Grants Advisory Committees

One highly effective method for involving volunteers in your grants quest is to develop an advisory committee focused on the need or problem your grant proposal will address. For example, while working for a university-affiliated hospital, I initiated one advisory committee on health promotion and wellness for children and another on research for children's diseases with different individuals on each committee. Even though you should think of your advisory committee as an informal affiliation of individuals you invite to take part in attracting grants to the problem area you have chosen, you may be able to recruit more members and support if you leave the word *grant* out of the committee's title. Include the problem instead. For example, I called one of the groups I initiated the Committee for Promoting Research on Children's Diseases instead of the Grants Committee for Promoting Research on Children's Diseases.

Invite fellow professionals, individuals from other organizations and the community, and corporate members who are interested in the area you have identified. By inviting a cross section of individuals to join your committee, you develop a wider base from which to draw support. Ask yourself who would care if you developed grants resources to solve a particular problem. The one common denominator for all the committee members should be their concern for positive change in the identified area of need. Develop a list of individuals, groups, and organizations you think would volunteer a little of their time to be instrumental in making progress in the problem area. Be sure to include

- individuals who might know foundation, government, or corporate grantors; and

- colleagues who may have previously prepared a proposal for the grantor you will be approaching or who may have acted as grant reviewers.

Also consider current and past employees, board of trustee members, and former clients.

Grant Resources

After you have identified individuals or groups that would be interested in seeing change in the area identified, make a list of skills and resources that would be helpful in developing your proposal. Match these with the types of individuals who might possess them. Your list of skills and resources may give you some ideas about whom you should recruit for your grants advisory committee. Consider the skills and resources and the types of individuals that could be useful in

- preparing your proposal (writers, experts in evaluation design or statistics, and individuals with computer programming skills),
- making preproposal contact (individuals with sales and marketing skills and people who travel frequently—especially to Washington, D.C.), and
- developing consortia or cooperative relationships and subcontracts (individuals who belong to other nonprofit groups with similar concerns).

All volunteers, including your advisory committee members, should be asked to review the Grant Resources Inventory (exhibit 7.1) and to indicate those resources they are willing to contribute. Tailor the list to include only what you need, and if you know of specific assets possessed by your volunteers, do not be afraid to ask.

How to Incorporate Advocates to Increase Grants Success

Specific activities to consider in relation to advocacy roles of individuals on your list are

- writing endorsement letters,
- contacting funding sources for you and setting up appointments or conference calls,
- providing expertise in particular areas (finance, marketing, and so on), and
- accompanying you to meetings with potential funders or even visiting a funding source for you.

Use the Advocacy Planning Sheet (exhibit 7.2) to organize your approach.

EXHIBIT 7.1
Grant Resources Inventory

Please indicate the resource areas you would be willing to help with. At the end of the list, provide more detailed information. In addition, if you are willing to meet with funding sources please list the geographic areas you travel to frequently.

___ Evaluation of Projects

___ Computer Equipment

___ Computer Programming

___ Spreadsheets on Methods and Protocols

___ Objectives, Hypothesis, Specific Aims

___ Budgeting, Accounting, Developing Cash Flow Forecasts, Auditing

___ Audiovisual Assistance (Equipment, DVDs, etc.)

___ Website Development

___ Travel to Make Contact with Grantors

___ Writing, Editing, Submission

___ Searching for Funding Sources

___ Equipment/Materials

___ Space for Program/Research

___ Other:

Description of Resources:

Areas Frequently Visited:

Endorsement Letters

One very effective way to use advocates is to request that they write endorsement letters related to your organization's credibility and accomplishments. Without guidance, however, many advocates will develop endorsement letters that focus on inappropriate aspects of your project or organization. To prevent this, spell out what you are looking for. Provide advocates with a draft endorsement letter that suggests what you would like them to consider including in their letters, such as

- pertinent facts or statistics that you may then quote or use in your proposal,

EXHIBIT 7.2
Advocacy Planning Sheet

Project Title:

Project Director:

Select from the following list of techniques you can suggest your advocates employ to advance your project.

- Endorsement letters
- Testimonials
- Letters of introduction to grantors
- Set appointments with granting officials
- Accompany you to see funding sources
- Go to see grantors for you

Techniques for This Project	Advocates To Be Used	Who Will Contact Advocate and When	Desired Outcome	Date Completed

- the length of time they have worked with you or your organization (for example, number of hours, consortia, or cooperative work relationships), and
- a summary of their committee work and their major accomplishments.

Advocates should almost be able to input your draft, print it on their stationery, and sign it. If the grantor has any special requirements concerning endorsement letters, make sure they are followed.

Contacts

Another way to involve your advocates is to present them with the names of potential grantors and their board members and to ask whether they know any of the grantors' key individuals. This approach is particularly useful if your advocates are reluctant to reveal all of their contacts and are holding back to see how serious you are in researching potential grantors.

If your advocates are trusting, you can ask them outright for a comprehensive list of their contacts. This includes asking your grants advisory committee members to reflect on their ability to contact a variety of potential grantors that may be helpful in your grants effort. To take this proactive approach, follow these steps:

1. Explain the advocacy concept to the individuals you have identified and how the information they provide will be used. Ask each participant to complete an Advocacy Webbing Worksheet (exhibit 7.3) and return it to you. Some organizations find they have better results in introducing the advocacy concept when they relate the concept to a major project of the organization that has widespread support.
2. Distribute the Advocacy Webbing Worksheet to the individuals you have identified as possible advocates. This may be done in a group or individually.
3. Input the advocacy information you collect from the completed worksheets in your computer, or file it.
4. When a match between a potential funder and an advocate is made, call your advocate and discuss the possibility of having him or her arrange a meeting for you with the funding source. Ask the advocate to attend the meeting with you to add credibility to your presentation.

Keep all completed Advocacy Webbing Worksheets on file and update them periodically. This is a good activity for volunteers. Be aware, however, that care should be taken to safeguard advocacy data. Advocacy data should be considered personal information that is privileged; you must not allow open access to the data or you will be violating your advocates' trust. Store the information on your personal computer, and keep a copy of your program/file in a safe place. This approach will ensure the privacy of this confidential information. When a potential funding source is identified, search your advocacy database to determine whether any of your advocates have a relationship to the potential funding source.

You may have an advocate who

- is a member of both your organization and the funding source's board,
- can arrange an appointment to get you in to talk to the funder,
- can write a letter to a "friend" on the funding source's board, or
- has worked for the grantor or been a reviewer for the funder's grant program.

Community Support

Advocacy can also play a valuable role in developing and documenting community support for your project. Some funding sources require that you demonstrate community support in the form of advisory committee resolutions and copies of the minutes of meetings, and more grantors are encouraging the development of consortia when applying for funding. Whether you are looking at a joint submittal for your proposal or just endorsement and support, it is important to start the process of applying for a grant early so that deadlines do not interfere with your ability to document your advisory committee's involvement and valuable work. To deal creatively with the area of community support,

- put together a proposal development workbook (see chapter 3) to focus on your problem area;
- organize an advisory committee to examine the problem area; and
- involve the advisory committee in brainstorming project ideas, examining needs assessment techniques, writing letters of endorsement, and providing links to funders.

Review the worksheet on Developing Community Support (see exhibit 7.4) to help you determine how to use community support to increase your fundability. Organize your supporters and maximize your chances for success by working through and with your volunteers. Involve those individuals who can be of service to your cause, from enhancing your resources to helping identify links to funders.

EXHIBIT 7.3
Advocacy Webbing Worksheet

Our organization's ability to attract grant funds is increased substantially if we can talk informally with a funding official (or board member) before we submit our formal proposal. However, it is sometimes difficult to make preproposal contact without having a link to the funding source. We need your help. By completing this worksheet, you will identify any links that you may have with potential grantors and increase our grants success dramatically.

If you have a link with a funding source that our research indicates may be interested in supporting one of our projects, we will contact you to explain the project and discuss possible ways you could help us. For example, you could write an endorsement letter, arrange an appointment, or accompany us to see the funding source. Even a simple phone call could result in our proposal actually being read and not just left in a pile. No matter what the case may be, you can rest assured that we will obtain your complete approval before any action is taken and that we will never use your name or link without your consent.

Links to foundations, corporations, and government funding sources are worth hundreds of thousands of dollars per year, and your assistance can ultimately help us continue our vital mission. Thank you for your corporation.

Your Name:
Your Phone No.:
Your Email:
Your Address:

1. What foundations or corporate boards are you, your spouse, or close friends on?

2. Do you know anyone who is on a foundation or corporate board? If so, who and what board?

3. Does your spouse know anyone on a foundation or corporate board? If so, who and what board?

4. Have you served on any government committees? If so, please list.

5. Do you know any government funding contacts? If so, please list.

EXHIBIT 7.4
Developing Community Support Worksheet

#	Techniques	Applicability of the Technique to This Project	Who Will Call Meeting	Members of Committee	Date
1	Use advisory committee to brainstorm uniquenesses of your organization				
2	Use advisory committee to work on setting up needs assessment				
3	Use advisory committee to brainstorm project ideas				
4	Use advisory committee to develop a public relations package and to produce it (printing, etc.) including newspaper coverage for your organization (press releases, interviews) and television coverage (public service announcements, talk shows)				
5	Have an artist perform or have an open house for key people in the community				
6	Other				

Involving Existing Boards, Advisory Groups, Volunteers, and Staff

Do not overlook the advantages of using the linkages that your organization's existing groups, volunteers, and staff may already have. These individuals and groups have already demonstrated an affinity for your organization and your programs. Participation in this opportunity should be voluntary, and while some administrators may express concern over asking paid staff to contribute names of friends and relatives who have connections to funding sources, they will be surprised at the voluntary response they receive. Involve your employee associations and unions, and initiate the idea by relating it to strong needs and well-accepted programs and projects that many people want to see developed or expanded.

Many nonprofit organizations already have boards and standing committees that can be invited to become involved in this webbing and linkage process. Most corporate people will be happy that they have been asked to participate in a game that the corporate world plays all the time. From my experience at universities, I have also found that department chairs, deans, and members of boards of institutes and centers usually respond favorably to the concept.

The key to acceptance of the webbing and linkage process is to assure those participating that linkages will not be contacted without their knowledge or approval and, in most cases, their assistance.

How to Use Webbing and Linkage Information

To help you get the most out of your newly discovered linkages, list them by linkage type. For example, foundation, corporate, federal, state, and so forth. Then use the funding source research tools described in chapters 11, 20, and 25 to look up the interest areas of the grantors to which you have a link. Review your organization's needs and projects and look for potential matches with the grantors. When a match is found, make preproposal contact through your linkage.

Where You Are

Once you have completed the proactive step of team and consortia building, you are faced with how to integrate the concept of webbing and linkages into your plan. First you must ask yourself if this concept fits with your grants plan for success. If it does, you must then determine where to insert it. Can you suggest it at a conference or meeting where your team/consortia members are in attendance? Can you add it to the agenda of one of your regularly scheduled meetings? Could the concept be the basis for a special retreat?

FIGURE 7.1
Action Steps' Chart: Creating Grant-Winning Teams

Your next step is to consider incorporating a grants advisory committee in your proactive planning. Consider the benefits of having such a committee and look at the roles the committee members could play in providing

- letters of endorsement,
- contact with funding officials,
- community support, and
- linkages to grantors.

Your job is to decide if you want to take advantage of the valuable strategies presented in this chapter and when. Figure 7.1 depicts the suggested system thus far.

Notes

1. Allen N. Fahden and Srinivasa Namakkal, *Team Dimension Profiles* (Minneapolis, MN: Inscape Publishing, Inc., 1995).

2. Christopher M. Avery, with Meri Aaron Walker and Erin O'Toole Murphy, *Teamwork Is an Individual Skill: Getting Your Work Done When Sharing Responsibility* (San Francisco: Berrett-Koehler Publishers, Inc., 2001).

3. Patrick Lencioni, *The Five Dysfunctions of a Team* (San Francisco: Jossey-Bass, 2002).

4. Patrick Lencioni, *Overcoming the Five Dysfunctions of a Team—A Field Guide* (San Francisco: Jossey-Bass, 2005).

5. Patrick Lencioni, *Death by Meeting* (San Francisco: Jossey-Bass, 2006).

8

Selecting the Right Marketplace
for Your Project

THE TWO MAIN SOURCES of support for universities and nonprofit organizations and their grant requests are public (government) and private philanthropy. Each marketplace and its subcategories are very different from one another in whom they fund, what they fund, the amount of support they provide, and what they will require of you and your organization.

Not only are there vast differences between the various types of grantors in each of the marketplaces, there are also differences in how the marketplaces are viewed in terms of prestige and credibility. When determining which grants marketplace is right for you and your project/research, you must take into consideration your career plan and how it may be affected by the grants marketplace hierarchy.

Whether you are using research grant funding to build your rationale for gaining tenure at a university or for a promotion in a nonprofit organization, peer-reviewed grant awards are viewed as the most prestigious and credible. Except for earmarked pork grants, most competitive federal grants (research and model projects) are peer reviewed and carry the highest regard in the grants world. Other peer-reviewed grants from state agencies, counties, and cities follow in a descending order.

Foundation grant awards are usually considered less prestigious than peer-reviewed government grant awards because most are decided by internal staff and board members who may not be experts in the field. Some private grantor decision makers may be knowledgeable in the field, but true peer review is used by only a very select few. The few that use peer review are considered more prestigious, but the system is much less refined than federal peer-reviewed grants. Being able to say you were funded by a foundation like the Robert Wood Johnson Foundation is more noteworthy than saying you were funded by a community foundation.

Grants made by nonprofit organizations, professional societies, service clubs, membership associations, and national and international groups in your field are viewed by many as the next most prestigious because they are reviewed and selected for funding by your peers. While these awards are usually for small amounts, they *are* credibility builders.

Corporate grantors are the lowest on the scale since they are viewed by many as pay or remuneration for services, research, or knowledge wanted by the grantor. With more and more university/corporate alliances, this formerly clear demarcation has become blurred. How a corporate grant is viewed in terms of credibility and prestige is linked to the project's objectivity and whether the research conducted was free from bias.

So, as you look at the major marketplaces, you must consider your career, your research/project, and your position in your field. Breaking through the glass ceiling to get a highly coveted federal grant may mean starting with a grant from a less prestigious marketplace sector, such as a foundation. This funding will allow you to gather preliminary data, test hypotheses, publish in journals, and build a track record that improves your image as well as that of your organization. Remember, where you work and the letterhead on your stationery *will* make a difference with each grantor segment.

Now that you have reviewed in a broad sense how the different grants marketplaces must be integrated into your career plan, it is time to get down to specifics. Start by reviewing the distinct characteristics of each marketplace, where the money is, and who your competition is.

General Grants Marketplace Information

I have administered a grants marketplace quiz as a pretest assessment instrument to over forty thousand grantseekers since 1975. These grantseekers attended one of my training seminars and, therefore, were not randomly selected and may not represent all grantseekers. However, they do vary widely in grants expertise and background. What is interesting and surprising is that more incorrect answers are given to the quiz today than thirty-five years ago. Why is this, when today's grantseekers are exposed to an abundance of information about grants and funding sources through the general media, professional journals, newsletters, conferences, grant databases, and e-mail alerts? I believe that improved grants information may, in fact, contribute to current misconceptions about the grants marketplace and, consequently, to faulty grant strategies.

Grantseekers, and the administrators they work for, read announcements about universities and nonprofit groups that attract large, million-dollar grant awards. These awards that make the news are usually exceptions to the rule. These awards unfortunately are often interpreted by well-meaning, motivated grantseekers and their administrators as the norm or average. Nonprofit leaders use these larger awards to shape their view of the marketplace. Judging the marketplace by larger grants that make headlines thus creates and reinforces misconceptions about grant making and influences unrealistic expectations about the level of grant support from each sector of the marketplace. As a result, many grantseekers end up basing their strategic grants decision making on fantasy or wishful thinking rather than on fact.

Both the private and public marketplaces reflect the global financial markets. While this most current recession and its impact on the stock market and unemployment is dramatic and has caused distress to people all around the world, it is not the first or the last that the grants marketplace will have to endure.

The 1980s experienced a recession that directly impacted the grants marketplace. While the federal government tried to stimulate the economic recovery in a number of ways, there was a concerted effort to reduce grants and hold programs at no growth. In addition, there were no increases in salaries and wages paid under federal grants. This included research and medical research. There was an effort to eliminate entire departments such as the Department of Education. Grantseekers generally overreacted to these cuts and no growth policies and often did not even apply. The result in some programs was a small reduction in funding (i.e., 5 percent) but a dramatic reduction in applications. The grants herd mentality scared off a lot of applicants. Because of this, grantseekers who applied to certain programs actually had an increased chance for funding. Eventually the budget was balanced and there were raises in pay ceilings on grants and actual increases in grant appropriations.

By extrapolating this phenomenon to the current situation, it is easy to understand the importance of looking beyond the news clips related to the government grant reductions to how these cutbacks will affect the applicant pool and the percentage of awards made.

Now we face another recession. In this instance, the federal government has not created a new bureaucracy to stimulate the economy as it did in the past with the Comprehensive Employment Training Act (CETA). Instead, the Economic Stimulus Act placed additional funds into existing grant programs in an attempt to avoid waste and duplication. In 2009 and 2010 many of the existing government granting agencies had special grants deadlines and extra review panels. This resulted in billions of dollars in new funded proposals. While some question the value of the stimulus funds, I believe that history will show that these funds/grants not only added to the employment of graduate students and researchers but also resulted in valuable research and projects that will benefit our society for decades. In addition, the Obama administration should get credit for not starting an entirely new system to distribute the grants related to stimulus funds. The use of existing programs and the peer review of grant funds, rather than the earmarking/pork process, will result in more good.

Before we see an increase in grant programs and appropriations, we will go through another balance the budget/trim the deficit cycle. As this book is being written the current administration is requesting a 5 percent cut in the 2011/2012 federal budget. Expect a constriction of the federal and state government grants marketplace. Be smart. If past behavior is any indication of future behavior, the bad news will travel fast and the herd mentality will take over. Do your homework and you may find that you actually have a better chance for success as many others will flee from the marketplace.

Private grantors (foundation and corporate) will continue to award billions in grant funds as well as equipment to nonprofits. However, keep in mind that this marketplace is heavily influenced by the economic situation in the United States as well as the global markets. Its growth depends on profits, sales, and stock markets. Since many foundations make their grants from the dividends in their stock portfolios, most grants experts base the growth or constriction of this marketplace on the Standard & Poor's 500 Index (the S&P 500). Many foundations and corporate foundations saw their assets decline at extraordinary rates. This has impacted their grant making, but a market improvement since 2008 has helped to improve the situation.

Considering the varying opinions on the pace of the economic recovery and the fluctuations in employment rates, this marketplace is likely to make retreats and advances for some time to come, but in general, I expect some growth from 2011 to 2015 unless there is a catastrophic economic event. What do you think? Remember, your perception of the grants marketplace has a tremendous impact on how you will conduct your grantseeking.

Take a minute to answer the following questions. This will help you develop your insight into who your competition is and where the money is—two critical areas to assist you in choosing the correct marketplace.

1. In the United States, approximately how many nonprofit organizations are eligible to receive gifts and grants?
   a. 50,000
   b. 500,000
   c. 1,500,000
   d. 850,000

2. What was the total amount of private money (nongovernment) donated to these nonprofit organizations (see question 1) as tax-deductible gifts in 2009?
   a. $10 billion
   b. $26 billion
   c. $133 billion
   d. $304 billion
3. The total amount of private money donated to nonprofit organizations came from the following four basic sources. Indicate the percentage attributed to each source.
   a. Foundation grants_____%
   b. Corporate grants_____%
   c. Bequests_____%
   d. Individual giving_____%
4. How much grant funding came from the federal marketplace in 2009?
   a. $75 billion
   b. $100 billion
   c. $200 billion
   d. $500 billion

Turn to the end of this chapter for the correct answers.

If taking this quiz reaffirmed what you already knew to be true, that is great. If your answers were incorrect, be thankful that you now know the correct answers and can avoid approaching the wrong marketplace and experiencing unnecessary rejection.

Most of my seminar participants guess that foundation grants account for 40 to 50 percent of the $304 billion donated in private money, with corporate grants at 30 to 35 percent, and bequests and individuals representing the balance of 15 to 30 percent.

I wish these misconceptions were correct. That would mean that foundations and corporations would have more grants funding than the federal government. However, wishful thinking will not get you a grant. Knowledge and a sound grants strategy will pay off in the end with a funded project.

The fact is that the foundation and corporate marketplace provides over $52 billion in grants, and their funding of projects can provide a catalyst in attracting the more plentiful government grant funds. However, these private grantors complain about the wild ideas and inappropriate monetary requests presented to them by grantseekers who have not done their homework and know little about the grants marketplace. To avoid this, I suggest you approach the marketplace in the following manner.

First, research the sector of the grants marketplace with the greatest amount of funds—the government marketplace (federal, state, county, and city). In order to approach these potentially valuable partners with knowledge and conviction, read through the government funding section (part 2) that follows. Take time to log on to the appropriate websites and do a search. Talking to a federal program official will often provide you with valuable insights into what you need to do to make you and your project more competitive and fundable.

Federal grantors fund great projects and research that have considerable preliminary data that promises results that work. They want data to take the guesswork out of grants. Once when I presented a dynamic grant idea one federal grant program officer told me she thought my project was fantastic and that her program liked to fund fantastic projects built on great ideas that had the potential to transform the field. However, she needed to see preliminary data to guarantee some degree of success. I asked her how I could get the data without grant money and she told me to get a foundation grant. Then she set me up with a private foundation director to discuss the project. The foundation funded us and turned a $175,000 feasibility study into a four-year multi-million-dollar federal grant. The foundation even applauded my effort to contact the larger federal granting source first to ascertain its interest because it knew that the federal grants program had more money than it did.

Approach the smaller marketplace after you can demonstrate that you have searched the government grants area and can show why the private marketplace (foundations, corporations, nonprofit organizations, membership groups, professional societies, and service clubs) provides your best opportunity. Keep in mind that foundations and corporations may provide valuable start-up funding to develop preliminary data, test hypotheses, and develop your consortia that will eventually result in larger grants from the government. See parts 3 and 4 of this book for a more detailed discussion of private funding opportunities.

Remember, if you can recognize when you have identified an inappropriate grantor for your proposal and you are requesting an inordinate amount of funding, by choosing not to apply you avoid positioning your institution and yourself negatively, and you keep your grants success rate up. Learning about each of the marketplaces and developing your strategies from the information provided in this book is bound to pay off for you.

Question	Correct Answer
1. In the United States, approximately how many nonprofit organizations are eligible to receive gifts and grants?	c. 1,500,000

2. What was the total amount of private money (nongovernment) donated to these nonprofit organizations (see question 1) as tax-deductible gifts in 2009?

   d. $304 billion

3. The total amount of private money donated to nonprofit organizations came from the following four basic sources. Indicate the percentage attributed to each source.

   Foundation grants   13% ($38.4 B)
   Corporate grants   4% ($14.1 B)
   Bequests   8% ($23.8 B)
   Individual giving   75% ($227.4 B)

4. How much grant funding came from the federal marketplace in 2009?

   d. $500 billion

9

Documenting Organizational Support for Your Proposal

Preproposal Summary and Approval

B EFORE YOU LAUNCH into your grantor search, you need to consider whether your application will be supported and approved by your sponsoring organization. While almost all colleges, universities, and other nonprofit organizations have a sign-off procedure for proposals, few have a sign-on requirement. The following Preproposal Summary and Approval Form (see exhibit 9.1) has been designed to help you with this issue. Exhibit 9.1 could be subtitled "The Grantseeker's Insurance Policy." When you have ideas you would like to seek funding for, fill out this form before writing your full-scale proposal. Then have the form reviewed by your grants/research office, proposal review committee, staff, or administrators, and have it returned to you with their criticisms and suggestions. Many organizations find it useful to make the preproposal summary and approval form available electronically to the appropriate individuals as an e-mail attachment.

The purpose of the preproposal summary and approval form is to elicit comments from your organization's leaders and to have them endorse your solution. The form actually provides a vehicle to test the acceptance of your idea or project with your superiors. This is important because they should agree on the use of institutional resources before you invest hours of your time on proposal development.

There are many benefits to using the preproposal summary and approval form at this point in the process. Since proposal developers have not yet invested a great deal of time writing their proposals, they are less defensive when their project summary is criticized, suggested improvements are easier to make, and if necessary, plans to deal with a lack of support can be developed.

EXHIBIT 9.1
Preproposal Summary and Approval Form

1. Proposed Proposal Director/Project Director:

2. Statement of the Problem:

3. Brief Statement of the Solution:

4. How the Project Relates to Our Mission/Goals:

5. Suggested Grantor:

   Special Grantor Requirements:
   _____ Matching Funds
   _____ Other

6. Estimated Cost of Project:

7. Proposed Project Personnel   Released Time/New Employee

   _____   _____
   _____   _____
   _____   _____

8. Facilities Required:
   Square Feet: _____   Desired Location: _____

9. Equipment Needed for Project (Note if equipment is on hand or is to be
   provided by grant, and if any special maintenance will be required):

10. Signature/Approval (Your signature represents approval of any institutional
    support outlined above): _____
    _____

11. Conditional Signature/Approval: _____
    _____

    Approval to proceed with full proposal development as long as the proposal
    developer meets the following conditions:

    Attach a brief summary/concept paper to this approval form and a list of
    potential/probable funding sources.

Using this form can also be beneficial when proposals must be approved before they are submitted. Make sure the form is reviewed by those people who will be signing the final proposal. This way these individuals will know in advance that the proposed project is coming. Have these key people comment on the areas they question or have a problem supporting. If they have no problems, they can endorse your idea by signing at number 10 of the exhibit. If they have a condition that must be met first, they can list the condition under number 11 of the exhibit and provide their conditional signature. This ensures that the time, money, and resources spent in your proposal preparation process will not be met with a negative response internally and result in failure to have your proposal signed when ready for submittal.

This preproposal summary and review process also enables decision makers to be made aware of important issues and the potential grantor's specific requirements and gives them an opportunity to comment on them. This includes, but is not limited to, the following:

- release time for project director/principal investigator to work on the grant when funded;
- matching funds commitment; and
- space, equipment, support personnel, and other resource allocations.

Because the form is generic and allows for the inclusion of the suggested grantor's specific requirements, it can be used with all of the grants market-places and with any grantor you uncover in the next three sections of this book.

Your grantseeking efforts are more likely to receive support and to provide a basis for matching funds and other resource allocations when you appraise your administration of your entrepreneurial grant effort and seek its endorsement in advance of submittal. This will reduce the chances of getting a grantor excited about your project and then you not being able to submit your proposal because of internal problems and a refusal to sign off by your administration later.

Review your action steps' chart to see where and when preproposal approval fits into your proactive grants plan (see figure 9.1).

FIGURE 9.1
Action Steps' Chart: Preproposal Approval

Part 2

PUBLIC/GOVERNMENT
FUNDING OPPORTUNITIES

10

Understanding the Government Grants Marketplace

The History of Federal and State Grants

THE CONCEPT OF transferring large tracts of land by making a grant predates our U.S. Constitution. Our founding fathers granted land to states to set up systems of public higher education. The colleges and universities set up within these systems were referred to as land grant institutions. The early colonial governments realized there was an educational void or problem in that few private colleges were able to develop the educated citizens the nation required. The economy was also agrarian based and few private colleges focused on agriculture. In an effort to fill that void, land grant colleges and universities were formed. This began the concept of focusing on a specific problem that federal and state governments wanted to impact. The public works projects from the Great Depression era used federal grants for funding. Educating farmers to end the dust bowl through the use of modern farming techniques was largely accomplished through a Department of Agriculture grant program to states to initiate a youth education program known as 4-H. The original purpose of the program was to have youth teach their parents new farming techniques.

While the use of a government grants mechanism was established early on in our country's history, the mechanism we twenty-first-century grantseekers know really took off in the 1940s, particularly during World War II. During the war the government stepped up grants primarily to deal with medical and scientific problems created by the war. These grants resulted in many advances, including the discovery of penicillin.

The 1950s witnessed the creation of the National Science Foundation and grants to close the gap in science created by the Soviet launching of *Sputnik.* The federal government expanded the use of the grants mechanism from health and science to education. Presidents began to utilize the grants mechanism to push for changes in their chosen areas of interest, and in many ways these grant programs became synonymous with their legacies. For example, President John F. Kennedy's New Frontier Initiative and President Lyndon B. Johnson's Great Society Initiative were both driven through a grants mechanism to improve education, health, and social programs. Historically, when there is a national problem the grants mechanism has been used to come up with a solution. For instance, the 1970s' recession gave birth to the Comprehensive Employment Training Act, a grant program to retrain and upgrade worker skills and increase employment.

Both Republican and Democratic administrations and Congress have used grant-related initiatives to create change and make a direct and often immediate impact on our cultural, social, health, education, and scientific/research infrastructure. An example is the Faith-Based Initiative, started under the George W. Bush administration, which allows religious-based organizations to apply for federal grants. The former separation of church and state requirements were lifted and in some government grant programs religiously affiliated groups actually got preferential treatment when competing with other nonprofit organizations. This was a dramatic departure from previous administrations' use of the grants mechanism. The Obama administration has kept the Office of Faith-Based Initiatives, but there are issues concerning the office's ability to restrict which faiths are eligible to apply for these grants.

While both Democrats and Republicans have used the grants mechanism, there are underlying philosophical differences as to the type of mechanisms that each group prefers. Republicans tend to favor local, regional, and state distribution of federal government grant dollars. Democrats tend to prefer national programs directed from Washington.

In the 1970s a growing trend developed on how to allocate federal grant dollars. The trend was based on federalism or the belief that the federal government should give funds back to state and local governments for them to distribute. The notion was that states should have the right to set their own agendas.

President Ronald Reagan used this new federalism or revenue sharing to cut and eliminate funding for programs that were previously controlled by federal agencies. Federal funds for categorical grants aimed at specific problems or areas were reduced, eliminated, or combined in an effort to support the administration's philosophy of "the government governs best which governs the least." It will be interesting to observe how the Tea Party and other conservative movements affect the use of the federal grants mechanism.

The idea of allowing states to grant funding to their priorities still has a lot of support. However, the concept is not tenable in the areas of research and model or demonstration grants. Even staunch conservatives agree that we must have a federal controlling management system for these types of grants or a wasteful duplication of efforts will occur.

The next section of this chapter describes the various mechanisms for distributing grants in more detail. It is important that you, the grantseeker, are familiar with these different types of mechanisms so that you can develop your grant strategies accordingly and recognize when to shift your grants research away from federal agencies and to state or local government agencies that control the moneys you desire.

Categorical Grants

As previously mentioned, categorical grants are designed to promote proposals within very specific, well-defined areas of interest. These grant opportunities address a specific area with which a federal program is concerned, such as arts, humanities, drug abuse, dropout prevention, nutrition for the elderly, or research on certain types of diseases and scientific advances. The House of Representatives and the Senate, using a system of committee hearings, select the problems to be addressed, provide for debate, vote on appropriations, and encourage prospective grantees to design approaches to solve or reduce the problem, or to increase knowledge in the area through research.

Project and research grants are awarded by various agencies under these congressionally authorized programs. Ideally, grants are awarded to the organizations (and individuals) whose proposals most clearly match the announced program guidelines. Most federal grant programs use nongovernmental review panels (often referred to as peer-review panels) to evaluate the projects. Peer review helps ensure that the best proposals are selected for funding. Because project design is left to the grantseekers, there is room for a wide variety of creative solutions, making the project and research grant approach very popular among grantseekers.

Government granting agencies require grantseekers to complete detailed applications. As categorical grants have increased, each federal agency that controls funds has developed its own grants system. Grants applications and the administration of grants differ in format from agency to agency, and sometimes from program to program within the same agency. Even with the use of online submittal through Grants.gov, the applications are tedious, complicated, and time consuming to complete. It is a challenge to tailor your proposal content to meet the requirements of the granting agency as well as your own needs. There is usually a three- to six-month review process, which may include an internal staff review by federal agency personnel and a peer review. Successful grantees are required to submit frequent reports, maintain accurate project records, follow Office of Management and Budget (OMB) guidelines, and agree to federal audits and site visits by government staff.

To be successful in research and project grants, grantseekers must be mindful of the constant changes in emphasis and appropriations. Hidden agendas and shifts in focus result from the funding agency's prerogative to interpret and be sensitive to changes in the field of interest, and to what Congress appropriates each year. Be mindful that while presidents may set priorities, Congress appropriates the funds. The federal budget changes dramatically from what the president presents, and generally, Congress likes the control that categorical grants provide.

Earmarked Grants

In grants earmarking, more commonly referred to as pork legislation, a project bypasses federal agency oversight and is placed in a bill that Congress is likely to pass. Bills that are popular or necessary to our country may have a number of very specific projects attached to them, projects that have little or nothing to do with the bills themselves. When passed, these specific projects do not have to go through an internal (agency) or peer-review process. In cases where a mandated review is required, the reviewers' comments, recommendations, and scores are irrelevant since the grant must be funded anyway. Once approved, the project must be handled by a federal agency (usually the most logical categorical program) that cannot question or alter the approved, funded project.

This process has become so widespread that most colleges, universities, local governments, and major nonprofit organizations spend millions each year to retain special lobbyists in Washington, D.C., to assist them in getting senators and congress people to insert earmarks for them in federal legislation. The practice is so pervasive that while working with a college to assist in getting federal funding for a researcher, I had to wait for permission from the university's earmarking consultant before I could contact a program officer to pursue competitive, peer-reviewed grant sources.

If not curtailed, the earmarking mechanism could eliminate entire categorical federal grants programs, especially since earmarked funding is frequently taken from the budgets of categorical programs. For example, one year the Fund for the Improvement of Postsecondary Education had *all* its appropriated funds earmarked for special projects.

Under earmarking, there is no internal staff or peer reviews to evaluate and select the highest quality projects and research. The only ones to be funded are those with the ability to push the other pigs out of their way at the federal grants trough. It is easy to see how this practice could be used to fund inferior research as well as poor model and demonstration grants, and devastate the peer-reviewed grants system. It is also easy to see why it is publicly criticized for funding wasteful projects such as the "bridge to nowhere" in Alaska.

The use of earmarking has increased so significantly that Congress has considered legislation to eliminate the practice, or shed so much public scrutiny on it that it is drastically reduced. Even with this new emphasis on reducing earmarking and promoting transparency by requiring the sponsor's name, it will be difficult to stop the pork process now that it has reached the current level. While earmarking appears at first to be very inviting and an easy way for your organization to get needed resources, there is a disadvantage to consider. Many of the federal officers whose jobs entail administering grant programs, ensuring that their programs accomplish their goals, and organizing peer review, see earmarking as a threat. Earmarking threatens their agency's credibility since they are the ones who will get blamed when these often ill-conceived projects are publicized. This is particularly frustrating since they have nothing to do with the choice of the grantee or the funding of the grant, but still have to administer it and send out the funds. Interviews with some program officers have revealed a lot of irritation with grantees who are subverting the grants system through earmarking. As a result, earmarked grantees can experience great difficulty in moving from a pork grant back to a peer-reviewed grant within the same agency and program.

Since control of the House and Senate has moved to the Democrats, earmarking has been in the spotlight and was supposed to be reduced. So far, this has not been the case. Like the other types of grants mechanisms, you need to understand earmarking so that you can determine the ramifications involved in using it.

Formula Grants

The term *formula grants* refers to granting programs under which funds are allocated according to a set of criteria (or a formula). The criteria for allocation of these grant funds may be census data, unemployment figures, number of individuals below the poverty level, number of people with disabilities, and the like, for a state, city, or region. Formula grant programs are generally specific to a problem area or geographic region and historically have been used to support training programs in the fields of health, criminal justice, and employment. They are rarely encountered in research areas but have been used to distribute funds for research equipment.

The formula grant funds must pass through an intermediary, such as a state, city, or county government, or a commission, before reaching the grantee. The formula grants mechanism is another example of the New Federalism that started developing in the early 1970s. While the general guidelines for formula grants are developed at the federal level, the rules are open to interpretation, and local input can significantly alter the intent of the original federal program. To encourage local control and input into how federal funds are spent, the formula grants mechanism requires a mandated review by local officials but usually very little accountability or evaluation of the actual impact of the funds. Because of this, it is difficult to substantiate the results of these programs at subsequent congressional appropriation hearings, which means that they (the programs placed in formula grant formats) are often easy targets for elimination.

Block Grants

The block grant concept was founded on the premise that it was not the purview of the federal government to force the states to follow categorical grant program priorities. Similar categorical grant programs were blocked, or synthesized into groups of related programs, and the federal funds were sent directly to the states. The states could set their priorities and grant the federal funds to the high priority areas and projects as they saw fit.

The block grant mechanism allowed the federal government to reduce staff formerly used to administer categorical grant programs. Decreases in staff were limited, however, because the federal government still had to direct the research component of categorical programs to avoid duplication and to coordinate research efforts.

Because of the federal government's continued involvement in the administration of grants (especially research grants), and Congress's desire to deal with problems in health research, education, employment, and crime, the late 1980s marked the decline of the block grant mechanism of the early Reagan years, and the use of categorical funding mechanisms increased. Virtually all of the new grant programs introduced from the 1990s to 2011 have been categorical grant programs designed to impact existing and new problems. Between the federal income tax cuts, the recession, the bank bailouts, the ongoing wars, and the growing federal deficits, new categorical grant areas will not be likely unless a major threat or new problem appears. As efforts are made to balance future budgets, categorical grant programs will probably be the first to be cut or condensed into block grants. The conservative agenda of George W. Bush's administration increased defense costs and the resulting deficit could result in more budget reductions, the blocking of more federal grant programs, and, in general, fewer grant dollars.

Contracts

No discussion of federal support would be complete without a discussion of government contracts. In recent years, the differences between a grant and a contract have become harder to discern. Indeed, after hours of negotiation with a federal agency on your grant, you may end up having to finalize your budget with a contract officer.

While there are several types of contracts, including fixed cost, cost reimbursable, and those that allow the contractor to add additional costs incurred during the contract, the basic difference between a grant and a contract is that a contract outlines precisely what the government wants done. You are supplied with detailed specifications, you propose a procedure to produce what the government agency has specified, and the contract is usually awarded on a lowest-bid basis. With a contract, there is decidedly less flexibility in creating the approach to the problem. To be successful in this arena, you must be able to convince the federal contracting agency that you can perform the contract at an acceptable level of competency and at the lowest bid. Contracts are also published or advertised in different ways than grants. Grant opportunities can be found in the *Catalog of Federal Domestic Assistance* and on Grants.gov while contracts are advertised in *Federal Business Opportunities* (FedBizOpps .gov). These resources will be explained in chapter 11.

The $500 billion in federal grants quoted in question 4 of the quiz in chapter 8 does *not* include government contract moneys. One reason that contract moneys are not included in federal grant statistics has to do with rollovers. Grant funds are appropriated and awarded in the federal budget year, which runs from October 1 to September 30. Grants awarded on a one-year time frame from award date may allow for a short, no-cost extension, but even multiyear grants contain a caveat that future funding is dependent on yearly budget allocations. While grantees can usually obtain an extension on expending their awarded grant funds beyond the end of their grant period, rollovers of unexpended federal agency funds are prohibited. Unexpended grant funds revert back to the federal treasury, except for federal contracts. For example, the Department of Defense may accrue rollover funds in certain contract areas for several years. The rollover variable makes it virtually impossible to estimate how much total contract funding is available from all of the federal agencies in any one year. However, it is safe to say that the variety, number, and dollar value of government contracts are staggering and go far beyond the $500 billion in government grants cited in chapter 8 and could be in the trillions of dollars.

Contracts have been increasingly pursued by nonprofit groups in recent years. For example, shifts away from domestic grant program funds have led some nonprofit organizations to look at Department of Defense contract opportunities for implementation of their programs and research. However, the contracts game requires a successful track record and documentable expertise. The best way to break into this marketplace is to identify a successful bidder and inquire as to whether you can work with them as a subcontractor. This way, you gain experience, confidence, and contacts with the contractor.

Many nonprofit groups have found that they can reduce the problems they routinely encounter in bidding contracts by developing separate profit and nonprofit entities for dealing with such issues as security agreements, academic freedom, patents, and copyrights. In addition, changes in the contracts area have been made to simplify government purchasing and to reduce paperwork. These changes, brought on by scandals over inflated prices for parts, have alleviated some of the problems associated with the administration of contract bids. Still, bidding on government contracts is a task for experienced grantseekers only.

State Government Grants

As a grantseeker, you will frequently discover a federal grant opportunity in which the eligible recipient must be a state agency. In these cases, federal funds are passed on for dissemination to the state agency that the state designates as best suited to do so. The federal program officers will know where the funds were directed in each state. States may also allocate their own funds into state grant programs. In some instances they may be required to put matching funds into the federal program as a requirement to receive the federal funds. Information on all federal funding must be accessible to the public and, therefore, are listed in the public grants resource Grants.gov (to be explained in chapter 11). Most states do not have a similar public database. To discover state grant opportunities you will need to look at state agency websites and talk to state officials. Many states appropriate grant funds to programs and projects their elected officials value. For example, states that have secured funding from the tobacco company settlement use these funds as their legislature and executives see fit. One state used the funds for grant opportunities related to the expansion of opportunities and employment in the technology sector, while a number of other states have used the funds to develop antismoking programs.

It is difficult to estimate how many grant dollars are awarded through individual state program initiatives. Many states develop their own initiatives in the social welfare and health areas, while few states deal in research funding. In most states, the majority of state grant funds are federal funds that must pass through the states to you, the grantseeker.

There are some grantseeker advantages to state control of grants. State-controlled grants funded by the federal government are easier to access than federal grants. They require less long-distance travel and allow you to use state and local politicians to make your case heard. These advantages are counterbalanced, however, by the fact that some states develop their own priorities for these pass-through federal funds. States may add additional restrictions and use a review system similar to the federal peer-review system, or use a system made up of state bureaucrats and political appointees. Although states have their own moneys, granting programs, and rules, if they distribute grant moneys obtained from the federal government, they must guarantee that the eventual recipient of those funds will follow all federal rules and circulars.

Many of the federal government grantseeking techniques found in the preceding chapters of this book also apply to accessing state grant funds. However, to determine which of the government sectors (federal or state) is best for your proposal, you must first learn how to research the government marketplace.

11

Researching the
Federal Government Marketplace

The Federal Grants System

FEDERAL GRANTS PROGRAMS are created by Congress, and federal funding is appropriated each year. Many federal grant programs are initiated as acts of Congress (for example, the Higher Education Act). While the acts may create programs that legally exist for a set number of years before they are reviewed, the funding for all government grant agencies and their programs is currently limited to one year. The federal budget year runs from October 1 to the following September 30.

At the time of this book's publication, the current federal grants calendar is the 2010/2011 budget year (October 1, 2010, through September 30, 2011). The president submits his preferred budget to Congress in the spring for the new fall budget year. Recent years have witnessed a Congress and a president that could not agree on the budget. When the budget does not get passed before the beginning of the new fiscal year (October 1), Congress passes a continuing resolution to keep the federal government operating while the parties work out their differences on what to cut and what to add. Continuing resolutions usually call for the level funding of current programs. Most recent federal budgets have had to operate on continuing resolutions from October 1 until January or February. During this four-month period there are deadline dates to deal with and peer reviews to conduct. Hence, federal program officers must operate as if they had the same budget as the previous year.

The key for you to remember is that a multiyear funded grant award is not guaranteed. Each year of that award is subject to changes based upon the agency's appropriation by Congress. Each yearly award is guaranteed for that year only.

To make matters more confusing, you may receive your grant award notice in June for a one-year grant. In this case, even though the federal fiscal year in which you were awarded will end on September 30, you are in essence given an extension from October to the following May to complete your research/ project. It all depends on the federal fiscal budget year that your funding is awarded under.

Federal Grants Research Form

The key to providing you and your organization with federal funding is a combination of determination, hard work, and homework. The homework consists of systematic research, record keeping, and follow-up. The Federal Grants Research Form (see exhibit 11.1) will allow you to keep track of each of the grant programs you investigate (that is, those that seem like your most logical grant sources) and will prevent your contacts and projects from being lost.

In exhibit 11.1 fill in the program information, agency contact person, website, and so on for each program that your research reveals may be a productive grants source. Procuring the items on the exhibit's checklist will help you analyze prospective funding sources and select the one most appropriate for you and your project/research. The information you gather will also help you develop a successful proposal. The Internet resources and database searching systems that are discussed in this chapter will provide much of the information on the checklist. Chapter 12 will supply you with more tips on making the preproposal contact needed to complete this form.

By knowing what information you are looking for, you will be ready to record it as you search the grantors and their websites. The first four items on exhibit 11.1's checklist deal with recording the grantor's contact information and program description.

The next item, the list of last year's grantees, is essential. All federal grant programs must provide a complete list of last year's grant recipients. This list is your first indication of your ability to be the principal investigator/project director and your organization's likelihood of being the successful recipient. Once you have obtained the list, review it and compare who were awarded grants last year, how much they were awarded, and where the money went geographically and by type of recipient.

Item 2 calls for background information on last year's reviewers. Record any information you can find on the program reviewers. What are their backgrounds? How are they selected? Item 3 requests information on the grants

EXHIBIT 11.1
Federal Grants Research Form

For (Your Project Reference or Title): _____

CFDA No. _____

Grants.gov Funding No. _____

Government Agency: _____

Deadline Date(s):_____

Create a file for each program you are researching and place all information you gather on this program in the file. Use this Federal Grants Research Form to:

- keep a record of the information you have gathered
- maintain a log of all contact made with the federal program

Agency Address: _____

Agency Director: _____   Program Director: _____

Name/Title of Contact Person: _____

Telephone Number: _____   Fax Number: _____

E-mail: _____   Website: _____

In order to prepare a professional proposal you need to gather the information listed below.

Place a check mark next to the information you have gathered and placed in the file.

_____ Program description from *CFDA*

_____ Synopsis from Grants.gov

_____ Subscription for automatic e-mail alert/notification for up-to-date program info.

_____ Copy of full announcement (link on Grants.gov)

1. _____ List of last year's grantees

2. _____ Background information on last year's reviewers

3. _____ Grant scoring system

4. _____ Sample funded proposal

5. _____ Federal Funding Staff Profile (exhibit 12.5)

Summary of each contact made (provide below and/or attach to form)

6. _____ Instructions on how to apply/submittal instructions (link on Grants.gov)

7. _____ Comments on rules/final rules from *Federal Register* or agency publication

scoring system to be used. Look for any information on the scoring rubric that has been applied to past applications.

The next item on the checklist is a sample funded proposal. You will need to see a successful proposal for style and format before you create your application. Review your list of last year's grantees for any possible contacts or relationships you may have with a successful recipient. Then contact the recipient to ask if he or she would be willing to share a copy of their funded proposal with you. (More on this in chapter 12.)

Item 5 is completion of the Federal Funding Source Staff Profile (see exhibit 12.5). You must make preproposal contact to increase your chances of success. Once you do so, record all of the contacts you make and all of the information you learn concerning the grantor's staff. Use exhibits 12.5, 12.6, and 12.7 in chapter 12 to help with this process.

Pay special attention to obtaining submittal instructions, log-on codes, and who in your organization is the single portal for submitting proposals to the agency of interest (see item 6, exhibit 11.1).

Item 7 asks that you obtain comments on the rules/final rules from the *Federal Register* or agency publication. Be alert for any changes or prospective changes in the grant program. You will run across requests for your input on last year's rules, interim rules, and rule changes that are being proposed based upon public comment.

If you are going after a federal grant opportunity and you cannot procure the items on this checklist you better stop now. You could be wasting your time.

As you look at examples of the resources available on funding opportunities, you will see that information necessary to complete the federal grants research form is usually readily available. In instances when it is not available on agency websites or program announcements, you can request it during preproposal contact. Do not stop with the first few funding sources that sound or look good. Remember, your goal is to locate the best funding sources for your project. Complete your research, then review and rate those funding sources you have identified using the Past Grantee Analysis Worksheet in chapter 12 (see exhibit 12.2).

Federal Research Tools

How do you research and track federal grant opportunities? Federal law requires the availability of public knowledge and opportunity for input regarding government grants. As such, there are several tools to help you find federal funding sources for your projects/research. By employing these tools you, the grantseeker, can proceed proactively, make intelligent preproposal contact and take control of the deadline and submittal process. The Federal Research Tools Table (see table 11.1) outlines some of the more useful resources for locating government funds.

Grants.gov

Grants.gov is a central storehouse for information on over one thousand grant programs and access to approximately $500 billion in annual awards. By registering once on this site, your organization can apply for grants from twenty-six federal grant-making agencies.

Grants.gov allows you to electronically find and apply for grant opportunities as well as track your application. The website also offers free subscriptions for e-mail notifications of new grant postings.

You do not have to register with Grants.gov if you want only to find grant opportunities. However, if you want to apply for a grant, you and your organization must complete the Grants.gov registration process, which takes three to five business days to complete. Most colleges and universities are registered on Grants.gov and have an Authorized Organization Representative (AOR). There may be more than one AOR for an organization. Check with your institution's grants office before beginning the registration process.

Once you have gained access to Grants.gov's home page (www.grants .gov) click "Find Grant Opportunities" to perform a search. Then follow the instructions on the screen. A basic search can be conducted using key words, the funding opportunity number, or the *CFDA* number. In the sample search (exhibit 11.2), the grantseeker performed a basic key word search for programs related to high school dropout prevention. The key word used was "dropout." Search results are shown in exhibit (11.3). By clicking one of the programs listed on the search results, the grantseeker can retrieve a synopsis of the grant opportunity (see exhibit 11.4), as well as

- links to the full announcement contained in either the *Federal Register* or one of the grant-making agency's publications, and
- application instructions.

In this particular example, clicking on "Full Announcement" will bring you to the full-text announcement in the *Federal Register.*

Catalog of Federal Domestic Assistance

The *Catalog of Federal Domestic Assistance (CFDA)* is another valuable resource for searching through available competitive and discretionary grant

TABLE 11.1
Federal Research Tools Table

Name	Description	Where to Get It
Grants.gov	Central storehouse for information on more than one thousand federal grant programs and access to $500 billion in annual awards (see sample entry)	Free online access at http://www.grants.gov
Catalog of Federal Domestic Assistance (CFDA)	A database of all federal programs created by law (see sample entry)	Free online access at http://www.cfda.gov If you wish to purchase a hard copy, call the U.S. Government Printing Office (GPO) at (202) 512-1800 in the DC metro area or toll-free at (866) 512-1800, or order from GPO's online bookstore at http://bookstore .gpo.gov. A hard copy can also be found at federal depository libraries throughout the United States (see below).
Federal Register	Official news publication for the federal government; makes public all meetings, announcements of granting programs, regulations, and deadlines (see sample entry)	Free online access at http://www.gpoaccess.gov/fr/index .html. A hard copy can found at federal depository libraries throughout the United States (see below).
FedBizOpps (Federal Business Opportunities)	This government database lists notices of proposed government procurement actions, contract awards, sales of government property, and other procurement information.	Free online access at http://www.fbo.gov.
Federal Depository Libraries	Public and university libraries that allow free access to government publications like the *CFDA*, *Federal Register*, and the *Congressional Record*.	To locate a library near you, visit http://www.gpoaccess .gov/libraries.html.

(continued)

TABLE 11.1
(*Continued*)

Name	Description	Where to Get It
Congressional Record	Day-to-day proceedings and debates of the Senate and the House of Representatives, including all grant program money appropriated by Congress. Published daily when Congress is in session.	Free online access at http://www.gpoaccess.gov/crecord/index.html.
		If you wish to purchase a hard copy, annual subscription you can do so by calling the U.S. Government Printing Office (GPO) at (202)512-1800 in the DC metro area or toll-free at (866)512-1800, or order from GPO's online bookstore at http://bookstore.gpo.gov.
		A hard copy is also available at federal depository libraries (see above).
Federal Staff Directory	Directory providing names, titles, telephone numbers, and e-mail addresses of senior and mid-level government officials in the executive office of the president, all cabinet-level federal departments, quasi-governmental agencies, U.S. Congress, and the federal court system	Fee-based print subscription available. Contact : CQ Press 2300 N Street NW, Suite 800 Washington, D.C., 20037 (866)427-7737, toll-free (202)729-1900, in the DC metro area
Agency Newsletters, Publications, RFPs, and Guidelines	Many federal agencies publish newsletters to inform you about the availability of funds and program accomplishments. You may also request application materials, guidelines, and so on.	Or order online version at http://www.cqpress.com. Usually free online availability from agency. See "Regulations, Guidelines, and Literature" in the *CFDA* entry.

EXHIBIT 11.2
Sample Search Grants.gov

opportunities. The primary purpose of the *Catalog* is to assist users in identifying programs that meet specific objectives of the potential applicant and to obtain general information on federal assistance programs.

The website www.cfda.gov is the primary means of disseminating the *Catalog*. However, the Government Printing Office continues to print and sell hardcopies of the *CFDA* to interested buyers. For information about purchasing the *CFDA* from the GPO, call (202) 512-1800 or toll-free at (866) 512-1800, or you may reach GPO's online bookstore at bookstore.gpo.gov.

The print edition of the *Catalog* contains seven indexes that can be used to help you identify your specific areas of program interest more efficiently. They are as follows:

- Agency Index Summary: Provides a description of the functions and activities of federal agencies responsible for administering programs in the *Catalog*.
- Agency Program Index: Lists all programs in the *Catalog* in numerical order by the five-digit program identification number, the program title, the federal agency responsible for administering the program, and

EXHIBIT 11.3
Grants.gov Search Results

GRANTS.GOV™

Contact Us   SiteMap   Help   RSS   Home

Home > Find Grant Opportunities > Search Grant Opportunities > Search Results

FOR APPLICANTS

Applicant Login

Find Grant Opportunities

Basic Search

Browse by Category

Browse by Agency

Advanced Search

Email Subscription

Get Registered

Apply for Grants

Track My Application

Applicant Resources

Search FAQs, User Guides and Site Information

APPLICANT SYSTEM-TO-SYSTEM

FOR GRANTORS

ABOUT GRANTS.GOV

HELP

CONTACT US

SITE MAP

Search Results

New Search

Sort: Relevance, Descending   Sort by Open Date   Sort by Relevance   Results 1 - 20 of 73

Close Date	Opportunity Title	Agency	Funding Number	Attachment
09/29/2010	Providing a Comprehensive Continuum of HIV/AIDS Care and Treatment Services in the Democratic Republic of Congo Under the President's Emergency Plan for AIDS Relief (PEPFAR)	Centers for Disease Control and Prevention	CDC-RFA-PS10-10132	Billing Code: , Billing Code: , Billing Code: ,
09/29/2009	Recovery Act - Pathways Out of Poverty	Employment and Training Administration	SGA-DFA-PY-08-19	Federal Register /Vol. 74, No. 139/Wednesday, July 22, 2009 ... , DEPARTMENT OF LABOR , Federal Register /Vol. 74, No. 156/Friday, August 14, 2009/Notices , Federal Register /Vol. 74, No. 120/Wednesday, June 24, 2009 ... , Federal Register /Vol. 74, No. 156/Friday, August 14, 2009/Notices ,
04/22/2010	OJJDP FY 10 Multi-State Mentoring Initiative	Office of Juvenile Justice Delinquency Prevention	OJJDP-2010-2547	OJJDP FY 2010 Multi-State Mentoring Initiative , OJJDP FY 2010 Multi-State Mentoring Initiative ,
09/07/2010	DoD PH/TBI Cognitive Rehabilitation For Traumatic Brain Injury Clinical Trial Award	Dept. of the Army -- USAMRAA	W81XWH-10-PH-TBI-RP-CR-CTA	Program Announcement , Program Announcement ,
06/02/2010	APHIAplus- PROGRAM DESCRIPTION	Kenya USAID-Nairobi	RFA-623-10-000009	USAID/KENYA FIVE YEAR IMPLEMENTATION FRAMEWORK FOR THE HEALTH ... , PROGRAM DESCRIPTION ,
08/03/2010	DoD Chiropractic Clinical Trial Award	Dept. of the Army -- USAMRAA	W81XWH-10-DHP-CCTA	Program Announcement , Program Announcement ,
07/28/2010	Office of Elementary and Secondary Education (OESE): High School Graduation Initiative CFDA Number 84.360	Department of Education	ED-GRANTS-061810-002	Federal Register /Vol. 75, No. 117/Friday, June 18, 2010/Notices ,
01/08/2010	Youth Education Program	Morocco USAID-Rabat	USAID-MOROCCO-608-10-002	Morocco Out-of-School Youth Education Project , SECTION A - GRANT APPLICATION FORMAT , APPLICATION FOR ,
08/02/2010	Race To The Top Fund CFDA Number 84.395A	Department of Education	ED-GRANTS-111809-002	Department of Education , Department of Education ,
05/14/2009	Suicide Prevention and Counseling Research (SPCR)	Dept. of the Army -- USAMRAA	W81XWH-08-MOMRP-SPCR2	Program Announcement , Program Announcement , Program Announcement ,
01/26/2010	AmeriCorps State and National Grants - FY 2010	Corporation for National and Community Service	CNCS-GRANTS-10062009-001	2010 AmeriCorps State and National APPLICATION INSTRUCTIONS , 1 Notice of Federal Funding Opportunity Overview Federal Agency ... , 2010 AmeriCorps State and National IONS APPLICATION

EXHIBIT 11.4
Grants.gov Opportunity Synopsis

GRANTS.GOV℠

Contact Us   SiteMap   Help   RSS   Home

Home > Find Grant Opportunities > Search Grant Opportunities > Search Results > Synopsis

FOR APPLICANTS

Applicant Login

Find Grant Opportunities

Basic Search

Browse by Category

Browse by Agency

Advanced Search

Email Subscription

Get Registered

Apply for Grants

Track My Application

Applicant Resources

Search FAQs, User Guides and Site Information

APPLICANT SYSTEM-TO-SYSTEM

FOR GRANTORS

ABOUT GRANTS.GOV

HELP

CONTACT US

SITE MAP

Office of Elementary and Secondary Education (OESE): High School Graduation Initiative CFDA Number 84.360

Synopsis	Full Announcement	Application

The synopsis for this grant opportunity is detailed below, following this paragraph. This synopsis contains all of the updates to this document that have been posted as of **06/21/2010** . If updates have been made to the opportunity synopsis, update information is provided below the synopsis.

If you would like to receive notifications of changes to the grant opportunity click send me change notification emails . The only thing you need to provide for this service is your email address. No other information is requested.

Any inconsistency between the original printed document and the disk or electronic document shall be resolved by giving precedence to the printed document.

Document Type:	Grants Notice
Funding Opportunity Number:	ED-GRANTS-061810-002
Opportunity Category:	Discretionary
Posted Date:	Jun 21, 2010
Creation Date:	Jun 21, 2010
Original Closing Date for Applications:	Jul 28, 2010 Applications Available: June 18, 2010. Deadline for Notice of Intent to Apply: July 7, 2010. We will be able to develop a more efficient process for reviewing grant applications if we have a better understanding of the number of entities that intend to apply for funding. Therefore, we strongly encourage each potential applicant to send a notification of its intent to apply for funding to hsgi@ed.gov by July 7, 2010. The notification of intent to apply for funding is optional. Applicants that do not supply this e-mail notification may still apply for funding. Deadline for Transmittal of Applications: July 28, 2010.
Current Closing Date for Applications:	Jul 28, 2010 Applications Available: June 18, 2010. Deadline for Notice of Intent to Apply: July 7, 2010. We will be able to develop a more efficient process for reviewing grant applications if we have a better understanding of the number of entities that intend to apply for funding. Therefore, we strongly encourage each potential applicant to send a notification of its intent to apply for funding to hsgi@ed.gov by July 7, 2010. The notification of intent to apply for funding is optional. Applicants that do not supply this e-mail notification may still apply for funding. Deadline for Transmittal of Applications: July 28, 2010.
Archive Date:	Aug 27, 2010
Funding Instrument Type:	Grant
Category of Funding Activity:	Education
Category Explanation:	
Expected Number of Awards:	50
Estimated Total Program Funding:	$45,000,000
Award Ceiling:	$3,000,000
Award Floor:	
CFDA Number(s):	84.360 -- School Dropout Prevention Program
Cost Sharing or Matching Requirement:	No

(*continued*)

EXHIBIT 11.4
(*Continued*)

Eligible Applicants

Others (see text field entitled "Additional Information on Eligibility" for clarification)

Additional Information on Eligibility:

Eligibility Information 1. Eligible Applicants: (a) SEAs to support activities in-- (i) schools that-- (A) serve students in grades 6 through 12; and (B) have annual school dropout rates that are above the State average annual school dropout rate; or (ii) middle schools that feed students into schools that serve students in grades 6 through 12 and have annual school dropout rates that are above the State average annual school dropout rate. (b) LEAS that operate-- (i) schools that-- (A) serve students in grades 6 through 12; and (B) have annual school dropout rates that are above the State average annual school dropout rate; or (ii) middle schools that feed students into schools serve students in grades 6 through 12 and that have annual school dropout rates that are above the State average annual school dropout rate. Note: Applicants must identify the specific schools that will receive project services and provide evidence that, using the most recent available data, those schools serve students in grades 6 through 12, and have annual school dropout rates that are above the State average annual school dropout rate or are middle schools that feed students into schools that serve students in grades 6 through 12 and that have annual school dropout rates that are above the State average annual school dropout rate.

Agency Name

Department of Education

Description

Note: Each funding opportunity description is a synopsis of information in the Federal Register application notice. For specific information about eligibility, please see the official application notice. The official version of this document is the document published in the Federal Register. Free Internet access to the official edition of the Federal Register and the Code of Federal Regulations is available on GPO Access at: http://www.access.gpo.gov/nara/index.html. Please review the official application notice for pre-application and application requirements, application submission information, performance measures, priorities and program contact information. Purpose of Program: The High School Graduation Initiative (formerly known as the School Dropout Prevention (SDP) program) awards grants to local educational agencies (LEAs) and State educational agencies (SEAs) to support the implementation of effective, sustainable, and coordinated dropout prevention and reentry programs in schools that serve students in grades 6 through 12 and that have event dropout rates that are above the State average event dropout rate or are middle schools that feed students into such schools.\1\ ---- -- \1\ According to the National Center for Education Statistics (NCES), in the 2007-08 school year, the most recent school year for which data are available, the national event dropout rate for public high schools in the 49 reporting States and the District of Columbia was 4.1 percent. The rate ranged from 1.7 percent in Indiana and New Jersey to 7.5 percent in Louisiana. Twenty-six States had event dropout rates for public high schools of 4 percent or less; four States had event dropout rates for public high schools of 6 percent or more (Stillwell, R. (2010). Public School Graduates and Dropouts From the Common Core of Data: School Year 2007-08 (NCES 2010-341)). -- Catalog of Federal Domestic Assistance (CFDA) Number: 84.360. Applications for grants under the High School Graduation Initiative--CFDA Number 84.360 must be submitted electronically using e-Application, accessible through the Department's e-Grants Web site at: http://e-grants.ed.gov. While completing your electronic application, you will be entering data online that will be saved into a database. You may not e-mail an electronic copy of a grant application to us.

Link to Full Announcement

Office of Elementary and Secondary Education (OESE): High School Graduation Initiative CFDA Number 84.360; Notice Inviting Applications for New Awards for Fiscal Year (FY) 2010

If you have difficulty accessing the full announcement electronically, please contact:

Julius Cotton
ED Grants.gov FIND Systems Admin.
Phone 202-245-6140
julius.cotton@ed.gov
Program Manager:
Theda Zawaiza
U.S. Department of Education
400 Maryland Avenue, SW., room 3E122
Washington, DC 20202
Telephone: (202) 205-3783 or by e-mail: e-Mail: Program Mailbox

whether the program offers financial assistance, no financial assistance, or a combination of both.

- Functional Index Summary: Groups programs into twenty basic functional categories, such as agriculture, education, health, and so on, and 176 subcategories that further identify specific areas of interest.
- Subject Index: The most commonly used index that provides a detailed listing of programs by various topics, popular name, general functional terms, categories of services, and selected beneficiaries.
- Applicant Eligibility Index: Allows you to look up a program to see whether you are eligible to apply. Because you must already know of the program to use this index, it is not a great help in identifying sources.
- Deadlines Index: Enables you to look up the deadline dates for programs to see whether the programs have a single or multiple deadline system.
- Authorization Index: Indexes the laws creating the funding.

Users should also be aware of the other sections of the *Catalog* that provide valuable information, such as

- programs added and deleted since the last edition of the *Catalog,*
- a crosswalk of changes to program numbers and titles,
- regional and local offices,
- intergovernmental review requirements,
- definitions of the types of assistance under which programs are administered, and
- a guide to proposal writing.

Using the CFDA *on the Internet*

Once you have gained access to the *CFDA*'s website, enter a key word or number in the "Find Programs" section to the right of the page. Then click "Search." In the sample search (exhibit 11.5), the grantseeker is again interested in high school dropout prevention and performed a key word search again using the term "dropout." Search results are shown in exhibit 11.6. By clicking on one of the programs listed on the search results, the grantseeker can retrieve a *CFDA* entry describing the program.

Reading the CFDA *Entry*

The sample *CFDA* entry (see exhibit 11.7) has been included to show the information provided in this valuable resource. All program descriptions/entries contain the following basic information.

EXHIBIT 11.5
Sample Search *Catalog of Federal Domestic Assistance (CFDA)*

| Home | Programs | Agencies | Regional Agency Offices | General Info | Privacy |

Search now! You do not need an account to search the catalog and view Federal assistance programs.

*CFDA contains detailed program descriptions for **2,075** Federal assistance programs. The following chart shows the program distribution for the top five issuing agencies.*

Keyword or Program Number
dropout

Select Assistance Type...

SEARCH

403	Department of Health and Human Services
238	Department of Agriculture
206	Department of the Interior
171	Department of Education
129	Department of Justice

Last updated July 12, 2010

Advanced Search Form
Find Programs by Number
Find Programs by Agency
Added Programs (since last publication date)

Download CFDA 2009 Print Edition

Catalog of Federal Domestic Assistance (CFDA) provides a full listing of all Federal programs available to State and local governments (including the District of Columbia); federally-recognized Indian tribal governments; Territories (and possessions) of the United States; domestic public, quasi- public, and private profit and nonprofit organizations and institutions; specialized groups; and individuals.

Download the CFDA User Guide (PDF format)

Click here *if you are responsible for managing CFDA program data.*

Login Here

Frequently Asked Questions
Search Historical Index
Federal Service Desk
CFDA 2009 Print Edition
CFDA 2008 Print Edition
Writing Grant Proposals
Types of Assistance
Overview of CFDA
LoanBenefits
GovBenefits
OMB Circular A-133 Compliance Supplement
Integrated Acquisition Environment
Federal Business Opportunities
Grants.gov
Recovery.gov
Whitehouse.gov/recovery/

User Guide   For Help: Federal Service Desk   Accessibility

Program Number and Title: Each program in the *Catalog* is preceded by a five-digit program identification number. The first two digits identify the federal department or agency that administers the program, and the last three numbers identify that agency's program. The numbers are assigned in a numerical sequence. The program title is the descriptive name given to a program. The popular name is the less descriptive name by which programs are commonly known.

EXHIBIT 11.6
CFDA Search Results

Agency: This is the branch of government administering the program, which is not much help to you except as general knowledge or for looking up programs and agencies in the *United States Government Manual.*

Authorization: You need this information to fill out some program applications or to look up the testimony and laws creating the funding (for the hard-core researcher and grantseeker only).

Objectives: Compare these general program objectives to your project. Do not give up if you are off the mark slightly; contact with the funding source may uncover new programs, changes, or hidden agendas.

Types of Assistance: Review and record the general type of support from this source, and then compare the information to your project definition.

EXHIBIT 11.7
Sample *CFDA* Entry

 School Dropout Prevention Program
Number: 84.360
Agency: Department of Education
Office: Office of Elementary and Secondary Education

PROGRAM INFORMATION

Authorization (040):

Elementary and Secondary Education Act of 1965, as amended, Title I, Part H.

Objectives (050):

To support effective, sustainable and coordinated dropout prevention and reentry programs in high schools with annual dropout rates that exceed their state average annual dropout rate. Middle schools that have students who continue on to these high schools are also supported.

Types of Assistance (060):

PROJECT GRANTS

Uses and Use Restrictions (070):

Grant recipients must implement proven strategies for reducing the number of students who drop out before completing secondary school and for assisting youth to reenter school after they have dropped out. These strategies may include: (1) identify students at risk of dropping out; (2) providing at-risk students with services designed to prevent them from dropping out; (3) identifying and encouraging youth who already have dropped out to reenter school; and (4)implementing other comprehensive approach. Specifically authorized activities may include: professional development; reduction in pupil-teacher ratios; counseling and mentoring for at-risk students; and implementing comprehensive school reform models.

Eligibility Requirements (080)

Applicant Eligibility (081):
State educational agencies (SEAs) and local educational agencies (LEAs) serving communities with dropout rates above the State's average annual dropout rate are eligible to apply for funding.

Beneficiary Eligibility (082):
School administrators, teachers, students, and parents are beneficiaries.

Credentials/Documentation (083):
Information to support annual dropout rate calculations. This program is excluded from coverage under OMB Circular No. A-87.

Application and Award Process (090)

Preapplication Coordination (091):

EXHIBIT 11.7
(Continued)

Preapplication coordination is required. Environmental impact information is not required for this program. This program is eligible for coverage under E.O. 12372, "Intergovernmental Review of Federal Programs." An applicant should consult the office or official designated as the single point of contact in his or her State for more information on the process the State requires to be followed in applying for assistance, if the State has selected the program for review.

Application Procedures (092):
This program is excluded from coverage under OMB Circular No. A-102. This program is excluded from coverage under OMB Circular No. A-110. Applications must be prepared and submitted in accordance with the notice published in the Federal Register. By the due date, eligible applicants must submit to the Department of Education, Application Control Center, a complete application that addresses the purposes of the program, the selection criteria, and includes all required assurances and signatures. Required assurances and certifications include: Group Application Certification (if applicable); Assurances for Non-Construction Programs (SF 422B); Certification regarding Lobbying, Debarment; Suspension and Other Responsibility Matter, and Drug-Free Workplace Requirements (ED Form 80- 0013); Disclosure of Lobbying Activities (SF LLL) (if applicable); Response to Notice to All Applicants (Section 427, GEPA). Applications should also include a Cover Page (SF424); the required Budget Form (ED Form 524); an itemized budget and other budget information; proof of eligibility; a project abstract; and a program narrative that includes responses to the selection criteria. Applicants are encouraged to submit (1) one original and (2) copies of their application.

Award Procedure (093):
The Department of Education notifies successful applicants of awards. Actual negotiations and awarding of grants is done by the Department's Grants and Contracts Service, in cooperation with the program staff. Contact the program office for more information.

Deadlines (094):
Contact the headquarters or regional office, as appropriate, for application deadlines.

Range of Approval/Disapproval Time (095):
Approximately 8-12 weeks.

Appeals (096):
Not Applicable.

Renewals (097):
Continuation funding is dependent upon future program appropriations, and demonstrated substantial progress toward meeting their goals and objectives.

Assistance Consideration (100)

Formula and Matching Requirements (101):
Statutory formulas are not applicable to this program.
Matching requirements are not applicable to this program.
MOE requirements are not applicable to this program.

Length and Time Phasing of Assistance (102):

(continued)

EXHIBIT 11.7
(*Continued*)

Grants are awarded for a period of not more than three years. Continuation awards are dependent on the availability of funding. See the following for information on how assistance is awarded/released: Electronic transfer.

Post Assistance Requirements (110)

Reports (111):
Grantees must submit performance reports annually. The program office will establish a due date. Final performance reports must be submitted within 90 days after the end of the grant award period. Cash reports are not applicable. Progress reports are not applicable. Expenditure reports are not applicable. Performance monitoring is not applicable.

Audits (112):
In accordance with the provisions of OMB Circular No. A-133 (Revised, June 27, 2003), "Audits of States, Local Governments, and Non-Profit Organizations," nonfederal entities that expend financial assistance of $500,000 or more in Federal awards will have a single or a program-specific audit conducted for that year. Nonfederal entities that expend less than $500,000 a year in Federal awards are exempt from Federal audit requirements for that year, except as noted in Circular No. A-133.

Records (113):
Records must be maintained for three years after the fiscal year in which the expenditure was made by the grantee, or until the grantee is notified of the completion of the Federal fiscal audit. In all cases of audit questions, records must be maintained until resolution has occurred.

Financial Information (120)

Account Identification (121):
91-0204-0-1-501.

Obligations (122):
(Project Grants) FY 09 not reported.; FY 10 est $50,000,000; FY 11 est not reported.

Range and Average of Financial Assistance (123):
No Data Available.

Program Accomplishments (130):
Fiscal Year 2009: No Current Data Available Fiscal Year 2010: No Current Data Available Fiscal Year 2011: No Current Data Available

Regulations, Guidelines, and Literature (140):
Education Department General Administrative Regulations (EDGAR), Parts 74, 75, 77, 79, 80, 81, 82, 85, 86, 97, 98, and 99. For further guidance and other information, contact the program office.

Information Contacts (150)

Regional or Local Office (151) :

EXHIBIT 11.7
(*Continued*)

None.

Headquarters Office (152):
Theda Zawaiza, Department of Education, OESE, 400 Maryland Ave., S.W. Room 3E122, Washington, District of Columbia 20202 Email: theda.zawaiza@ed.gov Phone: (202) 205-3783.

Website Address (153):
http://www.ed.gov/programs/dropout/index.html.

Related Programs (160):
Not Applicable.

Examples of Funded Projects (170):
Fiscal Year 2009: No Current Data Available Fiscal Year 2010: No Current Data Available Fiscal Year 2011: No Current Data Available

Criteria for Selecting Proposals (180):
Selection criteria are contained in the program guidelines. Contact the program office for more information.

Use and Use Restrictions: Compare your project to this description of the potential uses for the assistance provided to meet stated objectives, and the specific restrictions placed upon the use of the funds.

Eligibility Requirements: Be sure your organization is designated as a legal recipient (applicant eligibility). If it is not, find an organization of the type designated and apply as a consortium or under a cooperative arrangement. Determine whether your project can benefit those that the program is intended to benefit (beneficiary eligibility). Make sure you have the credentials or documentation required prior to, or along with, your application for assistance (credentials/documentation).

Application and Award Process: This section includes information on preapplication coordination, application procedure, award procedure, deadlines, range of approval or disapproval time, appeals, and renewals. Review this information and record it on your federal grants research form. Do not let the deadline data bother you. If the award cycle has passed, you should still contact the agency and position yourself for the following year by requesting copies of old applications and a list of current grantees and by asking to be a reviewer.

Assistance Considerations: This includes information on formula and matching requirements. It also includes a section describing the time period during which the assistance is normally available, whether there are many restrictions placed on the time permitted to use the funds awarded, and the time of the disbursements of the assistance, for example, lump sum, annually, quarterly, or as required. Record any information on any match you are required to provide. This will be useful in evaluating funding sources. Matching requirements may eliminate some funding sources from your consideration because your organization may not have any resources available for this purpose. In addition, assistance considerations will help you develop your project planner (see chapter 13). When you know about matching requirements in advance, you can identify what resources your organization will be required to provide. Watch for confusing comments such as this: "a match is not required, but is advised." You must find out from past grantees if this suggested match was actually a prerequisite.

Post Assistance Requirements: This section provides you with report, audit, and record requirements.

Financial Information: This section includes account identification, obligations, and range and average of financial assistance. It gives you an idea of what funds the agency program may have received, but do not take the information here as the last word. One entry I reviewed said the funding agency had $3 million for research. When contacted, the agency had over $30 million to disseminate under the program described and similar ones in the *CFDA*. Refer to the entry, but investigate it further.

Program Accomplishments: This section provides you with information on how many and what types of projects were funded during the past fiscal year and the current fiscal year, and includes projections for the coming fiscal year. The focus of this section is on program output, results achieved, and/or services rendered.

Regulations, Guidelines, and Literature: Download any materials that appear useful. Record and send for any information you can get on the funder.

Information Contacts: This section includes information on the contact at the regional or local office as well as the headquarters office. Record and use this information to begin contacting funders as outlined later in this book. If provided, note the name, phone number, and e-mail address of the contact person. While the contact person, phone number, or e-mail address may have changed, you will at least have a place to start.

Related Programs: Some *CFDA* entries include suggestions of other programs that are similar or related to your area of interest. This is like a free redefinition. While these suggestions are usually obvious, you may not have already uncovered the programs in your research. Therefore, review this section for leads.

Examples of Funded Projects: Compare your project with those listed and ask yourself how your project fits in.

Criteria for Selecting Proposals: Review and record the information here. Criteria are frequently listed with no regard to their order of importance and lack any reference to the point values they will be given in the review. Therefore, you should also obtain the rules from the *Federal Register*, agency publications, or a past reviewer.

Selecting the Best Funding Program

After you've reviewed the *CFDA* entries, select the best government funding program for your project. Contact the federal agency by using the information listed under "Information Contacts." Once you have found an assistance program you wish to apply for, follow the directions contained within that program. Each program is unique and has its own requirements and procedures. Unlike Grants.gov, you cannot apply for an assistance program on the *CFDA* website.

When researching federal grant opportunities it is necessary to search via both Grants.gov and the *CFDA*. These valuable resources sometimes use different key words (search terms). In addition, they sometimes categorize granting opportunities differently.

It is also necessary to look at both Grants.gov and the *CFDA* when searching for funding in the scientific fields. Again, funding opportunities are often categorized under different search terms. For example, when looking for grants in geophysics, one tool may list opportunities under the search term "geophysics," while the other may list geophysics opportunities under the search term "physics" and show no results under "geophysics."

Federal Register

The *Federal Register* is the official daily publication for rules, proposed rules, and notices of federal agencies and organizations, as well as exclusive orders and other presidential documents. Frequently requested materials from the *Federal Register* include grant information. However, not all funding agencies use the *Federal Register* as their public information vehicle. For instance, the National Science Foundation (NSF) and the National Institutes of Health (NIH) use their own agency publications to announce grant opportunities, program rules, and notices.

The *Register* can be accessed for free at www.gpoaccess.gov/fr/index.html. A hardcopy of this government publication is provided for free public use in federal depository libraries throughout the United States. Locate your nearest library by visiting www.gpoaccess.gov/libraries.html.

After you have used Grants.gov and/or the *CFDA* to select the best government funding program for your project, phone, fax, or e-mail the contact listed in the synopsis or entry to find out what vehicle the funding agency uses to post legal notices regarding its grant programs. If it is the *Federal Register*, find out the day(s) the *Federal Register* publishes notices, proposed rules, or final rules and regulations regarding the program you are interested in. Ask for the volume(s), the number(s), the issue date(s), and the page(s). The more information you have, the easier it will be for you to locate the information for which you are looking.

When accessing the *Federal Register* through the Internet, you can search online for the information you need. In the sample search shown in exhibit 11.8, the grantseeker asked to search the June 18, 2010, *Federal Register* for notices on page 34,716. Search results are shown in exhibit 11.9. By clicking on the second hit listed on the search results, the grantseeker retrieved the notice inviting applications for new awards for fiscal year 2010 under the High School Graduation Initiative CFDA No. 84.360 (see exhibit 11.10).

EXHIBIT 11.8
Sample Search *Federal Register*

EXHIBIT 11.9
Federal Register **Search Results**

The sample provided in exhibit 11.10 shows only pages 1 through 3 of this five-page, PDF-formatted notice. The notice in its entirety provides a full text of the announcement, including a funding opportunity description, award information, eligibility information, application and submission information, application review information, award administration information, agency contact information, and other miscellaneous information. However, contents of notices do vary.

As you can see in exhibit 11.8, "Notices" is not the only section of the *Federal Register* that can be searched. Grantseekers can also look at contents and preliminary pages, final rules and regulations, proposed rules, presidential documents, Sunshine Act meetings (before March 1, 1996), reader aids, and corrections.

EXHIBIT 11.10
Sample *Federal Register* Notice

Information Relay Service (FIRS) at 1–800–877–8339.

[FR Doc. 2010–14703 Filed 6–17–10; 8:45 am]

BILLING CODE 4000–01–P

DEPARTMENT OF EDUCATION

Office of Elementary and Secondary Education; Overview Information; High School Graduation Initiative; Notice Inviting Applications for New Awards for Fiscal Year (FY) 2010

Catalog of Federal Domestic Assistance (CFDA) Number: 84.360.

Dates:
Applications Available: June 18, 2010.
Deadline for Notice of Intent to Apply: July 7, 2010.
Deadline for Transmittal of Applications: July 28, 2010.

Full Text of Announcement

I. Funding Opportunity Description

Purpose of Program: The High School Graduation Initiative (formerly known as the School Dropout Prevention (SDP) program) awards grants to local educational agencies (LEAs) and State educational agencies (SEAs) to support the implementation of effective, sustainable, and coordinated dropout prevention and reentry programs in schools that serve students in grades 6 through 12 and that have event dropout rates that are above the State average event dropout rate or are middle schools that feed students into such schools.[1]

Priorities: This notice includes two priorities. In accordance with 34 CFR 75.105(b)(2)(v), Priority 1 is from the allowable activities specified in the statute (see section 1825(1) of the Elementary and Secondary Education Act of 1965, as amended (ESEA) (20 U.S.C. 6561d(1))). Priority 2 is from the notice of final priorities, requirements, definitions, and selection criteria for the SDP program, published in the **Federal Register** on July 8, 2005 (70 FR 39499) (2005 SDP program NFP).

Absolute Priorities: For FY 2010 and any subsequent year in which we make awards from the list of unfunded applicants from this competition, these priorities are absolute priorities. Under

[1] According to the National Center for Education Statistics (NCES), in the 2007–08 school year, the most recent school year for which data are available, the national event dropout rate for public high schools in the 49 reporting States and the District of Columbia was 4.1 percent. The rate ranged from 1.7 percent in Indiana and New Jersey to 7.5 percent in Louisiana. Twenty-six States had event dropout rates for public high schools of 4 percent or less; four States had event dropout rates for public high schools of 6 percent or more (Stillwell, R. (2010). Public School Graduates and Dropouts From the Common Core of Data: School Year 2007–08 (NCES 2010–341)).

34 CFR 75.105(c)(3) we consider only applications that meet these priorities. These priorities are:

Absolute Priority 1: Effective Early Identification, Prevention, and Intervention Programs.

This priority supports projects that propose to establish, enhance, or expand effective early intervention programs designed to identify at-risk students and prevent them from dropping out of school and encourage youth who have already dropped out of school to reenter school and complete their secondary education (20 U.S.C. 6561d(1)).

Absolute Priority 2: Collaboration with Other Agencies

Under this priority, an applicant must include in its application evidence that other public or private entities will be involved in, or provide financial support for, the implementation of the activities described in the application. Applicants may involve such State agencies as those responsible for administering postsecondary education, Title I of the Workforce Investment Act, Temporary Assistance for Needy Families, Medicaid, the State Children's Health Insurance Program, foster care, juvenile justice, and others. Applicants also may collaborate with business and industry, civic organizations, foundations, and community- and faith-based organizations, among other private-sector entities.

Acceptable evidence of collaboration is a memorandum of understanding or other document signed by the principal officer of each participating agency that identifies (1) how the agency will be involved in the implementation of the project or (2) the financial resources (cash or in-kind) that it will contribute to support the project, or both.

Definitions. In addition to the definitions in the authorizing statute and 34 CFR 77.1, the following definitions also apply to this program. These definitions are from the 2005 SDP program NFP.

High school dropout means an individual who—
(a) Was enrolled in a district in grades nine through 12 at some time during the preceding school year;
(b) Was not enrolled at the beginning of the current school year;
(c) Has not graduated or completed a program of studies by the maximum age established by a State;
(d) Has not transferred to another public school district, a nonpublic school, or a State-approved educational program; and

(e) Has not left school because of death, illness, or a school-approved absence.

State event dropout rate means the dropout rate calculated by dividing the number of high school dropouts (as defined elsewhere in this notice) in the State by the total number of students enrolled in grades 9 through 12 in public schools in the State during the current school year. This calculation is based upon the annual school event dropout rate calculation of the National Center for Education Statistics' Common Core of Data.

School event dropout rate means the dropout rate calculated by dividing the number of high school dropouts (as defined elsewhere in this notice) in a school by the total number of students enrolled in grades 9 through 12 in that school during the current school year.

Program Authority: 20 U.S.C. 6551 *et seq.* and the 2010 Consolidated Appropriations Act, Public Law 111–117.

Applicable Regulations: (a) The Education Department General Administrative Regulations (EDGAR) in 34 CFR parts 75, 77, 79, 80, 81, 82, 84, 85, 97, 98, and 99. (b) The notice of final priorities, requirements, definitions, and selection criteria for the SDP program, published in the **Federal Register** on July 8, 2005 (70 FR 39499).

II. Award Information

Type of Award: Discretionary grants.
Estimated Available Funds: $45,000,000.

Contingent upon the availability of funds and the quality of applications, we may make additional awards in FY 2011 from the list of unfunded applicants from this competition.

Estimated Range of Awards: $350,000–$3,000,000.

Estimated Average Size of Awards: $900,000.

Maximum Award: We will reject any application that proposes a budget exceeding $3,000,000 for a single budget period of 12 months. The Assistant Secretary for Elementary and Secondary Education may change the maximum amount through a notice published in the **Federal Register.**

Estimated Number of Awards: 50.

Note: The Department is not bound by any estimates in this notice.

Project Period: Up to 60 months.

III. Eligibility Information

1. *Eligible Applicants:*
(a) SEAs to support activities in—
(i) schools that—
(A) serve students in grades 6 through 12; and

EXHIBIT 11.10
(Continued)

(B) have annual school dropout rates that are above the State average annual school dropout rate; or

(ii) middle schools that feed students into schools that serve students in grades 6 through 12 and have annual school dropout rates that are above the State average annual school dropout rate.

(b) LEAS that operate—

(i) schools that—

(A) serve students in grades 6 through 12; or

(B) have annual school dropout rates that are above the State average annual school dropout rate; or

(ii) middle schools that feed students into schools serve students in grades 6 through 12 and that have annual school dropout rates that are above the State average annual school dropout rate.

Note: Applicants must identify the specific schools that will receive project services and provide evidence that, using the most recent available data, those schools serve students in grades 6 through 12, and have annual school dropout rates that are above the State average annual school dropout rate or are middle schools that feed students into schools that serve students in grades 6 through 12 and that have annual school dropout rates that are above the State average annual school dropout rate.

2. a. *Cost Sharing or Matching:* This program does not require cost sharing or matching.

b. *Supplement-Not-Supplant:* This program involves supplement-not-supplant funding requirements (*See* section 1823(b)(1)(F) of the ESEA (20 U.S.C. 6561b(b)(1)(F)). This restriction also has the effect of allowing projects to recover indirect costs only on the basis of a restricted indirect cost rate, according to the requirements in 34 CFR 75.563 and 34 CFR 76.564 through 76.569.

IV. Application and Submission Information

1. *Address to Request Application Package:* Theda Zawaiza, U.S. Department of Education, 400 Maryland Avenue, SW., room 3E122, Washington, DC 20202. *Telephone:* (202) 205–3783 or by *e-mail:* hsgi@ed.gov.

If you use a telecommunications device for the deaf (TDD), call the Federal Relay Service (FRS), toll free, at 1–800–877–8339.

Individuals with disabilities can obtain a copy of the application package in an accessible format (*e.g.,* braille, large print, audiotape, or computer diskette) by contacting the program contact person listed in this section.

2. *Content and Form of Application Submission:* Requirements concerning the content of an application, together

with the forms you must submit, are in the application package for this program.

Notice of Intent to Apply: July 7, 2010. We will be able to develop a more efficient process for reviewing grant applications if we have a better understanding of the number of entities that intend to apply for funding. Therefore, we strongly encourage each potential applicant to send a notification of its intent to apply for funding to hsgi@ed.gov by July 7, 2010. The notification of intent to apply for funding is optional. Applicants that do not supply this e-mail notification may still apply for funding.

Page Limit: The application narrative is where you, the applicant, address the selection criteria that reviewers use to evaluate your application. You must limit the application narrative to no more than 50 pages, using the following standards:

• A "page" is 8.5" x 11", on one side only, with 1" margins at the top, bottom, and both sides.

• Double space (no more than three lines per vertical inch) all text in the application narrative, including titles, headings, footnotes, quotations, references, and captions, as well as all text in charts, tables, figures, and graphs.

• Use a font that is either 12 point or larger or no smaller than 10 pitch (characters per inch).

• Use one of the following fonts: Times New Roman, Courier, Courier New, or Arial. An application submitted in any other font (including Times Roman or Arial Narrow) will not be accepted.

The page limit does not apply to the cover sheet; the budget section, including the narrative budget justification; the assurances and certifications; the one-page abstract, the resumes, the bibliography, or the letters of support. However, the page limit does apply to all of the application narrative section. We further encourage applicants to limit resumes to no more than three pages and all other attachments or appendices to no more than 20 pages.

Our reviewers will not read any pages of your application narrative that exceed the page limit.

3. *Submission Dates and Times:*

Applications Available: June 18, 2010.

Notice of Intent to Apply: July 7, 2010.

Deadline for Transmittal of Applications: July 28, 2010.

Applications for grants under this program must be submitted electronically using the Electronic Grant Application System (e-Application) accessible through the Department's e-

Grants site. For information (including dates and times) about how to submit your application electronically, or in paper format by mail or hand delivery if you qualify for an exception to the electronic submission requirement, please refer to section IV.7. *Other Submission Requirements* of this notice.

We do not consider an application that does not comply with the deadline requirements.

Individuals with disabilities who need an accommodation or auxiliary aid in connection with the application process should contact the person listed under **FOR FURTHER INFORMATION CONTACT** in section VII of this notice. If the Department provides an accommodation or auxiliary aid to an individual with a disability in connection with the application process, the individual's application remains subject to all other requirements and limitations in this notice.

4. *Intergovernmental Review:* This program is subject to Executive Order 12372 and the regulations in 34 CFR part 79. Information about Intergovernmental Review of Federal Programs under Executive Order 12372 is in the application package for this program.

5. *Funding Restrictions:* We reference regulations outlining funding restrictions in the *Applicable Regulations* section of this notice.

6. *Data Universal Numbering System Number, Taxpayer Identification Number, and Central Contractor Registry:* To do business with the Department of Education, (1) you must have a Data Universal Numbering System (DUNS) number and a Taxpayer Identification Number (TIN); (2) you must register both of those numbers with the Central Contractor Registry (CCR), the Government's primary registrant database; and (3) you must provide those same numbers on your application.

You can obtain a DUNS number from Dun and Bradstreet. A DUNS number can be created within one business day.

If you are a corporate entity, agency, institution, or organization, you can obtain a TIN from the Internal Revenue Service. If you are an individual, you can obtain a TIN from the Internal Revenue Service or the Social Security Administration. If you need a new TIN, please allow 2–5 weeks for your TIN to become active.

The CCR registration process may take five or more business days to complete. If you are currently registered with the CCR, you may not need to make any changes. However, please make certain that the TIN associated with your DUNS

(continued)

EXHIBIT 11.10
(*Continued*)

number is correct. Also note that you will need to update your CCR registration on an annual basis. This may take three or more business days to complete.

7. *Other Submission Requirements:* Applications for grants under this program must be submitted electronically unless you qualify for an exception to this requirement in accordance with the instructions in this section.

a. *Electronic Submission of Applications.*

Applications for grants under the High School Graduation Initiative— CFDA Number 84.360 must be submitted electronically using e-Application, accessible through the Department's e-Grants Web site at: *http://e-grants.ed.gov.*

We will reject your application if you submit it in paper format unless, as described elsewhere in this section, you qualify for one of the exceptions to the electronic submission requirement *and* submit, no later than two weeks before the application deadline date, a written statement to the Department that you qualify for one of these exceptions. Further information regarding calculation of the date that is two weeks before the application deadline date is provided later in this section under *Exception to Electronic Submission Requirement.*

While completing your electronic application, you will be entering data online that will be saved into a database. You may not e-mail an electronic copy of a grant application to us.

Please note the following:

• You must complete the electronic submission of your grant application by 4:30:00 p.m., Washington, DC time, on the application deadline date. E–Application will not accept an application for this program after 4:30:00 p.m., Washington, DC time, on the application deadline date. Therefore, we strongly recommend that you do not wait until the application deadline date to begin the application process.

• The hours of operation of the e-Grants Web site are 6:00 a.m. Monday until 7:00 p.m. Wednesday; and 6:00 a.m. Thursday until 8:00 p.m. Sunday, Washington, DC time. Please note that, because of maintenance, the system is unavailable between 8:00 p.m. on Sundays and 6:00 a.m. on Mondays, and between 7:00 p.m. on Wednesdays and 6:00 a.m. on Thursdays, Washington, DC time. Any modifications to these hours are posted on the e-Grants Web site.

• You will not receive additional point value because you submit your application in electronic format, nor will we penalize you if you qualify for an exception to the electronic submission requirement, as described elsewhere in this section, and submit your application in paper format.

• You must submit all documents electronically, including all information you typically provide on the following forms: the Application for Federal Assistance (SF 424), the Department of Education Supplemental Information for SF 424, Budget Information—Non-Construction Programs (ED 524), and all necessary assurances and certifications. You must attach any narrative sections of your application as files in a .DOC (document), .RTF (rich text), or .PDF (Portable Document) format. If you upload a file type other than the three file types specified in this paragraph or submit a password protected file, we will not review that material.

• Your electronic application must comply with any page limit requirements described in this notice.

• Prior to submitting your electronic application, you may wish to print a copy of it for your records.

• After you electronically submit your application, you will receive an automatic acknowledgment that will include a PR/Award number (an identifying number unique to your application).

• Within three working days after submitting your electronic application, fax a signed copy of the SF 424 to the Application Control Center after following these steps:

(1) Print SF 424 from e-Application.
(2) The applicant's Authorizing Representative must sign this form.
(3) Place the PR/Award number in the upper right hand corner of the hard-copy signature page of the SF 424.
(4) Fax the signed SF 424 to the Application Control Center at (202) 245–6272.

• We may request that you provide us original signatures on other forms at a later date.

Application Deadline Date Extension in Case of e-Application Unavailability: If you are prevented from electronically submitting your application on the application deadline date because e-Application is unavailable, we will grant you an extension of one business day to enable you to transmit your application electronically, by mail, or by hand delivery. We will grant this extension if—

(1) You are a registered user of e-Application and you have initiated an electronic application for this competition; and

(2) (a) E–Application is unavailable for 60 minutes or more between the hours of 8:30 a.m. and 3:30 p.m., Washington, DC time, on the application deadline date; or

(b) E–Application is unavailable for any period of time between 3:30 p.m. and 4:30:00 p.m., Washington, DC time, on the application deadline date.

We must acknowledge and confirm these periods of unavailability before granting you an extension. To request this extension or to confirm our acknowledgment of any system unavailability, you may contact either (1) the person listed elsewhere in this notice under **FOR FURTHER INFORMATION CONTACT** (*see* VII. Agency Contact) or (2) the e-Grants help desk at 1–888–336–8930. If e-Application is unavailable due to technical problems with the system and, therefore, the application deadline is extended, an e-mail will be sent to all registered users who have initiated an e-Application. Extensions referred to in this section apply only to the unavailability of e-Application.

Exception to Electronic Submission Requirement: You qualify for an exception to the electronic submission requirement, and may submit your application in paper format, if you are unable to submit an application through e-Application because—

• You do not have access to the Internet; or

• You do not have the capacity to upload large documents to e-Application; *and*

• No later than two weeks before the application deadline date (14 calendar days or, if the fourteenth calendar date before the application deadline date falls on a Federal holiday, the next business day following the Federal holiday), you mail or fax a written statement to the Department, explaining which of the two grounds for an exception prevents you from using the Internet to submit your application. If you mail your written statement to the Department, it must be postmarked no later than two weeks before the application deadline date. If you fax your written statement to the Department, we must receive the faxed statement no later than two weeks before the application deadline date.

Address and mail or fax your statement to: Theda Zawaiza, U.S. Department of Education, 400 Maryland Avenue, SW., room E3122, Washington, DC 20202. *Fax:* (202) 205–4921.

Your paper application must be submitted in accordance with the mail or hand delivery instructions described in this notice.

b. *Submission of Paper Applications by Mail.*

FedBizOpps

FedBizOpps (FBO) lists notices of proposed government procurement actions, contract awards, sales of government property, and other procurement information over $25,000—all updated daily. Thousands of separate contracting offices and numerous grant programs advertise billions in government contracts each year through FBO. These contracts may total hundreds of billions and are in addition to the $500 billion cited in Grants.gov. Currently you can search more than 31,700 active federal opportunities on FBO.

Many successful nonprofit organizations have used the list of successful bidders to develop subcontracts and form consortia that work with the successful bidder to perform some aspect of the contract cost effectively. In the process they develop a track record of successful performance that will provide the basis for their own successful bid in the future. Through subcontracts and consortia, these organizations are able to build a track record and gain familiarity with both the contracts process and federal contract offices. The FBO also advertises notices of meetings that assist bidders in developing insight into upcoming contracts. FedBizOpps is available online, free of charge, at www.fbo.gov.

Grants Databases

GrantSelect

GrantSelect is an online grants database that provides information on more than 13,000 funding opportunities available from state and federal governments, corporations, foundations, and associations. Subscriptions to the *GrantSelect* database allows unlimited access to all of the targeted segments offered: arts and humanities, biomedical and health care, children and youth, community and economic development, education, environment/energy/agriculture/animal, faith-based grants, international programs, minority populations, operating grants, research, and scholarships and fellowships. Subscriptions include an e-mail alerts service that will notify you immediately of new and changed records in its database. Pricing information for colleges and universities, libraries, K–12 schools/districts, municipalities, and nonprofit organizations is available online at grantselect.com. You can order online via *GrantSelect*'s web form or off-line by downloading the appropriate forms and sending or faxing the subscription order to:

ATTN: Accounts
Schoolhouse Partners
P.O. Box 2059
Nashville, IN 47448-2059
Fax: (812) 988-6479

BIG Online America

BIG Online (bigdatabase.com) is the flagship product of Metasoft Systems, Inc., a private corporation headquartered in Vancouver, British Columbia. It is a membership-based key word and field searchable database with detailed information and profiles on 25,000 American and Canadian foundations, corporate donors, matching gift programs, in-kind donations, and government grant makers. Membership also includes access to geographic giving analysis, funder news, searchable IRS form 990 information, writing resources, and a deadline calendar. *BIG Online* has recently released a new program called Director Connections. This is a mapping product designed to show users the diverse network of connections between foundations and the various boards their members sit on. It also offers Director Connections for Corporations. For membership information or to take a free online tour of *BIG Online* call (888) 638-2763 or e-mail info@bigdatabase.com.

Sponsored Programs Information Network (SPIN)

SPIN is a widely used funding opportunity database produced by InfoEd International, Inc. In fact, nearly five hundred institutions worldwide subscribe to *SPIN*. Originally developed by the Research Foundation of the State University of New York (SUNY), the database tracks the funding programs (e.g., research grants, fellowships, publication support, sabbatical support, curriculum development) of over 6,000 government, private, and nonprofit funding sources worldwide. *SPIN*'s search engine allows users to query the database with either basic key word or advanced Boolean searches. The *SPIN* service also includes SMARTS (the SPIN Matching and Research Transmittal Service), an automated alerts system that notifies investigators of new programs that match their research interests. *SPIN* is also integrated with InfoEd's proposal development module that generates electronic proposal templates that are preloaded with relevant sponsor and program details from *SPIN. GENIUS*, a CV/biosketch database, is also available through InfoEd. You can find more information about InfoEd's products and *SPIN* memberships by calling (800) 727-6427 or visiting www1.infoed.org.

Illinois Researcher Information Service (IRIS)

IRIS, a unit of the University of Illinois Library at Urbana-Champaign, offers colleges and universities three fee-based online funding and research services:

- IRIS Database, which is updated daily, contains over nine thousand federal and private funding opportunities in the sciences, social sciences, and arts and humanities. In addition to funding opportunities for faculty, the database also contains fellowships and scholarships for graduate students and undergraduates. Users can search IRIS by sponsor, deadline, date, key word, and other criteria.

- IRIS Alert Service, which allows subscribers to create their own IRIS search profiles and select their preferred frequency, delivery method (e-mail or web), and key words. The program runs the user's profile against the IRIS Database and delivers the search results automatically.
- IRIS Expertise Service, which enables researchers at subscribing institutions to create detailed electronic CVs (biosketches) and post them to a web-accessible database for viewing by colleagues at other institutions, program officers at federal and private funding agencies, and private companies. The biosketches can also be used in the electronic submission of grant proposals.

The IRIS office does not sell subscriptions to individual researchers. Subscriptions are available to colleges and universities for an annual subscription fee. You can try IRIS for two weeks by having a representative from your institution, such as your librarian, research officer, grants administrator, and so forth contact the IRIS office at (217) 333-9893. For more information about IRIS and IRIS subscriptions, visit www.library.illinois.edu/iris/.

Community of Science (COS)

Community of Science (COS) is a global registry of information about scientists and the funding of science and is designed to meet the needs of the research and development community. *COS* uses a broad definition of science and therefore provides information on a wide variety of granting programs including those in humanities, health, and education. The *COS* system includes the following:

- *COS* Funding Opportunities—a database of announcements for grants, fellowships, awards, and more, comprising more than 25,000 records worth over $33 billion.
- *COS* Funding Alert—a weekly e-mail notification with a customized list of funding opportunities based on specified criteria provided by the individual *COS* member.
- *COS* Expertise—a knowledge management system for individuals and institutions, containing more than 480,000 first-person profiles of researchers from over 1,600 institutions worldwide. *COS* users, including researchers, scholars, and other professionals with expertise in their

fields, have the opportunity to create profiles to showcase and share their research and expertise among researchers and scholars from universities, corporations, and nonprofits in more than 170 countries.

- *COS* Scholar Universe—a searchable, editorially controlled database of nearly two million published scholars in a variety of disciplines.
- *COS* Public View of Expertise (PVE)—a user-friendly interface to make selected information from an institution's research expertise available to key external constituencies and the general public.
- *COS* Workbench—an easy-to-use web workspace with many features to help you promote your work, manage your saved funding searches and tracked funding records, and maintain your resume or CV.

COS offers three types of memberships that provide a wide range of benefits; these types include individual researchers, universities and research institutions, and corporations. (For smaller nonprofits and nonresearch individuals, I suggest you involve university faculty and staff on your advisory committee and ask them to access *COS* and other grants-related resources for you.) For more information on *COS* and to contact its membership team, visit www.cos.com/.

Federal Agency Internet Mailing Lists

Several federal agencies have established Internet mailing lists to electronically disseminate news about their activities and services. Subscribing to these will help you keep up to date on federal funding opportunities. The following is a list of some of the federal agencies that provide this type of service.

- National Science Foundation: National Science Foundation Update, formerly MyNSF, allows you to receive e-mail notifications about new content posted on the NSF website. You can subscribe at service.govdelivery.com/service/multi_subscribe.html?code=USNSF&custom_id=823.
- National Institutes of Health: The National Institutes of Health (NIH) Office of Communications and Public Liaison offers a free e-mail subscription service that allows you to receive e-mail when new information is available. With a subscription profile, you get the updated information on the items of interest to you automatically without having to return to the website and check for changes. For instructions on how to sign up for these free NIH e-mail updates visit www.nih.gov/email.htm.
- Centers for Disease Control and Prevention (CDC): At the Centers for Disease Control and Prevention, you can subscribe to receive e-mail

alerts about new information related to your topics of interest. For a list of available topics, and to subscribe, go to www.cdc.gov/emailupdates/index.html.

- U.S. Department of Justice: *JustInfo*, sponsored by the U.S. Department of Justice National Criminal Justice Reference Service (NCJRS), is a biweekly newsletter containing information about new publications, funding and training opportunities, events, and web-based resources available from NCJRS federal sponsors. View previous issues and subscribe at www.ncjrs.org/justinfo/dates.html/.
- U.S. Department of Education (DOE): The Department of Education offers subscriptions to electronic mailing lists for several of its newsletters, including the following:
  - *EDInfo*: new teaching resources and ED grant opportunities
  - *ED Review*: biweekly update on ED activities
  - *Education Innovator*: promising innovations in education
  - *ED RSS*: daily feed of ED news, funding, and teaching resources
  - *IESNews*: education research, evaluation, and statistics
  - *Research e-News*: newsletter of the Institute of Education Sciences
  - *Thursday Notes*: technical assistance information, and adult education and literacy news
  - *Touching Base*: newsletter for the military community
  - *PreventionED*: updates on substance abuse and violence prevention education issues, legislation, and funding opportunities
  - *OVAE Connection*: research, evaluation, and technical assistance on career and technical education, adult education, and community colleges

  For links to these newsletters and instructions on how to subscribe to their electronic mailing lists, visit www.ed.gov/news/newsletters/.
- National Institute for Standards and Technology (NIST) provides NIST news releases and the *NIST Tech Beat* newsletter in an electronic format. *NIST Tech Beat* is a newsletter containing recent research results and other NIST news and is published biweekly. For links to NIST news releases and *NIST Tech Beat*, visit www.nist.gov/public_affairs.

Assessing the information you need to locate available government funding is not difficult or expensive. Whether you use the Internet, a commercial database, or hardcopies of government publications, the key to locating federal grant funds and to commanding the respect of the bureaucrats you will interact with in your quest for grants is to do your homework and learn all you can about each program you are thinking about approaching.

Now you must find the time to complete your search for federal grant opportunities. Review your action steps' chart to see where and when you can fit this task into your busy schedule. Review figure 11.1 and commit to a deadline.

FIGURE 11.1
Action Steps' Chart: Researching Federal Grant Opportunities

12

Contacting Government Grantors, Past Grantees, and Past Reviewers

A T THIS POINT YOU HAVE RESEARCHED several government grant programs and you can almost smell the grant money. But hold on for the most important step of all—contacting the federal program officer or state grants staff. Because government grants are based on tax revenues there are freedom of information laws that require transparency and public disclosure related to grant programs. However, information on state and local grantors may be difficult to obtain. You are now aware of the resources the Internet provides and the advantages that federal grantseeking has over state and local grantseeking with respect to locating grant opportunities. These same disparities will be encountered as you seek to apply the preproposal contact strategies that follow. This is not to say that the information you are encouraged to obtain is any less important or useful on state and local proposals. It just may not be possible to get. Try to follow the suggested strategies with *all* government grantors. Even if a state grant program does not have the information you need available, they will usually respect you for asking the right questions.

The following preproposal contact strategies are not intended to provide you with an unfair advantage over your competition. The information should be available to everyone. For example, it is imperative to have access to the grantor's priorities and the scoring rubric that the reviewers will use in evaluating and recommending proposals for funding. But I know from experience that some state grant programs develop their scoring system after the submittal deadline.

Do not be put off by my suggestion to contact grantors to augment your grants research even though many of my grant fellows have trouble with preproposal contact. They are awarded travel money and in some programs they are required to visit Washington, D.C., to meet with a program officer. Still, most hesitate and some even refuse to go. So I am not surprised that you may not be convinced of the importance of preproposal contact with a federal program officer, especially if you have bookmarked the program's website, registered, and already have its application form and guidelines. Like many other prospective grantseekers, you probably do not see the need to talk to government bureaucrats. However, you should remember that your goal is not to *apply* for a grant; it is to be *awarded* a grant. Therein lies the reason for making preproposal contact. In fact, after forty years in the grants field, I can assure you that the principal investigators and project directors who are consistently funded across the board, from health research to humanities, actually contact government grantors several times a year, and not just during the preproposal period.

Several years before the first edition of this book was created, a study of ten thousand federal grant applicants documented that those grantseekers who had made contact with federal program staff before submitting their applications experienced a threefold increase in success over those who simply submitted the application. The key to their success was the opportunity to ask questions that may not have been covered in the *Catalog of Federal Domestic Assistance (CFDA)* program descriptions or agency publications.

When the successful grantees were asked what they discussed with the federal program officers, many said they asked questions that helped them to more closely meet the program guidelines. While this was the most frequent response, I believe they really asked questions aimed at uncovering what the program was actually interested in funding.

You can meet with program officers at conferences and professional meetings, as well as in their offices. Ask them what conferences are on their calendars and if they are speaking on any panels. Go to their presentations and ask if you could have a few minutes alone with them to ask questions. Some agencies have regional meetings that may be less expensive for you to attend. No harm can come from asking, only good!

When contacting a program officer make no mistake about your intention. It is to confirm your grantor research and provide a more complete picture of what the grant program seeks to create and fund in your field. Your contact is professional, not personal. Even if you have very limited resources and no money for travel, do not be frustrated. While the study of ten thousand federal grantees was done years before e-mail was possible, it revealed no differences between telephone and face-to-face contact. The crucial point is that while you have done your homework, you need to make preproposal contact to confirm what you do know and to find out more about the projects funded, how the submitted proposals will be evaluated, and by whom in order to prepare a winning proposal.

When to Make Preproposal Contact

The timing of contact is critical. Each of the thousand-plus federal programs has a similar sequence of events related to its granting cycle. Review the diagram of the federal grants clock to help you determine where each of your prospective federal agency programs is in the grants process (see figure 12.1).

1. The first step involves the dissemination of information regarding the agency's grant opportunity and a request to the public to help the agency develop the rules that will govern the grant program. In subsequent program cycles, the request is made to comment on last year's rules. This process may entail developing proposed rules, interim rules, and final rules. With each request, interested prospective grantees are usually given thirty days to submit their comments on the rules. The comments are published, the final rules are printed, and the announcements of deadlines

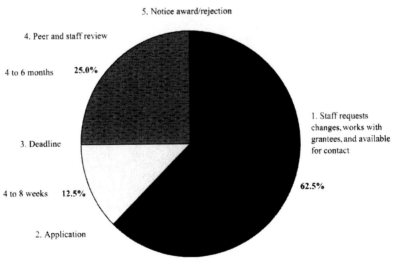

FIGURE 12.1
Federal Grants Clock

are made in such publications as the *Federal Register, NIH Guide,* and *National Science Foundation E-Bulletin.*

2. The federal program officer then develops the actual application package and places it on the agency's website for public access. This package is referred to as the Request for Proposal (RFP) or the Request for Application (RFA).

3. The deadline for submissions is published.

4. Once proposals have been submitted through Grants.gov they are forwarded to selected peer reviewers for evaluation. In some cases, the reviewers are required to go to a specified site to receive and review the proposals. In other cases, they may review them at home or in their offices. The reviewers must follow the agency's evaluation system and score each proposal according to the published guidelines. There is usually a staff review that follows the peer review. In all cases, the staff reviewers provide the head of the agency with a list of proposals recommended for funding. The actual decision to fund is made by the director of the agency (or staff) and usually reflects the peer-review score but changes may be made for other reasons. For example, I was once told by a granting staff person that if the top scorers were all in one state, the agency might fund a high-ranking proposal from another state to provide a more equitable geographic distribution. (However, this information was presented during a casual conversation and therefore the actual process or variables used by the agency cannot be confirmed.)

5. The notices of award and rejection are made and the cycle starts again. Some federal programs with multiple deadlines repeat the process in four- and six-month cycles.

Getting the Most from Past Grantees

You will find it beneficial to discover who has previously received funding by the program that interests you. In many cases you can locate a list of past grantees on the agency's website. You can use the sample e-mail in exhibit 12.1 to request a list of past grantees as well as guidelines and other relevant information. E-mail the contact person identified in your research or the program announcement. You may have to request the list of past grantees again by phoning the contact person. If you get his or her phone mail, leave a message about what you want and leave your phone number and your e-mail address. Access to this list and the valuable information it provides is your right. If you do not receive a response to your initial request, request the list again, making sure to let the funding source know why you want it and also that you

EXHIBIT 12.1
Sample E-mail to a Federal Agency Requesting List of Past Grantees, Guidelines, and Other Relevant Information

From: <grantseeker@proactive.edu>
To: <contactperson@feds.gov>
Cc:
Sent: Date, Time
Subject: Information Request

Dear [Contact Person]:

I am interested in receiving information on [*CFDA#*, Program Title]. Please email relevant web site information and Internet addresses for application forms, guidelines, etc.

In order to increase my understanding of your program, I would also appreciate a list of last year's grant recipients. If this list is available on the Internet please provide the address. If it is not, please email the list to me as an attachment.

Thank you for your assistance.

Name
Title
Organization/Institution
Address
Telephone Number

---

are aware that you are entitled to this list under the Freedom of Information Act. If all else fails, you may be able to get this information from the public information office of the agency, or you can ask your congressperson to get the list for you. By law, federal bureaucrats have to respond to a congressperson's request. He or she *will* get the list. Be aware, though, that bureaucrats may react negatively to the intervention of elected officials. Therefore, you should ask the elected official not to reveal for whom he or she is getting the list.

Several databases provide grantee information. For example, the *COS (Community of Science)* provides abstracts of grantees' proposals. NSF's Award Search provides abstracts that describe the research, the names of principal investigators, and their institutions. The FastLane server offers a list of Recent Awards, and the Budget Internet Information System provides summaries of award amounts by states, awardee institution, and NSF Directorate.

With your past grantee list in hand, you are now ready to begin the analysis of your chances for success. Place the information you have obtained on the

Past Grantee Analysis Worksheet (exhibit 12.2) and analyze the information contained in the list of grantees. When this worksheet is completed, you will be able to approach the grantor with knowledge and insight into its granting program. You may need to contact the program officer to get data on the number of applications. When you request information on the number of applications, let the program officer know you already have information on the number of awards. What you are trying to do is evaluate your chances of success by determining the overall success rate (number of applications versus number of awards).

Contacting a Past Grantee

Successful grant recipients can be approached and, while they are not required to, will generally share helpful information with you. Grantees will generally feel flattered that you called. By and large, they are not competing with you for funds because you will be seeking first-year funding and they will be seeking a continuation grant. Select a past grantee to contact. Choose one outside of your geographic area and one who is less likely to view you as a competitor. If you have a colleague at that grantee institution, contact him or her to help you connect with the principal investigator/project director. Tell the grantee how you got his or her name, congratulate him or her on the award, and then ask to speak to the person who worked on the proposal.

Ask the principal investigator/project director for a copy of his or her funded proposal. Assure them that you are just looking for a successful model to follow. You are interested in style, format, how they articulated the literature search, and how they developed the budget. For example, many proposal formats use their own vocabulary and seeing how a successful grantee arranged his or her winning proposal will be of great benefit to you. An example of a winning hypothesis and successful specific aims, primary objectives, methods, and protocols is much more useful to you than trying to interpret the guidelines and read between the lines.

I suggest you obtain at least two or three copies of funded proposals before you create yours. You are probably thinking that no one will share one, right? Well, you will be pleasantly surprised. I challenge my grant fellows on this matter all the time and I have never been proven wrong yet. One fellow sent an e-mail request for copies of funded proposals to five grant recipients as I instructed. He handpicked the five icons in his field to prove me wrong. To his amazement, three of the five responded within one week without even a follow-up request. One sent it in forty-eight hours and asked if the grantseeker would also like a copy of the reviewers' comments to increase his (the grantseeker's) insights into what the reviewers liked and disliked. Even

EXHIBIT 12.2
Past Grantee Analysis Worksheet

1. Applications
    • How many applications were received? _____
    • How many applications were funded? _____

2. Award Size
    • What was the largest award granted? _____
    • For what type of project? _____
    • For how many years? _____
    • What was the smallest award granted? _____
    • For what type of project? _____
    • For how many years? _____

3. Grantor Type
    • What characteristics or similarities can be drawn from last year's list of grant recipients?

    • What is the size and type of grantee organization (i.e., public, private, college)?

    • What are the geographic preferences or concentrations?

4. Project Director/Principal Investigator
    • What title or degrees appear most frequently on the list of last year's recipients?

    • Does there seem to be a relationship between award size and project director degree?

5. From the list of last year's grantees, select two to contact for more information. Select grantees that you may have a link with and/or organizations that you are familiar with.

6. Based on the information gathered in questions 1–4, rate how well your proposal idea matches the prospective grantor's profile.
    _____ very well   _____ good   _____ fair   _____ not well

7. What programs can you now ask the program officer/contact person about as a result of your analysis?

though the proposal was funded, some elements cost the grantee points and the reviewers wanted him to be aware of them so he would not make the same mistakes again.

I learned something from my fellow's experience. Now I always ask for a copy of the reviewers' comments in addition to a copy of the funded proposal.

You can also check with your organization's grants office to see if there have been any proposals submitted in the past to the agency/program you are interested in. If there are any, you should contact the principal investigator or project director to see if he or she would be willing to share a copy of the proposal and the reviewers' comments with you. It does not matter whether the proposal was accepted or rejected. You can learn from either scenario.

Remember, awarded federal and state proposals are public property. Rejected proposals are not public property and ownership is retained by the rejected grantee. Reviewing rejected proposals is still of value because you can compare them to the awarded ones and focus on the differences. However, when asking for copies of rejected proposals and reviewers' comments you should be extra polite and diplomatic and explain exactly why you are asking to see them.

Select a few questions from the following list to ask the person who worked on the proposal, or ask any other questions that will help you learn more about the funding source:

- Did you call or go to see the funding source before writing the proposal?
- Whom did you find most helpful on the funding source's staff?
- Did you use your advocates or congressperson?
- Did the funding source review your idea or proposal before submission?
- Did you use consultants to help you on the proposal?
- Was there a hidden agenda to the program's guidelines?
- When did you begin the process of developing your application?
- When did you first contact the funding source?
- What materials did you find most helpful in developing your proposal?
- Did the funding source come to see you (site visit) before or after the proposal was awarded? Who came? What did they wear? How old were they? Would you characterize them as conservative, moderate, or liberal? Did anything surprise you during their visit?
- How close was your initial budget to the awarded amount?
- Who on the funding source's staff negotiated the budget?
- How did you handle matching or in-kind contributions?
- What would you do differently next time?

Understanding the Proposal Review Process

To prepare the best possible proposal, you must know the background of who will be reviewing it and how it will be reviewed. Request information on the review process from the federal program officer. This can be done in writing, by phone, by e-mail, or in person. I suggest sending an e-mail and then following up with the other methods if necessary. Exhibit 12.3 provides a sample e-mail you may use.

You want a profile of last year's reviewers or criteria related to what the grantor looks for in a reviewer so you can write a proposal based on the reviewers' expertise, educational degrees, publications, and so forth.

EXHIBIT 12.3
Sample E-mail to a Federal Agency for Information on Reviewers and the Review Process

From:	\<grantseeker@proactive.edu\>
To:	\<contactperson@feds.gov\>
Cc:	
Sent:	Date, Time
Subject:	Request for List of Reviewers

Dear [Contact Person]:

I am presently developing a proposal under your _____ program. I would like information on the composition of your program's peer reviewers and the areas of expertise represented on the review committee. This information will help me prepare a quality proposal based upon the level of expertise, and diversity of the reviewers.

Information on the scoring rubric and process would also be helpful in that it would help me perform a quality circle or mock review of my proposal before submittal.

The information you provide will be appreciated and will help me produce a quality proposal.

Name
Title
Organization/Institution
Address
Phone Number
Fax Number

There is no harm in asking the program officer if you could observe a peer-review session as a learning experience. If you have the correct credentials/background to be a reviewer but lack the grant award experience, you could volunteer your services. Ask if you can submit your credentials and be of service to the program officer if there is ever a last-minute need for a reviewer. You could also ask the program officer if he or she could recommend a past reviewer you could talk with to increase your understanding of the process and avoid errors resulting in a rejected proposal. Inform the program officer that the information you gather from this contact will help you perform a mock review of your proposal before submitting it. Remember, they like receiving quality proposals and working with grantseekers who are proactive. Some federal programs use the same reviewers each year and may be reluctant to give you any names. If this is the case, tell the federal bureaucrat that you would like to know at least the background and credentials of the reviewers so that you can prepare the best possible proposal by writing toward their level. You would ultimately like to know the types of organizations the reviewers come from, their titles and degrees, and, if possible, the selection criteria for choosing them and whether the reviewers meet in Washington, D.C., or review proposals at home or work.

You may also ask colleagues or your grants office if they have the name, e-mail address, and/or phone number of a past reviewer. You can also ask your grants office for any contact information they may have on a staff or faculty member at your institution/organization who has been a reviewer for the program. If you know any of the awarded grantees, contact them since programs frequently use past grantees as reviewers.

If the system that the reviewers must adhere to has been published in the *Federal Register* or an agency publication, request a copy or the date of the publication so you can look it up. Again, let the funding source know that you will be using a quality circle (see chapter 14) to perform a mock review of your proposal before submission and that you would like to mirror the actual review process as closely as possible. Request a copy of their reviewer training materials or the scoring system that was used.

Contacting a Past Reviewer

When contacting a past reviewer, explain that you understand he or she was a reviewer for the program you are interested in and that you would like to ask a few questions about his or her experience as a reviewer for the program. Select a few questions to ask from the following list, or make up your own:

- How did you get to be a reviewer?
- Did you review proposals at a funding source location or at home?

- What training or instruction did the funding source give you?
- Did you follow a point system? What system? How did you follow it? What were you told to look for?
- How would you write a proposal differently now that you have been a reviewer?
- What were the most common mistakes you saw?
- Did you meet other reviewers?
- How many proposals were you given to read?
- How much time did you have to read them?
- How did the funding source handle discrepancies in point assignments?
- What did the staff members of the funding source wear, say, and do during the review process?
- Did a staff review follow your review?

Telephoning and E-mailing Federal and State Funding Sources

Contacting public funding sources is an experience in itself. Your initial research should yield a contact name, e-mail address, phone number, and fax number. Because of personnel changes and reassignments the contact listed may not be the best person to assist you. However, he or she should be able to tell you who at the agency/program could best answer your questions. You can also check the agency's/program's website to make sure your contact information is current. If your research does not yield the information you need, you could use the *United States Government Manual* (see list of resources) to track down the phone number or e-mail address of the office likely to handle the funds you are seeking.

After you have identified the appropriate program officer, my first choice is to go see him or her in person. However, if this is not possible, I recommend a combination of phone and e-mail contact. The purpose of this contact is twofold.

1. You want to confirm the validity of the program information you have and ask intelligent questions that demonstrate your understanding of the program's grant system while eliciting information that will assist you in developing your proposal. You also need to complete your Past Grantee Analysis Worksheet (exhibit 12.2).
2. You want to position yourself and your institution or organization as thorough and capable.

Demonstrate that you have done your homework (research) and know about the program, and then ask a question or make a request to further your knowledge of the grant opportunity. For example, if you are requesting information on matching funds, state what you know from your research, and then ask your question. Do not ask what the matching requirements are when you already uncovered this information in Grants.gov, the *CFDA,* or a program announcement. Instead, let the program officer know, for example, that you are aware that a match is not *required* (if this is the case), and then ask if past applicants that ultimately became grantees volunteered to provide one anyway and, if so, what was the average size or range.

What really bothers federal program officers is when they get calls or e-mails from grantseekers asking what kinds of projects they are funding this year or what they are looking for this year. These are what I call flavor of the month questions and are indicative of the types of questions asked by lazy, unsophisticated grantseekers.

In addition, several federal and state program officers have told me that they are overwhelmed with questions and requests from grantseekers for information that is readily available from other sources such as the *CFDA, Federal Register,* Grants.gov, program guidelines, and so on. One way they deal with these lazy grantseekers is to ignore their e-mail and telephone requests. One federal program officer told me that his simple solution is to never respond to a first request for information unless it is an intelligent question that demonstrates that the grantseeker has done his or her home-work (research). He then went on to say that 80 percent of the prospective grantseekers he does not respond to initially do not call or e-mail a second time. His rationale for not responding initially is how critical could the information be if the grantseeker does not even call or e-mail back. On the upside, he stated that he always responds to a second request. So the moral of the story is select intelligent questions to ask that demonstrate your knowledge of the program, be persistent, phone first, and then follow up with an e-mail or vice versa.

Be careful not to ask too many questions or to make several requests at one time. Determine which of your possible questions will be the most critical in helping you determine your proposal approach, and ask one or two. If you do not get a response the first time, try again. In your follow-up contact, refor-mat the questions, note the date of your initial request, and ask again. Let the program officer know that you respect his or her time and understand how busy he or she is, but you need to know the answers to your questions and that you will recontact him or her another time if necessary.

Once contact is made with the program officer (whether it is by phone or e-mail) you should gather the same information as you would face-to-face. Since it may be difficult for the funding official to discuss your idea and ap-proaches without seeing a written description of your project, ask whether you could mail, fax, or e-mail him or her a one-page concept paper and then recontact him or her for the purpose of discussion.

Although it may be difficult for you to "read" what the funding source is really saying through phone or e-mail contact, you must at least try to uncover any hidden agenda so that you can meet the grantor's needs and to increase your chances of success. Review the list of questions in the Questions to Ask a Program Officer section of this chapter.

Making an Appointment with a Public Funding Source Official

The objective of seeking an appointment is to get an interview with an administrator of the program. Start by sending or e-mailing a letter requesting an appointment. Exhibit 12.4 provides a sample e-mail you may use. You may not get a response to this e-mail/letter. Its intent is to show that you mean business. Then follow the next few steps.

1. Call and ask for the program officer or information contact.
2. Record the name of whomever you speak to and ask if he or she is the correct person to contact. If he or she is not, ask who is, and how and when that person can be reached.
3. Call back. Ask whether anyone else can answer technical questions about the program. You may get an appointment with an individual whose job is to screen you, but this is still better than talking to yourself. As an alternative, try to get an advocate to help you set up an appointment, or try going in cold early in the week to set up an appointment for later in the week. Do not be surprised if this results in an immediate appointment. Staff members may decide they would prefer to deal with you on the spot rather than later. Be careful using elected officials to make appointments for you or to accompany you on an appointment. Bureaucrats and politicians often do not get along well and you may appear as a candidate for future earmarking.
4. When you get the program person on the phone, introduce yourself and give a brief (ten-word) description of your project. Explain that
   - the need to deal with the specific problem your project addresses is extreme,
   - your organization is uniquely suited to deal with this problem,
   - you understand that the grantor's program deals with this need, and
   - you would like to make an appointment to talk about program priorities and your approach.

EXHIBIT 12.4
Sample E-mail to a Federal Agency Requesting an Appointment

From: <grantseeker@proactive.edu>
To: <contactperson@feds.gov>
Cc:
Sent: Date, Time
Subject: Request for an Appointment

Dear [Contact Person]:

My research on your funding program indicates that a project we are developing
would be appropriate for consideration by your agency for funding under

_____.

I would appreciate five to ten minutes of your time to discuss the project and
how it matches your program. The development of the project has created
questions that I would like to discuss with you. Your insights and knowledge will
help us in our focus.

My travel plans call for me to be in your area on _____. I will phone
to confirm the possibility of a brief meeting during that time to discuss this
important proposal.

Name
Title
Organization/Institution
Address
Phone Number
Fax Number

When you get an appointment, stop and hang up. If an appointment is
not possible, tell the program representative that you have some questions and ask about the possibility of asking them now or arranging a
ten-minute phone call in the future. Fill in any information you get
(names, phone numbers, and so on) on the Federal Grants Research
Form (exhibit 11.1).

Visiting Public Funding Sources

A meeting is vital to getting the input you need to prepare a proposal that is
tailored to the funding source. A visit also will provide you with the oppor-

tunity to update any information you have gathered on the funding source through your research.

The objective of this preproposal visit is to find out as much as possible about the funding source and how it perceives its role in the awarding of grants. Then you can use the newly acquired information to produce a proposal that reflects sensitivity to the funding source's needs and perception of its mission. According to the theory of cognitive dissonance, the more the funding source perceives a grantseeker as different from what the funding source expects, the greater the problems with communication, agreement, and acceptance. We want the funder to love us, so we need to produce as little dissonance as possible by looking and talking as the funder thinks we should. Just remember, Washington, D.C., is one of the most conservative areas in the country for dress. By dressing accordingly, you can avoid not getting heard because your attire creates dissonance. Asking a past grantee how the program officer dresses and how his or her office is laid out will give you insight into what the program officer likes.

Plan Your Visit

When planning for a personal visit, remember that it is better to send two people than one and that an advocate, advisory committee member, or graduate of your program has more credibility than a paid staff member. In deciding who to send, try to match the age, interests, and other characteristics of your people with any information you have on the funding official. Before the visit, role-play your presentation with your team members and decide who will take responsibility for various parts of the presentation and what questions each will ask.

What to Take

It may be helpful to bring the following items with you on the visit:

- Materials that help demonstrate the need for your project.
- Your proposal development workbook (Swiss cheese book).
- A short DVD shown on your laptop, complete with sound, that documents the problem and the unique attributes that make you a logical choice as a grantee. The DVD could also summarize your approach to solving the problem, but the entire presentation should be short (no longer than three minutes) and simple. You do not need a projection system and a PowerPoint presentation unless you will be meeting with five or more grantor staff members.

- Information on your organization that you can leave with the funding official. However, never leave a proposal. Remember, at this point you are there to gather information to produce a better proposal.

Questions to Ask a Program Officer

Review the following list of possible questions to ask a program officer and select two or three that are critical to your proposal.

- I have located the program application on your website and found references to (*rules, announcements, and so on*). Are there any other sources of information I should review?
- The (*CFDA, Grants.gov, or agency publication*) lists the program funding level at (*$$$$$*). Do you expect that to change?
- My research shows that there are several different types of awards that fall under your program and this area of interest. What are the differences in the success rates (applications versus awards) in the granting mechanisms your program uses? (In addition to research and demonstration grants, many programs have special awards for young or new researchers or career awards to initiate and shape a career. The rules for qualifying for each type of granting mechanism vary, as does the funding. All these variables must be taken into consideration when deciding to apply to a program for a specific type of grant award.)
- How will successful grantees from last year affect the chances for new or first applicants? Will last year's grantees compete with new grantees, or have their funds been set aside? If their funds have been set aside, how much is left for new awards?
- Are there any unannounced program or unsolicited proposal funds in your agency to support an important project like ours?
- The required matching portion is X percent. Would it improve our chances for funding if we provide a greater portion than this?
- The program announcement states that matching funds are suggested but not mandatory. I need to give my institution/organization an idea of how much match is needed to meet the "suggested" amount. Could you provide me with a figure, or select three past grantees at random, and tell me how much match they (the grantees) provided?
- If no match is required, would it help our proposal if we volunteered to cost share?
- What is the most common mistake or flaw in the proposals you receive?

- We have developed several approaches to this needs area. From your vantage point, you may know whether one of our approaches has been funded but not yet published. Could you review our concept paper and give us any guidance?
- Would you review or critique our proposal if we get it to you early?
- Would you recommend a previously funded proposal for us to read for format and style? (Remember, you are entitled to see funded proposals, but be cool.)
- What changes do you expect in type or number of awards this year (for example, fewer new awards versus continuing awards)?
- Is there a relationship between the type of project or proposal and the amount awarded? Is there a sequence or progressions in the type of grant awarded? For example, do you suggest getting a consultant grant before we apply for a demonstration grant or an evaluation grant?
- We will conduct a quality circle (mock review) to improve our proposal before we submit it. Could we get more information on the review process your office will conduct? Can we get a reviewers' package including instructions, scoring information, weighting of criteria, and so on? What is the background of the reviewers? How are the reviewers selected? Could one of our team members be a reviewer? How many proposals do reviewers read? How much time do they take to read and score each proposal?

Immediately after your visit, record any information you have gathered about the funder on the Funding Source Staff Profile (exhibit 12.5). Record the results of your visit on the Public Funding Source Contact Summary Sheet (exhibit 12.6).

Making Your Decision to Develop a Proposal

So far you have not invested a tremendous amount of time writing your proposal. You have taken time to gather data and contact potential grantors. Now you must decide which federal grant program you will apply to.

Your best project is the grant program that provides the closest match between the project you want to implement and the profile you have developed of the grantor. Seldom is there a perfect fit between your project and the grantor's program, and some tailoring and changes in your program will likely add to your chances of success. Use the Tailoring Worksheet (exhibit 12.7) to analyze each grant or program you are interested in and to select the closest match. After reviewing your answers on the worksheet, rate your prospect.

EXHIBIT 12.5
Funding Source Staff Profile

Before each visit to a funding source, review this sheet to be sure you are taking the correct materials, advocates, and staff.

Agency Director: _____ E-mail: _____

Program Director: _____ E-mail: _____

Contact Person: _____ E-mail: _____

Education: College _____

                 Postgraduate: _____

Work Experience: _____

Military Experience: _____

Service Clubs:_____

Interests/Hobbies: _____

Publications: _____

Comments:

Note: Do not ask the staff person direct questions related to these areas. Instead, record information that has been volunteered or gathered from comments or observations made in the office.

Remember that the competition (alluded to in question 1) and the award rejection ratio (alluded to in question 2) are critical to calculating your chances of success. After careful analysis, what chance do you think you have of attracting a grant from this prospect? A 25 percent chance? A 50 percent chance? A 75 percent chance?

Once you are fairly sure you are going to apply to a specific federal grant program, review its advertised procedures carefully. Many federal programs request that prospective applicants submit a letter of intent to alert them of your plan to submit a full proposal. This letter has no legal implications. In other words, you could change your mind and not apply. Its purpose is to help the granting agency estimate how many proposals it will receive and thus how many reviewers may be required for the peer-review process that will follow submittal. The letter needs to state that you are considering developing a proposal for their competition and should include the exact title of the program as stated in the announcement, its *CFDA* number, and its deadline(s).

EXHIBIT 12.6
Public Funding Source Contact Summary Sheet

Project Title:_____

Complete a public funding source contact summary sheet each time you contact a public funding source.

Agency Name:_____

Program Officer: _____

Contacted On (Date):_____

By Whom: _____

Contacted By: _____ Letter _____ Phone _____ E-mail _____ Personal Visit

Staff or Advocate Present: _____

Discussed:

Results:

The letter of intent is considered a courtesy, and I always side with being courteous with those who control money! Those who submit the letter of intent may also be those who perform quality circles/mock reviews and submit early. I do not know whether any agencies keep track of the grantors who try to make their jobs easier. But if some do, I want to be on the courteous list.

Now that you have read about the importance of preproposal contact, how will you integrate it into your action steps' chart (see figure 12.2)?

EXHIBIT 12.7
Tailoring Worksheet

CFDA # _____   Prospect Rating   A. Excellent
Program Title _____   B. Good
Amount Requested _____   C. Fair
Percent Match/In-Kind _____.

                                       Estimated Success   A. 75%
                                                           B. 50%
                                                           C. 25%

1. How does your grant request match with the average award size to your
   type of organization? _____
   size of organization?_____
   location of organization? _____
   proposal focus?_____

2. What was the number of applications received versus the number of grants
   awarded in your area of interest?
   applications received _____
   grants awarded _____

3. How does your organization compare to the previous grantees relative to
   expertise of key individuals? _____
   publications and previously funded proposals?_____
   access to special equipment, space, etc.?_____
   access to subjects?_____

4. How would you rate the funding staff's interest in your concept?
   _____ very interested
   _____ interested
   _____ not interested
   _____ unknown

5. From the information you obtained on the reviewers and the review process,
   what should your writing strategy include?

6. Based on the information you obtained on the review process, how will
   points be distributed in the funding source's evaluation process?

   Area   Point Value
   _____   _____
   _____   _____
   _____   _____

FIGURE 12.2
Action Steps' Chart: Contacting Grantors, Past Grantees, and Past Reviewers

13

Planning the Successful Federal Proposal

T HE PURPOSE OF THIS CHAPTER is to help the serious government grantseeker prepare a credible proposal in a proactive manner. In order to take advantage of the strategies and insights contained in this chapter, you must obtain the application package for the most appropriate government granting agency. Read the agency's guidelines and review this chapter to ensure that you have integrated the best techniques into your proposal. This material is designed to assist you with all federal grants, and as such, it is to be of general use.

Each federal agency has its own proposal format to which applicants must adhere. If you have been successful in obtaining a copy of a previously funded proposal, you have a quality example of what the funding source expects. After reading exemplary proposals for forty years, I have learned that really excellent proposals do stand out. One does not have to be an expert in a proposal's particular area of interest to determine whether the proposal is of high quality. The required components or sections of each type of proposal—a research proposal or a proposal for a demonstration or model project—are remarkably similar. In general, federal applications include sections on

- search of relevant literature/documentation of need: to demonstrate that you have a command of the relevant studies and knowledge in the field;
- what you propose to study, change, or test (for a research project, the hypothesis and specific aims; for a model project, the measurable objectives);

- proposed intervention: the activities, methods, or protocol that state what you will do and why you have selected these methods or activities;
- budget: the cost of the project broken down by category of expenditure;
- evaluation: how you will establish the levels of change that constitute success and demonstrate that your intervention worked; and
- grantee credibility: unique qualities and capabilities that you possess and believe are relevant to support and complete the project.

Most federal grantors will also require a summary or abstract, a title, an agreement to comply with federal assurances, and the attachment of pertinent materials that the reviewer may want to refer to while evaluating the proposal. Sections on future funding and dissemination of the research finding or model may also be included.

While the inclusion of these general components seems logical, the differences in terminology, space restrictions, and order or sequence from one federal application to another can be very perplexing. The novice grantseeker frequently asks why there is not a standard federal grant application form for all programs. It seems that this would make sense, but due to the variety of federal programs and the deep-seated conviction that each area of interest is distinct, this type of standardization will probably never happen. The point is that you must follow each agency's format exactly, make no changes and no omissions and give each agency what it calls for, not just what you want to give. Even when you think you have already addressed an issue or question and that the agency's guidelines are redundant, repeat what the agency asks for and remember the golden rule of grantseeking—he or she who has the gold, makes the rules! So follow them exactly.

Each federal agency has its own preferences concerning the components and order. What is similar from agency to agency is that in one way or another, the grantseeker's proposal must establish that he or she has a project that needs to be carried out in order to advance the field of research, knowledge, or service. Chapter 14 on conducting a quality circle or proposal improvement exercise will discuss in more detail the federal agencies' systems for evaluating and scoring proposals, including how the different sections of the proposal compare in terms of importance in the final decision. When applying to a specific agency, it is expected that you will procure a copy of the desired proposal format and develop specific insights into the agency's scoring system and an idea of what an outstanding proposal looks like by obtaining a copy of a funded proposal.

Work through this chapter and collect the materials suggested. Then develop or rearrange your proposal in the format and order required by the grantor.

Documentation of Need

Most grantseekers begin their proposal with *what* they propose or want to do. Government grantors want to know *why* there is a need to do anything at all. To gain the reviewer's respect, you must show that you are knowledgeable about the need in a particular area. Your goal in this section of the proposal is to use articles, studies, and statistics to demonstrate a compelling reason or motivation to deal with the problem now.

The grantor invariably must choose which proposals to fund this year and which to reject or put on hold; therefore, you must demonstrate the urgency to close the gap between what exists now and what ought to be in your special field (see figure 13.1). Your proposed project will seek to close or reduce this gap.

In a research proposal, need documentation involves a search of relevant literature in the field. The point of the literature search is to document that there is a gap in knowledge in a particular area. Currently in the scientific community it is necessary to enhance the motivation of the reviewer to fund your research project by suggesting the value of closing the gap, in monetary terms or in terms of increased knowledge, and by proposing what this new knowledge can lead to.

In proposals for model projects and demonstration grants, this section is referred to as the needs statement or need documentation. To be successful in grantseeking, you must produce a clear, compelling picture of the current situation and the desired state. Grantors are buying an altered or better state of affairs.

Creating a sense of urgency depends on how well you document the needs. Since not all proposals can be funded, you must make the funding source believe that movement toward the desired state cannot wait any longer. Those proposals that do not get funded did not do a good job of

- documenting a real need (perceived as important),
- demonstrating what ought to be (for clients) or the field of interest, or

THE GAP

What exists now. What is real. What the present situation is.	_____	What could be. The goal. The desired state of affairs, level of achievement.

FIGURE 13.1
The Gap Diagram

- creating the urgent need to close the gap by demonstrating that each day the need is not addressed the problem grows worse or that there is unnecessary suffering, confusion, or wasted efforts.

Documenting What Is

Use the following steps to document a need in a model or demonstration grant:

1. Review the section on performing a needs survey (chapter 2) to assess whether any of the methods described could help document the need.
2. Use statistics from articles and research (for example, "Approximately ___ women in the United States were murdered by their husbands or boyfriends last year").
3. Use quotes from leaders or experts in the field (for example, "Dr. Flockmeister said children who are raised in a family with spouse abuse have a ___ percent chance of being abused or of abusing their partners").
4. Use case statements (for example, "John Quek, a typical client of the Family Outreach Center, was abused as a child and witnessed his mother and aunt being abused").
5. Describe a national need and reduce it to a local number that is more understandable (for example, "It is estimated that ___ percent of teenagers are abused by their boyfriend or girlfriend by the time they reach age seventeen; this means that at West Side High School, ___ seniors in the graduating class may have already experienced abuse").
6. State the need in terms of one person (for example, "The abused spouse generally has . . .").
7. Use statements from community people such as police, politicians, and clergy.

When documenting what exists in a research grant, include the following:

1. The latest studies, research articles, and presentations to demonstrate your currency in the field.
2. Studies that demonstrate the scope and sequence of work in the field and its current state, and the necessity to answer your proposed research question before the field can move ahead.
3. A thorough literature search that does not focus only on a few researchers or data that reinforce your research position. Show how the diversity or conflict in the field reinforces the need to search for an answer to your question.

4. A logical flow of reference to the literature. The flow may consist of a chronological and conceptual demonstration that builds to the decision to fund your work. Remember, the literature search should not be a comprehensive treatise in the field that includes references to every contributor but, rather, a convincing documentation of significant works.

Demonstrating What Ought to Be

To establish what ought to be, proven statistics may be difficult or impossible to find. Using experts' statements and quotes to document what ought to be is much more credible than using your opinion. Do not put your opinion in the needs statement. In this section you are demonstrating your knowledge of the field and showing that you have surveyed the literature.

Avoid terms that point to a poorly documented needs statement. They include the words *many* and *most* and expressions like *a great number* and *everyone knows the need for*. Make sure your needs statement does not include any of these types of words or expressions.

It is relatively easy to say what ought to be when discussing areas such as family violence or drug abuse but more difficult when dealing with bench or pure research. However, it is still important to demonstrate the possible uses your research could be related to even if you are working in the hard sciences. Documenting the other side of the gap is a necessity if you want to close the gap of ignorance in your field.

Creating a Sense of Urgency

The needs section should motivate the prospective funding source. One way to do this is to use the funding source's own studies, surveys, or statistics. The same basic proposal can be tailored to two different funding sources by quoting different studies that appeal to each source's own view of the need. By appealing to the views of individual sources, you will appear to be the logical choice to close the gap and move toward reducing the problem.

Capabilities of the Project Investigator/Project Director and the Unique Contributions That the Applicant/Consortia Will Provide

Most government grants programs will ask the applicant to substantiate the credibility of the applicant's key personnel who will deal with solving the established problem. This can be accomplished by referring to previous work of the project director and codirectors, or by referring to studies, research, or publications citing the work of the director and codirectors and consultants' contributions to the field.

Review chapter 6, "Why Grant Funds to You and Your Organization," to refresh yourself with the credibility builders of your personnel that you can work into your proposal. In the same way, review the assets that your organization and your partners' organizations bring to bear on your ability to compete with other applicants to carry out the methods/activities that you will be describing to close the gap you have identified.

If the proposal format required by the funding source does not have a section that deals with your capabilities, the end of the needs statement is the best place to put your credentials. To make a smooth transition from the need to your capabilities, do the following:

- State that it is the mission of your organization to deal with this problem.
- Summarize the unique qualities of your organization that make it best suited for the job. For example, your organization has the staff or facilities to make the project work.
- Capitalize on the similarities you share with other organizations. For instance, "Our project will serve as a model to the other agencies that face this dilemma each day." Such statements will help the prospective grantor realize that the results of your project could affect many.
- Emphasize that the needs are urgent and that each day they go unmet the problem grows. For example, "Each year that teacher education colleges do an inadequate job of integrating comprehensive computer education into their curriculum, a new group of teachers with limited computer skills enters our schools unable to utilize the Internet and the problem grows."

What You Propose to Study or Change

Objectives provide the basis for the steps you propose to take to narrow or close the gap created in the needs statement. Objectives follow the needs statement because they cannot be written until the need has been documented.

Since the accomplishment or attainment of each objective will help to close the gap, you must write objectives that are measurable and can be evaluated. It is critical to be able to determine the degree to which the objectives have been attained and, thus, demonstrate the amount of the gap that has been closed. Grantseekers preparing research proposals should note that the objective of a research proposal is to close the gap of ignorance or lack of understanding.

Government grantors have been putting increasing pressure on researchers to explain how their research can be used on a very practical level.

Philosophical (and the author's) arguments aside, there are conservative elements that want a component of even basic research grants to deal with such issues as dissemination of results and how findings can be applied to benefit the general public.

Objectives versus Methods

Objectives tell the grantseeker and the funding source what will be accomplished by this expenditure of funds and how the change will be measured. *Methods* state the means to the end or change. They tell how you will accomplish the desired change. Naturally, the ability to accomplish an objective depends on the methods or activities chosen.

When in doubt as to whether you have written an objective or method, ask yourself whether there is only one way to accomplish what you have written. If your answer is yes, you have probably written a method. For example, once a participant at one of my seminars told me that his objective was to build a visitors center for his organization's museum. When asked why he wanted to build a visitors center, he responded, "To help visitors understand the relationship between the museum buildings so that they can more effectively use the museum." Once he stated this out loud, he realized that his objective was really the effective utilization of the museums and that building a visitors center was just one method for accomplishing this objective. In other words, building the visitors center was a means to an end, just one way that my seminar participant could attempt to accomplish his objective. In fact, the reason a funding source might give money to support his project would be to help people use and appreciate the museum, not to build the visitors center. The bricks and mortar that make up the visitors center simply do not lend themselves to the kind of measurement that the issue of effective utilization does.

The following is a technique for writing objectives:

1. Determine result areas. Result areas are the key places you will look for improvement or change in the client population. Examples include the health of people over sixty-five years of age in St. Louis, better educated minority students, and more efficient use of a museum.
2. Determine measurement indicators. Measurement indicators are the quantifiable parts of your result areas. By measuring your performance with these indicators, you will be able to determine how well you are doing. Examples include the number of hospital readmissions of people over sixty-five years of age, scores on standardized tests, and the number of people who understand the relationship between museum buildings.

Brainstorm a number of measurement indicators for each of your result areas, and then select the ones that reflect your intent and are the least difficult to use.

3. Determine performance standards. Performance standards answer the question "How much (or how little) of a change do we need to consider ourselves successful?" Using our above example, we might determine the following performance standards: a 10 percent drop in hospital readmissions, scores rising from the 80th to the 90th percentile for freshman on the Flockman reading scale, or a 50 percent reduction in requests by visitors for directions from museum staff.

4. Determine the time frame. The time frame is the amount of time in which you want to reach your performance standards. It is your deadline. You might decide you want to see a 10 percent drop in hospital readmissions within six or eighteen months. Usually, this time frame is determined for you by the funding source. Most grants are for twelve months. In setting your deadlines, use months 1 through 12 instead of January, February, and so on because you seldom will start the grants when you expect, and seldom do they start in January.

5. Determine the cost frame. This is the cost of the methods or activities you have selected to meet your objectives. (This cost estimate can be obtained retrospectively from the project planner, the document you will fill out next.)

6. Write the objective. This step combines the data you have generated in the previous five steps. The standard format for an objective is as follows: "To [action verb and statement reflecting your measurement indicator] by [performance standard] by [deadline] at a cost of no more than [cost frame]." For example, "To increase the reading scores of freshmen from the 80th to the 90th percentile on Flockman's reading scale in twelve months at a cost of $50,000."

7. Evaluate the objective. Review your objective and answer the question: "Does this objective reflect the amount of change we want in the result area?" If your answer is yes, you probably have a workable objective. If your answer is no, chances are that your measurement indicator is wrong or your performance standards are too low. Go back to steps 2 and 3 and repeat the process.

When writing program objectives, you should follow the same seven steps.

Again, remember to emphasize results, not tasks or methods. Do not describe how you are going to do something; instead, emphasize what you will accomplish and the ultimate benefit of your program's work.

Hypothesis and Research Question

In a research proposal, the section on what the researcher proposes to study or change is referred to as the research question and hypothesis to be tested. The development of research proposals follows an analogous route to model and demonstration grants. There must be a clearly defined problem, question, or gap to be addressed.

Researchers are inoculated with the same virus that all grantseekers share—the "why" virus. (Why does this happen? What can we do to change it?) The researcher asks a question and then must search the literature in the field to determine what is already known and who would care if the question was answered. (What is the value or benefit? Who would value the closing of the gap?) For example, the question of whether treatment X or Y influences the healing time of a pressure sore (bedsore) is subject to a search of the literature to see what work has already been done in this area and to determine the importance of the question. (What exists now? What is the incidence or extent of the problem, and what is the future impact of not addressing the question?) If there is no compelling or motivating reason to use grant moneys to answer the question, the researcher is not likely to be successful.

The research question must be specific and focused. Many researchers are overly optimistic and select too broad a question or too many questions to investigate. This sets them up for failure because they cannot control the situation. In other words, they have too many forces or variables to deal with that can influence the outcome.

Researchers must develop their questions into either a null hypothesis or an alternative hypothesis. In a *null hypothesis*, the researcher

- predicts that there is no basic difference between the two selected areas. For example, "There is no difference between pressure sores treated with X or Y."
- sets up the study to measure the outcome, or the *dependent* variable (increased healing of pressure sores).
- manipulates or changes the intervention, or the *independent* variable (use of treatment X or Y), to observe the effects of the two treatments on the dependent variable.
- selects a statistical evaluation model before data are collected, which will be used to evaluate the differences in the intervention.

When there are significant differences between two treatments, the null hypothesis is disproved and the results are based on differences in treatment rather than on chance. A common level is .01 significance, which means the chances of this result occurring randomly is less than 1 in 1,000.

The alternative hypothesis predicts that there is indeed a difference between the two treatments and suggests the direction of that difference. For example, "Treatment X will result in a healing rate that is 50 percent faster than treatment Y." The research protocol then seeks to prove that there is a difference at the level that is substantiated by the evaluation design to be used.

Proposed Intervention

The methods, activities, or protocol section is the detailed description of the steps you will take to meet the objectives. Methods identify

- what will be done,
- who will do it,
- how long it will take, and
- the materials and equipment needed.

The protocol of a research proposal details how each experiment or trial will be carried out. The methods or protocols are all a function of what you set out to accomplish. The best order to follow is to write your objectives first and then develop your methods to meet them. In making up a realistic estimate of your project costs, avoid inflating the budget. Instead, consider adding several more methods to this section to ensure that your objectives are met. When you negotiate the final award, you will gain much more credibility with the funding source by eliminating methods instead of lowering the price for the same amount of work. The basic idea is that eliminating methods or steps impacts the ability to prove or create the desired change at the level of certainty wanted by both you and the grantor.

Historically, final awards for research proposals and model project proposals were followed by a letter that included a dollar amount significantly less that what was applied for. Criticism of this practice led many major grantors to announce that the methods for research and model/demonstration proposals should be cost analyzed and negotiated. Now both demonstration and research proposals must include an estimate of the cost of each method or activity and must show each activity's effect on the outcome.

Your methods section should

- describe your program activities in detail and demonstrate how they will fulfill your objectives or research study;
- describe the sequence, flow, and interrelationship of the activities;
- describe the planned staffing for your program and designate who is responsible for which activities;

- describe your client population and method for determining client selection;
- state a specific time frame;
- present a reasonable scope of activities that can be accomplished within the stated time frame with your organization's resources;
- refer to the cost-benefit ratio of your project;
- include a discussion of risk (why success is probable); and
- describe the uniquenesses of your methods and overall project design.

The Project Planner (exhibit 13.1) provides you with a format to ensure that your methods section reflects a well-conceived and well-designed plan for the accomplishment of your objectives. A copy of the project planner programmed to work with Microsoft Excel can be downloaded free of charge at www.dgbauer.com.

The Project Planner

An outcome of my forty years of work in grant and contract preparation, the project planner is a spreadsheet planning tool designed to assist you in several important ways. It will help you

- create a budget narrative that describes expenditures;
- develop your budget by having you clearly define which project personnel will perform each activity for a given time frame, with the corresponding consultant services, supplies, materials, and equipment;
- defend your budget on an activity-by-activity basis so that you can successfully negotiate your final award;
- project a monthly and quarterly cash forecast for year 1, year 2, and year 3 of your proposed project; and
- identify matching or in-kind contributions.

The project planner will also help you develop job descriptions for each individual involved in the project and a budget narrative or written explanation documenting your planned expenses. Several federal granting agencies have been criticized for not negotiating final awards with grantees. Their practice has been to provide grantees with a statement of the final award with no reference or discussion of how the award differs from the amount budgeted in the application or how the reduction will affect the methods and outcome. As more importance is placed on the budget negotiation and the planning of project years, the more valuable the project planner will become.

EXHIBIT 13.1
The Project Planner

PROJECT PLANNER

PROJECT TITLE:

A. List project objectives or outcomes A. B.
B. List methods to accomplish each objective as A-1, A-2, ... B-1, B-2 ...

	MONTH		TIME	PROJECT PERSONNEL	PERSONNEL COSTS		
	Begin	End			Salaries & Wages	Fringe Benefits	Total
		C/D	E	F	G	H	I
					$		.
					$		.
					$		.
					$		.
					$		.
					$		.
					$		.
					$		.
					$		.
					$		.
					$		.
					$		.
					$		.
					$		.
					$		.
					$		.
					$		.

Total Direct Costs or Costs Requested From Funder   0
Matching Funds, In-Kind Contributions, or Donated Costs
Total Costs   0

(continued)

EXHIBIT 13.1
(Continued)

Proposal Developed for _____

Project Director: _____

Proposed Start Date _____

Proposal Year _____

	CONSULTANTS CONTRACT SERVICES			NON-PERSONNEL RESOURCES NEEDED SUPPLIES - EQUIPMENT - MATERIALS				SUB-TOT ACTIVITY COST	MILESTONES PROGRESS INDICATORS	
Time	Cost/Week	Total	Item	Cost/Item	Quantity	Tot cost	Total J,L,P	Item	Date
J	K	L	M	N	O	P	Q	R	S

% of Total

You will find the following explanations of each project planner column helpful as you review the blank project planner in exhibit 13.1 and the sample project planner in exhibit 13.2.

1. Project objectives or outcomes (column A/B): List your objectives or outcomes as A, B, C, and so on. Use the terms the prospective grantor wants. For example, grantors may refer to the objectives as *major tasks*, *enabling objectives*, or *specific aims*.

2. Methods (column A/B): Also in the first column, list the methods or protocol necessary to meet the objectives or outcomes as A-1, A-2, B-1, B-2, C-1, C-2, and so on. These are the tasks you have decided upon as your approach to meeting the need.

3. Month (column C/D): Record the dates you will begin and end each activity in this column.

4. Time (column E): Designate the number of person-weeks (you can use hours or months) needed to accomplish each task.

5. Project personnel (column F): List the key personnel who will spend measurable or significant amounts of time on this activity and the accomplishment of this objective or specific aim. The designation of key personnel is critical for developing a job description for each individual. If you list the activities for which the key personnel are responsible, and the minimum qualifications or background required, you will have a rough job description. Call a placement agency to get an estimate of the salary needed to fill the position. The number of weeks or months will determine full- or part-time classification.

   This column gives you the opportunity to look at how many hours of work you are providing in a given time span. If you have your key personnel working more than 160 hours per month, it may be necessary to adjust the number of weeks in column E to fit a more reasonable time frame. For example, you may have to reschedule activities or shift responsibility to another staff member.

6. Personnel costs (columns G, H, I): List the salaries, wages, and fringe benefits for all personnel. Special care should be taken in analyzing staff donated from your organization. The donation of personnel may be a requirement for your grant or a gesture you make to show your good faith and appear as a better investment to the funding source. If you do make matching or in-kind contributions, place an asterisk by the name of each person you donate to the project. Be sure to include your donation of fringes as well as wages. As you complete the remaining columns, put an asterisk by anything else that will be donated to the project.

EXHIBIT 13.2
Sample Project Planner

PROJECT PLANNER

PROJECT TITLE: A Contract for Educational Cooperation - Parents, Teachers, and Students Charting AS Course for Involvement   A Course for Involvement

A. List project objectives or outcomes A. B.
B. List methods to accomplish each objective as A-1, A-2, ... B-1, B-2 ...

| | MONTH | | TIME | PROJECT PERSONNEL | PERSONNEL COSTS | | |
| | Begin | End | | | Salaries & Wages | Fringe Benefits | Total |
		C/D	E	F	G	H	I
Objective A: Increase educational cooperation of parents, teachers, and students as measured on the responsible educational practices survey in 12 months at a cost of $64,705.00							$ -
							$ -
A-1 Develop the responsible educational practices survey with the advisory committee	January	February	4 weeks	PD Smith & 2 Graduate Students (GS)	West State University		$ -
a. Write questions and develop a scale of responsibility for parents, teachers, and students							$ -
A-2 Administer the survey to the target population	February	March	4 weeks	2 GS	West State University		$ -
a. Develop procedure			4 weeks	PD Smith &	West State University		$ -
b. Get human subjects approval thru West State University							$ -
c. Graduate students to administer survey			4 weeks	2 GS	West State University		$ -
d. Input survey data			4 weeks*	Sec'y	$800	$160	$960*
e. Develop results			1 week	PD Smith	West State University		$ -
A-3 Develop curriculum	March	June					$ -
a. Review results of pre-test given to parents, teachers, and students			1 week	PD Smith	West State University		$ -
b. Develop a curriculum on responsibility concepts in education for each group (includes workbook and DVD on each area of curriculum):			5 weeks	PD Smith	West State University		$ -
responsible use of time			8 weeks*	Sec'y	$1,600	$320	$1920*
homework responsibility			8 weeks	Senior High Film Club	Jones Corporation Facility		$ -
communication skills							$ -
A-4 Promote and carry out program	June	December	24 weeks	PD Smith	West State University		$ -
a. Use advisory group to announce program			24 weeks	Sec'y	$4,800	$960	$5760*
b. Public service spots on radio and television							$ -
c. Develop and send home a program							$ -
d. Schedule meetings with parent							$ -
e. Develop a student DVD							$ -
							$ -
							$ -
							$ -
							$ -
							$ -
							$ -
							$ -
							$ -
Total Direct Costs or Costs Requested From Funder							0
Matching Funds, In-Kind Contributions, or Donated Costs							8,640

EXHIBIT 13.2
(Continued)

Proposal Developed for

| Project Director: | D. Smith | | | Proposed Start Date | January | | | | Proposal Year | 2011 |

	CONSULTANTS CONTRACT SERVICES		NON-PERSONNEL RESOURCES NEEDED SUPPLIES - EQUIPMENT - MATERIALS				SUB-TOT ACTIVITY COST	MILESTONES PROGRESS INDICATORS	
Time	Cost/Week	Total	Item	Cost/Item	Quantity	Tot cost	Total I,L,P	Item	Date
J	K	L	M	N	O	P	Q	R	S
	$ -	$ -				$ -	$ -		
2 weeks	$1,000	2,000.00	micro/word			2,500.00	4,500.00		
2 weeks	$500	1,000.00	printer/modem			175.00	1,175.00		
		-	phone expense			150.00	150.00		
4 weeks	$500	2,000.00				-	2,000.00		
4 weeks	$1,000	4,000.00				-	4,000.00		
		-	travel allowance			800.00	2,800.00		
4 weeks	$500	2,000.00	modem/phone			150.00	$1,110.00		
		-	micro processor			-	1,000.00		
1 week	$1,000	1,000.00				-	1,000.00		
1 week	$1,000	1,000.00	layout & print			1,250.00	6,250.00		
5 weeks	$1,000	5,000.00				-	$1,920.00		
			workbooks	$10	200	*2000.00	2,000.00		
			blank DVDs	$2	20	40.00	40.00		
			video studio	$5,000	5 hours	*25,000.00	25,000.00		
			camera edit			-			
			character			-	5,760.00		
			generation			-			
			video camera	$1,000	6 hours	*6,000.00	6,000.00		
		18,000				5,065	23,065	36%	% of Total
		0				33,000	41,640	64%	

7. Consultants and contract services (columns J, K, L): These three columns are for the services that are most cost-efficiently supplied by individuals who are not in your normal employ. They may be experts at a skill you need that does not warrant your training a staff member or hiring an additional staff person (you may need someone skilled in evaluation, computers, commercial art, and so forth). There are no fringes paid to consultants or contract service providers.

8. Nonpersonnel resources needed (columns M, N, O, P): List the components that are necessary to complete each activity and achieve your objective, including supplies, equipment, and materials. Many a grantseeker has gone wrong by underestimating the nonpersonnel resources needed to successfully complete a project. Most grantseekers lose out on many donated or matching items because they do not ask themselves what they really need to complete each activity. Travel, supplies, and telephone communications are some of the more commonly donated items.

Equipment requests can be handled in many ways. One approach is to place total equipment items as they are called for under your plan under column M (item) and to complete the corresponding columns appropriately—cost per item (column N), quantity (column O), and total cost (column P). However, this approach may cause problems in the negotiation of your final award. The grantor may suggest lowering the grant money by the elimination of an equipment item that appears as though it is related to the accomplishment of only one activity, when in actuality you plan to use it in several subsequent activities. Therefore, I suggest that if you plan to list the total cost of equipment needed in your work plan next to one particular activity, designate a percentage of usage to that activity and reference the other activities that will require the equipment. This way you will show 100 percent usage and be able to defend the inclusion of the equipment in your budget request.

In some cases, you may choose to allocate the percentage of the cost of the equipment with the percentage of use for each activity. If you allocate cost of equipment to each activity, remember that if you drop an activity in negotiation you may not have all the funds you need to purchase the equipment.

9. Subtotal cost for each activity (column Q): This column can be completed in two ways. Each activity can be subtotaled, or you can subtotal several activities under each objective or specific aim.

10. Milestones, progress indicators (columns R, S): Column R should be used to record what the funding source will receive as indicators that you are working toward the accomplishment of your objectives. Use

column S to list the date on which the funding source will receive the milestone or progress indicator.

Please note that you might want to develop a computer-generated spreadsheet version of the project planner so that your objectives or other information can be easily added, deleted, or changed. This would be especially useful when the grant amount awarded is less than the amount requested, because you could experiment with possible changes without too much trouble. Remember, a downloadable Microsoft Excel version is available free of charge at www.dgbauer.com.

Indirect Costs

An aspect of federal grants that is critically important yet poorly understood by many grantseekers and other individuals connected with grants is the concept of indirect cost. Indirect costs involve repaying the recipient of a federal grant for costs that are difficult to break down individually but are indirectly attributable to performing the federal grant. These costs include such things as

- heat and lights,
- building maintenance,
- payroll personnel, and
- purchasing.

Indirect costs are calculated by using a formula that is provided by the Federal Regional Controller's Office and are expressed as a percentage of the total amount requested from the funding source (total from column Q of your project planner), or as a percentage of the personnel costs (total from column I of your project planner).

Recent developments in the area of indirect costs have led the federal government to strictly enforce the definition of costs eligible for reimbursement under a grant's direct expenditures versus those eligible under its indirect expenditures. Under the Office of Management and Budget's guidelines, costs related to the handling of increased grant-supported payroll, increased purchasing, or grant-related travel reimbursement are already covered under indirect costs. Therefore, any added personnel that fall under the category of secretarial support are not eligible to be added to your grant. All personnel in your grant should have a special designation and job description showing that their duties are not secretarial but rather extraordinary and thus eligible to be funded under the grant.

Budget

While preparing the budget may be traumatic for unorganized grantseekers, you can see that the project planner contains all the information you need to forecast your financial needs accurately. No matter what budget format you use, the information you need to construct your budget lies in your project planner. The project planner, however, is not the budget; it is the analysis of what will have to be done and the estimated costs and time frame for each activity.

In most government proposal formats, the budget section is not located near the methods section. Government funders do not understand why you want to talk about your methods when you talk about money. As you know, the budget is a result of what you plan to do. If the money you request is reduced, you know you must cut your project's methods. Draw the public funding source back into your project planner during any budget negotiations so that they too can see what will be missing as a result of a budget cut. If you must cut so many methods that you can no longer be sure of accomplishing your objectives, consider refusing the funds or reducing the amount of change (reduction of the need) outlined in your objectives when negotiating the amount of your award. The sample budget in exhibit 13.3 is provided for your review. In a research proposal, show how limiting your intervention or protocol will affect the reliability and validity of your research.

If you are required to provide a quarterly cash forecast, use the grants office timeline in exhibit 13.4. The project activities/methods (A-1, A-2, B-1, B-2) from your project planner should be listed in the first column. The numbered columns across the top of the timeline indicate the months of the duration of the project. Use a line bar to indicate when each activity/method begins and ends. Place the estimated cost per method in the far-right column. Use a triangle to indicate where milestones and progress indicators are to occur (taken from columns R and S of your project planner). By totaling costs by quarter, you can develop a quarterly forecast of expenditures. Complete a separate grants office timeline and project planner for each year of a continuation grant or multiyear award.

One of the more common federal budget forms for nonconstruction projects is Standard Form (SF) 424A (see exhibit 13.5). The instructions for completing SF-424A are shown in exhibit 13.6. As with other budget forms, if you have completed a project planner, you already have all the information you need to complete SF-424A.

Many grantors also require that you submit a narrative statement of your budget, explaining the basis for your inclusion of personnel, consultants, supplies, and equipment. This is known as a budget narrative. Again, your completed project planner will help you construct the budget narrative and explain the sequence of steps. The budget narrative gives you the opportunity

EXHIBIT 13.3
A Sample Project Budget

PROJECT NAME:

Nutrition Education for Disadvantaged Mothers through Teleconferencing

	Expenditure Total $148,551	Donated/In-Kind $85,122	Requested from This Source $63,429
I. PERSONNEL			
A. Salaries, Wages			
Project Director @$2,200/mo × 12 mos. × 50% time	13,200	13,200	
Administrative Assistant @ $1,600/mo. × 12 mos. × 100% time	19,200		19,200
Data Input Specialist @ $1,300/mo × 12 mos. × 100% time	15,600		15,600
Volunteer time @ 9.00 × 10 mos. × 400 hours	36,000	36,000	
B. Fringe Benefits			
Unemployment Insurance (3% of first $18,600)	1,400	450	990
FICA (6.2% of first $87,000 of each employee salary)	2,976	953	2,023
Health Insurance ($150/mo. per employee × 12 mos.)	5,400	1,800	3,600
Workmen's Compensation (1% salaries paid—$48,000)	480	144	336
C. Consultants/Contracted Services			
Copy Editor ($200/day × 5)	1,000		1,000
PR Advisor ($200/day × 10)	2,000		2,000
Accounting Serv. ($250/day × 12)	3,000	3,000	
Legal Services ($500/day × 6)	3,000	3,000	
Personnel Subtotal	103,296	58,547	44,749
II. NONPERSONNEL			
A. Space Costs			
Rent (1.50/sq. ft. × 400 sq. ft. × 12 mos.)	7,200	7,200	
Utilities ($75/mo. × 12 mos.)	900	900	

(continued)

EXHIBIT 13.3
(Continued)

B. *Equipment*			
Desk ($275 × 1)	275		275
Computer, Printer, Copy Machine, Rental ($300/mo x 12 mos.)	3,600		3,600
Office Chairs ($50 × 3)	150		150
File Cabinets ($125 × 3)	375	375	
Electronic Blackboard & Misc.	7,200		7,200
Equip. for Teleconferencing			
C. *Supplies (Consumables)*			
(3 employees × $200/yr.)	600	600	
D. *Travel*			
Local			
Project Director ($.40/mile × 500 miles/mo × 12 mos.)	2,400		2,400
Administrative Assistant ($.40/mile × 750 miles/mo. × 12 mos.)	3,600		3,600
Out-of-Town			
Project Director to Nutrition Conference in St. Louis			
Airfare	450		450
Per Diem ($75/day × 3)	225		225
Hotel ($100/nt. × 3)	300		300
E. *Telephone*			
Installation ($100/line × 3)	300	300	
Monthly Charges ($25/line × 3 lines × 12 mos.)	900	900	
Long Distance ($40/mo x 12 mos.)	480		480
F. *Other Nonpersonnel Costs*			
Printing ($.30 × 25,000 brochures)	7,500	7,500	
Postage ($.34 × 25,000)	8,500	8,500	
Insurance ($25/mo. × 12 mos.)	300	300	
Nonpersonnel Subtotal	$45,255	$26,575	$18,680
Personnel Subtotal	$103,296	$58,547	$44,749
Project Total	$148,551	$85,122	$63,429
Percentage	100%	57%	43%

EXHIBIT 13.4
Grants Office Timeline

Activity Number	1	2	3	4	5	6	7	8	9	10	11	12	Total Cost of Activity

	1st Quarter		2nd Quarter		3rd Quarter		4th Quarter		Total
Quarterly Forecast of Expenditures									

EXHIBIT 13.5
Standard Form (SF) 424A

SECTION A - BUDGET SUMMARY

Grant Program Function or Activity (a)	Catalog of Federal Domestic Assistance Number (b)	Estimated Unobligated Funds		New or Revised Budget		
		Federal (c)	Non-Federal (d)	Federal (e)	Non-Federal (f)	Total (g)
1.		$	$	$	$	$ 0.00
2.						0.00
3.						0.00
4.						0.00
5. Totals		$ 0.00	$ 0.00	$ 0.00	$ 0.00	$ 0.00

SECTION B - BUDGET CATEGORIES

6. Object Class Categories	GRANT PROGRAM, FUNCTION OR ACTIVITY				Total (5)
	(1)	(2)	(3)		
	$	$	$	$	$ 0.00
a. Personnel					0.00
b. Fringe Benefits					0.00
c. Travel					0.00
d. Equipment					0.00
e. Supplies					0.00
f. Contractual					0.00
g. Construction					0.00
h. Other					0.00
i. Total Direct Charges (sum of 6a-6h)	0.00	0.00	0.00		0.00
j. Indirect Charges					0.00
k. TOTALS (sum of 6i and 6j)	$ 0.00	$ 0.00	$ 0.00		$ 0.00
7. Program Income	$	$	$	$	$ 0.00

EXHIBIT 13.5
(Continued)

SECTION C - NON-FEDERAL RESOURCES

(a) Grant Program	(b) Applicant	(c) State	(d) Other Sources	(e) TOTALS
8.	$	$	$	0.00
9.				0.00
10.				0.00
11.				0.00
12. TOTAL *(sum of lines 8-11)*	$ 0.00	$ 0.00	$ 0.00	$ 0.00

SECTION D - FORECASTED CASH NEEDS

	Total for 1st Year	1st Quarter	2nd Quarter	3rd Quarter	4th Quarter
13. Federal	$ 0.00	$	$	$	$
14. Non-Federal	0.00				
15. TOTAL *(sum of lines 13 and 14)*	$ 0.00	$ 0.00	$ 0.00	$ 0.00	$ 0.00

SECTION E - BUDGET ESTIMATES OF FEDERAL FUNDS NEEDED FOR BALANCE OF THE PROJECT

(a) Grant Program	FUTURE FUNDING PERIODS (Years)			
	(b) First	(c) Second	(d) Third	(e) Fourth
16.	$	$	$	$
17.				
18.				
19.				
20. TOTAL *(sum of lines 16-19)*	$ 0.00	$ 0.00	$ 0.00	$ 0.00

SECTION F - OTHER BUDGET INFORMATION

21. Direct Charges:	22. Indirect Charges:

23. Remarks:

EXHIBIT 13.6
Instructions for Standard Form (SF) 424A

Public reporting burden for this collection of information is estimated to average 180 minutes per response, including time for reviewing instructions, searching existing data sources, gathering and maintaining the data needed, and completing and reviewing the collection of information. Send comments regarding the burden estimate or any other aspect of this collection of information, including suggestions for reducing this burden, to the Office of Management and Budget, Paperwork Reduction Project (0348-0044), Washington, DC 20503.

PLEASE DO NOT RETURN YOUR COMPLETED FORM TO THE OFFICE OF MANAGEMENT AND BUDGET. SEND IT TO THE ADDRESS PROVIDED BY THE SPONSORING AGENCY.

General Instructions

This form is designed so that application can be made for funds from one or more grant programs. In preparing the budget, adhere to any existing Federal grantor agency guidelines which prescribe how and whether budgeted amounts should be separately shown for different functions or activities within the program. For some programs, grantor agencies may require budgets to be separately shown by function or activity. For other programs, grantor agencies may require a breakdown by function or activity. Sections A, B, C, and D should include budget estimates for the whole project except when applying for assistance which requires Federal authorization in annual or other funding period increments. In the latter case, Sections A, B, C, and D should provide the budget for the first budget period (usually a year) and Section E should present the need for Federal assistance in the subsequent budget periods. All applications should contain a breakdown by the object class categories shown in Lines a-k of Section B.

Section A. Budget Summary Lines 1-4 Columns (a) and (b)

For applications pertaining to a *single* Federal grant program (Federal Domestic Assistance Catalog number) and *not requiring* a functional or activity breakdown, enter on Line 1 under Column (a) the Catalog program title and the Catalog number in Column (b).

For applications pertaining to a *single* program *requiring* budget amounts by multiple functions or activities, enter the name of each activity or function on each line in Column (a), and enter the Catalog number in Column (b). For applications pertaining to multiple programs where none of the programs require a breakdown by function or activity, enter the Catalog program title on each line in *Column* (a) and the respective Catalog number on each line in Column (b).

For applications pertaining to *multiple* programs where one or more programs require a breakdown by function or activity, prepare a separate sheet for each program requiring the breakdown. Additional sheets should be used when one form does not provide adequate space for all breakdown of data required. However, when more than one sheet is used, the first page should provide the summary totals by programs.

Lines 1-4, Columns (c) through (g)

For new applications, leave Column (c) and (d) blank. For each line entry in Columns (a) and (b), enter in Columns (e), (f), and (g) the appropriate amounts of funds needed to support the project for the first funding period (usually a year).

For continuing grant program applications, submit these forms before the end of each funding period as required by the grantor agency. Enter in Columns (c) and (d) the estimated amounts of funds which will remain unobligated at the end of the grant funding period only if the Federal grantor agency instructions provide for this. Otherwise, leave these columns blank. Enter in columns (e) and (f) the amounts of funds needed for the upcoming period. The amount(s) in Column (g) should be the sum of amounts in Columns (e) and (f).

For supplemental grants and changes to existing grants, do not use Columns (c) and (d). Enter in Column (e) the amount of the increase or decrease of Federal funds and enter in Column (f) the amount of the increase or decrease of non-Federal funds. In Column (g) enter the new total budgeted amount (Federal and non-Federal) which includes the total previous authorized budgeted amounts plus or minus, as appropriate, the amounts shown in Columns (e) and (f). The amount(s) in Column (g) should not equal the sum of amounts in Columns (e) and (f).

Line 5 - Show the totals for all columns used.

Section B Budget Categories

In the column headings (1) through (4), enter the titles of the same programs, functions, and activities shown on Lines 1-4, Column (a), Section A. When additional sheets are prepared for Section B, provide similar column headings on each sheet. For each program, function or activity, fill in the total requirements for funds (both Federal and non-Federal) by object class categories.

Line 6a-I - Show the totals of Lines 6a to 6h in each column.

Line 6j - Show the amount of indirect cost.

Line 6k - Enter the total of amounts on Lines 6i and 6j. For all applications for new grants and continuation grants the total amount in column (5), Line 6k, should be the same as the total amount shown in Section A, Column (g), Line 5. For supplemental grants and changes to grants, the total amount of the increase or decrease as shown in Columns (1)-(4), Line 6k should be the same as the sum of the amounts in Section A, Columns (e) and (f) on Line 5.

Line 7 - Enter the estimated amount of income, if any, expected to be generated from this project. Do not add or subtract this amount from the total project amount, Show under the program

EXHIBIT 13.6
(*Continued*)

INSTRUCTIONS FOR THE SF-424A (continued)

narrative statement the nature and source of income. The estimated amount of program income may be considered by the Federal grantor agency in determining the total amount of the grant.

Section C. Non-Federal Resources

Lines 8-11 Enter amounts of non-Federal resources that will be used on the grant. If in-kind contributions are included, provide a brief explanation on a separate sheet.

> **Column (a)** - Enter the program titles identical to Column (a), Section A. A breakdown by function or activity is not necessary.
>
> **Column (b)** - Enter the contribution to be made by the applicant.
>
> **Column (c)** - Enter the amount of the State's cash and in-kind contribution if the applicant is not a State or State agency. Applicants which are a State or State agencies should leave this column blank.
>
> **Column (d)** - Enter the amount of cash and in-kind contributions to be made from all other sources.
>
> **Column (e)** - Enter totals of Columns (b), (c), and (d).

Line 12 - Enter the total for each of Columns (b)-(e). The amount in Column (e) should be equal to the amount on Line 5, Column (f), Section A.

Section D. Forecasted Cash Needs

Line 13 - Enter the amount of cash needed by quarter from the grantor agency during the first year.

Line 14 - Enter the amount of cash from all other sources needed by quarter during the first year.

Line 15 - Enter the totals of amounts on Lines 13 and 14.

Section E. Budget Estimates of Federal Funds Needed for Balance of the Project

Lines 16-19 - Enter in Column (a) the same grant program titles shown in Column (a), Section A. A breakdown by function or activity is not necessary. For new applications and continuation grant applications, enter in the proper columns amounts of Federal funds which will be needed to complete the program or project over the succeeding funding periods (usually in years). This section need not be completed for revisions (amendments, changes, or supplements) to funds for the current year of existing grants.

If more than four lines are needed to list the program titles, submit additional schedules as necessary.

Line 20 - Enter the total for each of the Columns (b)-(e). When additional schedules are prepared for this Section, annotate accordingly and show the overall totals on this line.

Section F. Other Budget Information

Line 21 - Use this space to explain amounts for individual direct object class cost categories that may appear to be out of the ordinary or to explain the details as required by the Federal grantor agency.

Line 22 - Enter the type of indirect rate (provisional, predetermined, final or fixed) that will be in effect during the funding period, the estimated amount of the base to which the rate is applied, and the total indirect expense.

Line 23 - Provide any other explanations or comments deemed necessary.

---

to present the rationale for each step, piece of equipment, and key person that your proposal calls for.

Keep foremost in your mind that these federal funds are the result of taxes paid by individuals like you, as well as corporations. It is your responsibility to make the plan for how you propose to spend these moneys as precise and as clearly related to the project outcome as possible. The tendency to "round up" numbers and pad budgets is a threat to your credibility and could affect your ability to gain the peer reviewers' and federal staff's confidence.

Remember, do not leave anything to chance. All required forms must be completed precisely.

Evaluation

Federal and state funding sources generally place a much heavier emphasis on evaluation than most private sources do. While there are many books written on evaluation, the best advice is to have an expert handle it. I suggest enlisting the services of a professional at a college or university who has experience in evaluation. Professors will generally enjoy the involvement and the extra pay and can lead you to a storehouse of inexpensive labor—undergraduate and graduate students. A graduate student in statistics can help you deal with the problem of quantifying your results inexpensively, while he or she gathers valuable insight, experience, and some much-needed money.

Irrespective of who designs your evaluation, writing your objectives properly will make the process much simpler. Most grantseekers have little problem developing objectives that deal with cognitive areas or areas that provide for results that can be easily quantified. The problems start when they move into the affective domain, because values, feelings, and appreciation can be difficult to measure. Use consultants to assist you. You will gain credibility by using an independent third party to carry out your evaluation analysis.

If you use the techniques presented in this chapter for writing objectives and ask yourself what your client population will do differently after the grant, you should be able to keep yourself on track and develop an evaluation design that will pass even the most critical federal and state standards. For example, a grant to increase appreciation of opera could be measured by seeing how many of the subjects pay to attend an inexpensive performance after the free ones are completed.

The Summary or Abstract

The summary or abstract is usually written after the proposal is completed. After the title, the summary is the second most often read part of a proposal. The summary must be succinct, clear, and motivating so the reader (reviewer) does not lose interest. It is important to determine whether the grantor uses summaries or abstracts. These terms may not be interchangeable and, therefore, could require different consideration.

In a sense, the summary or abstract has a dual purpose. Its first purpose is to provide the peer reviewer with a clear idea of what the proposed research or project entails. Its second purpose is to provide prospective grantseekers with an example of the type of research or project the federal agency funds. This second purpose occurs after the proposal is accepted, when the summary or abstract becomes public information and is placed on the funding source's website and in databases that are Internet accessible.

Unfortunately, some applicants do not devote enough time to preparing their summary or abstract and the description that is made public does not do the funding agency or the grantee's project/research justice. In order to get grantseekers to pay more attention to this section of their proposals, some federal agencies score the summary or abstract in the overall proposal evaluation. Whether this area is scored or not, it plays a critical role in setting up the expectations of the reviewer before he or she gets into the body of your proposal.

In general terms, the summary/abstract is a much-abbreviated version of your proposal and should contain a concise description of the need for your project, your project's goal or hypothesis, objectives or specific aims, approach or protocol, and evaluation design. Use your summary or abstract to show readers that they will find what they want in your proposal (since you have the scoring system), and try to follow the same order in the summary or abstract as you do in your proposal. You can determine which components to emphasize in your summary or abstract by reviewing the point or evaluation system the funding source will apply. Place more emphasis by devoting more space in the abstract or summary to the components that will be weighted more heavily in the scoring/review process. Make sure your abstract or summary is arranged so that it is easy to read. Do not crowd the contents by using every inch of space designated for this area. Instead, highlight important parts with bullets, bold print, or underlining as long as these visual aids are allowed.

Many funding sources have explicit requirements concerning the summary or abstract. Some designate the space and number of words or characters that can be used, while others require potential grantees to underline a certain number of key words or phrases. Exhibit 13.7 defines what the National Science Foundation (NSF) expects to be found in a project summary and provides very specific instructions in terms of what person the summary should be written in and what it should include. The NSF's guidelines even go so far as to state that the project summary should *not* be an abstract of the proposal. Be sure to verify your funding source's rules before constructing this critical part of your proposal.

Title Page

Federal granting programs have a required face sheet or title page that must be included in your federal grant applications or proposals. The most common is Standard Form (SF) 424 (exhibit 13.8; instructions for completing the form are included in exhibit 13.9). Remember, you are dealing with a bureaucracy and, therefore, should double-check all requirements and make sure all necessary forms are completed per instructions.

The title of a proposal is very important. It is the first part of your proposal to be read by reviewers, and, if unclear or misleading, it may be the only part read! Take the time to develop a title that ensures your proposal will get attention.

EXHIBIT 13.7
National Science Foundation Profile Summary

From the National Science Foundation Grant Proposal Guide
NSF 1-1 January 2010

2. Sections of the Proposal

b. Project Summary

The proposal must contain a summary of the proposed activity suitable for
publication, not more than one page in length. It should not be an abstract of
the proposal, but rather a contained description of the activity that would result
if the proposal were funded. The summary should be written in the third person
and include a statement of the objectives and methods to be employed. It must
clearly address in separate statements (within the one-page summary):

• the intellectual merit of the proposed activity; and
• the broader impacts resulting from the proposed activity.

It should be informative to other persons working in the same or related fields
and, insofar as possible, understandable to a scientifically or technically literate
lay reader. Proposals that do not separately address both merit review criteria
within the one-page Project Summary will be returned without review.

(To obtain information about NSF program deadlines, to download copies of
NSF publications, and/or to access abstracts of awards, visit the NSF website at
www.nsf.gov.)

The title of your proposal should

• describe your project,
• express your project's results, not methods,
• describe your project's benefits to clients, and
• be short and easy to remember.

The best titles are like newspaper headlines, descriptive and to the point.
Titles that try to entice the reader by giving only part of the story or creating
a mystery seldom work. Do not use jargon, buzzwords, biblical characters, or
Greek gods in your proposal title since you cannot be sure that the funding
source will be familiar with your reference. For example, calling your solar energy project "Apollo's Flame" could work to your disadvantage if the reviewer
does not know who Apollo is or fails to make the connection.

EXHIBIT 13.8
Standard Form (SF) 424

Application for Federal Assistance SF-424		Version 02

*1. Type of Submission:	*2. Type of Application	* If Revision, select appropriate letter(s)
☐ Preapplication	☐ New	
☐ Application	☐ Continuation	*Other (Specify)
☐ Changed/Corrected Application	☐ Revision	

3. Date Received:	4. Applicant Identifier:

5a. Federal Entity Identifier:	*5b. Federal Award Identifier:

State Use Only:

6. Date Received by State:	7. State Application Identifier:

8. APPLICANT INFORMATION:

*a. Legal Name:

*b. Employer/Taxpayer Identification Number (EIN/TIN):	*c. Organizational DUNS:

d. Address:

*Street 1: _____

Street 2: _____

*City: _____

County: _____

*State: _____

Province: _____

*Country: _____

*Zip / Postal Code _____

e. Organizational Unit:

Department Name:	Division Name:

f. Name and contact information of person to be contacted on matters involving this application:

Prefix: _____	*First Name: _____

Middle Name: _____

*Last Name: _____

Suffix: _____

Title:

Organizational Affiliation:

*Telephone Number:	Fax Number:

*Email:

(*continued*)

EXHIBIT 13.8
(*Continued*)

Application for Federal Assistance SF-424	Version 02

*9. Type of Applicant 1: Select Applicant Type:

Type of Applicant 2: Select Applicant Type:

Type of Applicant 3: Select Applicant Type:

*Other (Specify)

*10 Name of Federal Agency:

11. Catalog of Federal Domestic Assistance Number:
_____

CFDA Title:
_____

*12 Funding Opportunity Number:
_____

*Title:
_____

13. Competition Identification Number:
_____

Title:
_____

14. Areas Affected by Project (Cities, Counties, States, etc.):

*15. Descriptive Title of Applicant's Project:

EXHIBIT 13.8
(Continued)

Application for Federal Assistance SF-424	Version 02

16. Congressional Districts Of:

*a. Applicant: *b. Program/Project:

17. Proposed Project:

*a. Start Date: *b. End Date:

18. Estimated Funding ($):

*a. Federal   _____

*b. Applicant   _____

*c. State   _____

*d. Local   _____

*e. Other   _____

*f. Program Income _____

*g. TOTAL   _____

*19. Is Application Subject to Review By State Under Executive Order 12372 Process?

☐ a. This application was made available to the State under the Executive Order 12372 Process for review on _____

☐ b. Program is subject to E.O. 12372 but has not been selected by the State for review.

☐ c. Program is not covered by E. O. 12372

*20. Is the Applicant Delinquent On Any Federal Debt? (If "Yes", provide explanation.)

☐ Yes   ☐ No

21. *By signing this application, I certify (1) to the statements contained in the list of certifications** and (2) that the statements herein are true, complete and accurate to the best of my knowledge. I also provide the required assurances** and agree to comply with any resulting terms if I accept an award. I am aware that any false, fictitious, or fraudulent statements or claims may subject me to criminal, civil, or administrative penalties. (U. S. Code, Title 218, Section 1001)

☐ ** I AGREE

** The list of certifications and assurances, or an internet site where you may obtain this list, is contained in the announcement or agency specific instructions

Authorized Representative:

Prefix: _____   *First Name: _____

Middle Name: _____

*Last Name: _____

Suffix: _____

*Title:

*Telephone Number: Fax Number:

* Email:

*Signature of Authorized Representative: *Date Signed:

EXHIBIT 13.9
Instructions for Standard Form (SF) 424

Public reporting burden for this collection of information is estimated to average 60 minutes per response, including time for reviewing instructions, searching existing data sources, gathering and maintaining the data needed, and completing and reviewing the collection of information. Send comments regarding the burden estimate or any other aspect of this collection of information, including suggestions for reducing this burden, to the Office of Management and Budget, Paperwork Reduction Project (0348-0043), Washington, DC 20503.

PLEASE DO NOT RETURN YOUR COMPLETED FORM TO THE OFFICE OF MANAGEMENT AND BUDGET. SEND IT TO THE ADDRESS PROVIDED BY THE SPONSORING AGENCY.

This is a standard form (including the continuation sheet) required for use as a cover sheet for submission of preapplications and applications and related information under discretionary programs. Some of the items are required and some are optional at the discretion of the applicant or the Federal agency (agency). Required items are identified with an asterisk on the form and are specified in the instructions below. In addition to the instructions provided below, applicants must consult agency instructions to determine specific requirements.

Item	Entry:	Item	Entry:
1.	**Type of Submission:** (Required): Select one type of submission in accordance with agency instructions. • Preapplication • Application • Changed/Corrected Application – If requested by the agency, check if this submission is to change or correct a previously submitted application. Unless requested by the agency, applicants may not use this to submit changes after the closing date.	10.	**Name Of Federal Agency:** (Required) Enter the name of the Federal agency from which assistance is being requested with this application.
		11.	**Catalog Of Federal Domestic Assistance Number/Title:** Enter the Catalog of Federal Domestic Assistance number and title of the program under which assistance is requested, as found in the program announcement, if applicable.
2.	**Type of Application:** (Required) Select one type of application in accordance with agency instructions. • New – An application that is being submitted to an agency for the first time. • Continuation - An extension for an additional funding/budget period for a project with a projected completion date. This can include renewals. • Revision - Any change in the Federal Government's financial obligation or contingent liability from an existing obligation. If a revision, enter the appropriate letter(s). More than one may be selected. If "Other" is selected, please specify in text box provided. A. Increase Award B. Decrease Award C. Increase Duration D. Decrease Duration E. Other (specify)	12.	**Funding Opportunity Number/Title:** (Required) Enter the Funding Opportunity Number and title of the opportunity under which assistance is requested, as found in the program announcement.
		13.	**Competition Identification Number/Title:** Enter the Competition Identification Number and title of the competition under which assistance is requested, if applicable.
		14.	**Areas Affected By Project:** List the areas or entities using the categories (e.g., cities, counties, states, etc.) specified in agency instructions. Use the continuation sheet to enter additional areas, if needed.
3.	**Date Received:** Leave this field blank. This date will be assigned by the Federal agency.	15.	**Descriptive Title of Applicant's Project:** (Required) Enter a brief descriptive title of the project. If appropriate, attach a map showing project location (e.g., construction or real property projects). For preapplications, attach a summary description of the project.
4.	**Applicant Identifier:** Enter the entity identifier assigned buy the Federal agency, if any, or the applicant's control number if applicable.		
5a.	**Federal Entity Identifier:** Enter the number assigned to your organization by the Federal Agency, if any.	16.	**Congressional Districts Of:** (Required) 16a. Enter the applicant's Congressional District, and 16b. Enter all District(s) affected by the program or project. Enter in the format: 2 characters State Abbreviation – 3 characters District Number, e.g., CA-005 for California 5th district, CA-012 for California 12th district, NC-103 for North Carolina's 103rd district. • If all congressional districts in a state are affected, enter "all" for the district number, e.g., MD-all for all congressional districts in Maryland. • If nationwide, i.e. all districts within all states are affected, enter US-all. • If the program/project is outside the US, enter 00-000.
5b.	**Federal Award Identifier:** For new applications leave blank. For a continuation or revision to an existing award, enter the previously assigned Federal award identifier number. If a changed/corrected application, enter the Federal Identifier in accordance with agency instructions.		
6.	**Date Received by State:** Leave this field blank. This date will be assigned by the State, if applicable.		
7.	**State Application Identifier:** Leave this field blank. This identifier will be assigned by the State, if applicable.		
8.	**Applicant Information:** Enter the following in accordance with agency instructions:		
	a. Legal Name: (Required): Enter the legal name of applicant that will undertake the assistance activity. This is ththat the organization has registered with the Central Contractor Registry. Information on registering with CCR may be obtained by visiting the Grants.gov website.	17.	**Proposed Project Start and End Dates:** (Required) Enter the proposed start date and end date of the project.
	b. Employer/Taxpayer Number (EIN/TIN): (Required): Enter the Employer or Taxpayer Identification Number (EIN or TIN) as assigned by the Internal Revenue Service. If your organization is not in the US, enter 44-4444444.	18.	**Estimated Funding:** (Required) Enter the amount requested or to be contributed during the first funding/budget period by each contributor. Value of in-kind contributions should be included on appropriate lines, as applicable. If the action will result in a dollar change to an existing award, indicate only the amount of the change. For decreases, enclose the amounts in parentheses.

EXHIBIT 13.9
(Continued)

	c. Organizational DUNS: (Required) Enter the organization's DUNS or DUNS+4 number received from Dun and Bradstreet. Information on obtaining a DUNS number may be obtained by visiting the Grants.gov website.	19.	**Is Application Subject to Review by State Under Executive Order 12372 Process?** Applicants should contact the State Single Point of Contact (SPOC) for Federal Executive Order 12372 to determine whether the application is subject to the State intergovernmental review process. Select the appropriate box. If "a." is selected, enter the date the application was submitted to the State.
	d. Address: Enter the complete address as follows: Street address (Line 1 required), City (Required), County, State (Required, if country is US), Province, Country (Required), Zip/Postal Code (Required, if country is US).	20.	**Is the Applicant Delinquent on any Federal Debt?** (Required) Select the appropriate box. This question applies to the applicant organization, not the person who signs as the authorized representative. Categories of debt include delinquent audit disallowances, loans and taxes. If yes, include an explanation on the continuation sheet.
	e. Organizational Unit: Enter the name of the primary organizational unit (and department or division, (if applicable) that will undertake the assistance activity, if applicable.	21.	**Authorized Representative:** (Required) To be signed and dated by the authorized representative of the applicant organization. Enter the name (First and last name required) title (Required), telephone number (Required), fax number, and email address (Required) of the person authorized to sign for the applicant. A copy of the governing body's authorization for you to sign this application as the official representative must be on file in the applicant's office. (Certain Federal agencies may require that this authorization be submitted as part of the application.)
	f. Name and contact information of person to be contacted on matters involving this applicat required), organizational affiliation (if affiliated with an organization other on: Enter the name (First and last name than the applicant organization), telephone number (Required), fax number, and email address (Required) of the person to contact on matters related to this application.		

9.	Type of Applicant: (Required) Select up to three applicant type(s) in accordance with agency instructions.
	
	A. State Government M. Nonprofit
	B. County Government N. Nonprofit
	C. City or Township O. Private Institution of
	    Government Higher Education
	D. Special District Government P. Individual
	E. Regional Organization Q. For-Profit Organization
	F. U.S. Territory or Possession (Other than Small
	G. Independent School District Business)
	H. Public/State Controlled R. Small Business
	    Institution of Higher S. Hispanic-serving
	    Education Institution
	I. Indian/Native American T. Historically Black
	    Tribal Government Colleges and
	    (Federally Recognized) Universities (HBCUs)
	J. Indian/Native American U. Tribally Controlled
	    Tribal Government (Other Colleges and
	    than Federally Recognized) Universities (TCCUs)
	K. Indian/Native American V. Alaska Native and
	    Tribally Designated Native Hawaiian Serving
	    Organization Institutions
	L. Public/Indian Housing W. Non-domestic (non-US)
	    Authority Entity
	     X. Other (specify)		

Acronyms should be used only if the funding source has a preference for them. Trying to develop a title that describes the benefits of your project is difficult enough without trying to use specific words that will result in a catchy acronym.

Since you have written the proposal, it is easy for you to develop tunnel vision and attribute more meaning to the words in the title than a person reading it for the first time would. To make sure this does not happen, read your title to other people who know little or nothing about your proposal, and then ask them what they think the proposal is about based on the title. You may find that you are not the best person to write the title. Have friends read the proposal and ask them for title suggestions.

Titles can vary in length and can be up to ten or thirteen words. Some federal programs have rules on the number of characters or spaces used in a title. Check the rules.

The key to writing a good title is to ask funding officials what they prefer and to examine a list of titles used by past grantees. This will give you a more accurate idea of what the funding source really likes.

Future Funding

Most funding sources are buying a piece of the future. It is in their best interest to see any project they fund continue even though their guidelines may prohibit them from supporting continuation. If the project continues they are able to take credit for it and its benefits over a greater length of time. Unfortunately, many grantseekers ignore the funding source's interest in keeping the investment alive and neglect to mention a future financing plan in their proposals. If you cannot think of ways to finance your project after your federal grant funds run out, try brainstorming with your advisory committee. Perhaps you could continue your project through

- service fees,
- membership fees,
- support from agencies like the United Way,
- big gift campaigns aimed at wealthy individuals,
- an endowment program,
- foundation and corporate grants,
- a direct-mail campaign, or
- other fund-raising mechanisms.

Include the cost of one or more of these activities in your expenses and budget them in the grant. You are not automatically considered an ingrate for doing this; rather, you may come across as a good executor of the funding source's estate. You are planning for continuation.

Dissemination

In addition to the good that will come from meeting the objectives and closing the gap established in your needs statement, much good can come from letting others know what you and the funding source have accomplished. Others in your field will come to know your name and ask you to enter into consortia with them. In addition, other funding sources will have knowledge of your application and possibly look at ways to extrapolate it to their program. The idea is to get more PR and mileage out of your work in addition to that which you will derive from having an article published in a journal in your field.

Explore how you could disseminate the results of your grant by

- mailing a final report, quarterly journal, or a newsletter to others in your field;

- sponsoring a seminar or conference on the topic;
- attending a national or international conference to deliver the results of the project (many government funding officials cannot travel to conferences, but they can fund you to go and disseminate the results);
- providing a satellite downlink to others in your field;
- producing a DVD of the project; and/or
- creating a website and allowing others to download parts of your work.

Activities aimed at disseminating project results are viewed positively by most funding sources. In general, they want their agency and program name up in lights and are willing to pay for it. So build the costs related to dissemination into your budget. Remember, you can always negotiate down the cost for dissemination in your budget, but you may be surprised at how much the grantor will want to keep in.

Attachments (Appendix)

The attachments can provide the winning edge when your proposal is compared to a competitor's. Throughout the proposal development process, you should be gathering materials that could be used in the attachment section of your proposal. Your final task is to select which materials to include. Naturally, you want to choose those that will best support your proposal and build credibility. Whether the funding source skims over them or examines them in detail, attachments may include

- studies or research, tables, charts, and graphs;
- vitae of key personnel;
- minutes of advisory committee meetings;
- a list of board members;
- an auditor's report or statement;
- letters of recommendation or endorsement;
- a copy of your IRS tax-exempt designation;
- pictures or architect's drawings;
- copies of your agency's publications; and
- a list of other funding sources you will approach for support.

Check funding source rules to determine what is required and the regulations regarding how long your attachments section can be. Guidelines usually state the maximum number of pages it can have. Many funding sources will not want you to include the full vitae of key staff and will specify that you attach abbreviated resumes or biosketches instead.

Also check funding source rules for the appropriate appendix format. Provide a separate table of contents for your appendix, and number the pages for easy reference.

Writing Your Federal or State Proposal

Your proposal must reflect what the funding source wants and what the reviewers will be looking for. To create a winning proposal

- follow the guidelines exactly (even when they seem senseless, or when you think you are repeating yourself),
- fill in all the blanks (if not applicable mark NA),
- double-check all computations, and
- include anything the funding source asks for, even if you think you already provided the information under another section of your proposal.

When writing your proposal, keep in mind that it must be readable and easy to skim. Place special emphases on vocabulary, style, and visual attractiveness and, above all, consider the intended audience (the reviewer).

Vocabulary

Your research on the probable reviewer will have given you an idea of the reviewers' level of expertise and their depth of knowledge in your subject area. Be sure your proposal uses language appropriate to the reviewers. Shorter words are generally better than long, complex words, and avoid buzzwords unless you are sure the reviewer expects them. Define all acronyms, or avoid them completely. You want to avoid using language that is under or over their level. In most cases I have had to simplify proposals because the reviewers were technically literate lay readers rather than experts in the field.

Writing Style

By now you should have some idea of the background of the typical reviewer selected by the grantor agency and how much time the reviewers spend reading each proposal. These peer reviewers are under pressure to use their time efficiently, so you must produce a proposal that is poignant, yet organized and easy to read. Your best aid here is to review two or three successful proposals. After all, they followed the golden rule—they got the gold! When you analyze them, I bet you will find that they adhere to the following grant winner techniques:

- Use simple sentences (no more than two commas) and short paragraphs (five to seven lines).
- Begin each section with a strong motivating lead sentence.
- Make sure your writing style cannot be construed as cute or offensive to the reader.
- Avoid stating the obvious and talking down to the reviewer.
- Develop a user-friendly proposal. One of the peer reviewers may be chosen to defend your proposal to the rest of the review panel. In this case, you want to be certain to make the reviewer your friend by organizing and referencing attachments in such a way that they can be used to mount a good defense and to answer the other panelists' questions.

Visual Attractiveness

Due to the formats required under electronic submission, your creativity is severely limited in terms of visual attractiveness. However, the need still exists to make your proposal stand out from the rest of the pile. Depending upon submission rules, the application of allowable techniques is designed to make your proposal more interesting, draw reviewers to the salient points, and make the areas that are part of the scoring rubric stand out. While space is always a problem, you are better off to edit your proposal to keep it from looking crowded and to make it more readable and reviewer friendly.

Reviewers usually must struggle through several proposals. In addition, their reading is frequently interrupted and they often have to return to a proposal in the middle of a section. Tired reviewers need all the help you can give them to locate and score the important sections of your proposal. For example, if you use "1, 2, and 3" to explain the order of your methods or protocols, it is easier to see the numbers if they are justified to the left margin rather than burying them in a paragraph. Also, it has been noted by funding sources that there are often more "firsts" than "seconds" and "thirds." Reviewers can get frustrated when there is a "first" with no following points. Reviewers may also take you to task for using an ordinal approach (1, 2, and 3) when there is no reason for "3" to follow "2" and could, in fact, be presented first. You will understand how important readability, writing style, and visual attractiveness are after you read several samples of funded proposals followed by your own.

Even scientific research need not look boring to the reviewer. Again, review any electronic submittal rules and then look to enhance the "readability" of your proposal by making your points stand out through

- underlining,
- bullets,

- different fonts,
- various margins and s p a c i n g,
- **bold headings,**
- pictures and graphics, and/or
- charts and tables.

While you must follow the grantor's rules regarding type font, number of characters per inch, line spacing, and so on, your computer and laser printer can provide you with a wealth of creative ways to make your proposal more readable. Avoid creativity for its own sake, but think of the reviewer and your goal to hit those review criteria as you write your proposal.

Online Proposal Preparation

The advent of Grants.gov has hastened compliance with Congress's paperless environment. While there are variations in applications between agencies and even programs within the same federal agency, the Grants.gov portal governs all proposal submissions. Proposal creation is governed by this system as well. Not only are you required to transmit your proposal electronically, the creation or writing of your proposal is also accomplished on the agency's website. Electronic submission then moves the proposal from the creation/writing status to submission, and then to a pending or under review status.

Grants.gov not only supplies the grantseeker with the ability to search for grantors in twenty-six federal agencies and over one thousand grant programs, but also allows you to procure an application online once you have located the best program.

While you do not have to log on to search, you do have to get registered in order to apply for and submit a grant. You or your organization must complete the Grants.gov registration process. Once registered, it is possible for you and your coprincipal investigators and project directors to work on separate sections of your proposal simultaneously. However, you must retain the access code given to you through the registration process to retrieve your proposal.

Discuss the proposal development online process with a successful grantee if at all possible. You can gain invaluable insights by asking successful grantees about the online application problems they encountered and how they overcame them. For example, you could discover through conversation with a successful grantee that the federal agencies are not licensed to provide software programs with spell or grammar check and that to perform these functions you must download the proposal, clean it up, and upload it back into the agency's application program. Even this relatively simple process can become fraught with difficulties, especially if you are doing it at the last minute. When the deadline is looming and hundreds, if not thousands, of proposal creators/writers are changing and transmitting tens of thousand of documents, problems occur. So the more you know early on in the process, the better.

If you are fortunate enough to have an institutional grants office, you can check with it for its recommended submittal procedures. Most colleges, universities, and major nonprofit organizations have a central office to deal with proposal development. In fact, it is even common for universities to have colleges, departments, or centers with their own policies and procedures dealing with federal, electronic submission.

Starting out by contacting the offices in your organization that are involved with the submittal process is smart and polite. In addition, keep in mind that you will ultimately need these people for submission. If your organization has obtained federal grant funds recently they probably already have designated a person who is the only one allowed to move a proposal from the creation/ writing part of proposal development to the actual submittal state (more about that later). Find out how your institution's system is set up so you do not hit any snags later.

The Grants.gov website states that the registration process can take between three to five business days, but if all the steps are not completed in a timely manner the process could take as long as four weeks. So I suggest you or your organization register early, submit early, and verify that your submissions are received on time and validated successfully.

When will you create your actual proposal using the strategies in this chapter? Review your action steps' chart to determine when you will set aside the time to write your federal proposal. Use figure 13.2 to place this action step in your plan.

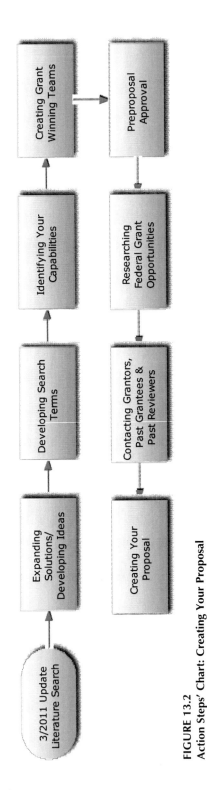

FIGURE 13.2
Action Steps' Chart: Creating Your Proposal

14

Improving Your Federal Proposal
The Grants Quality Circle

T HE MOST IMPORTANT CHANGE in this book since the last edition is the inclusion of the techniques outlined in this chapter, which have had a dramatic impact on the quality of proposals and, thus, on the success rates of those institutions who have embraced these strategies. Fellows who are accepted into my grants/research development programs are trained in the quality circle concept, required to put their proposals through the quality circle process, and expected to take part in and lead quality circles for the other fellows.

The dramatic transformation that occurs in the proposal development environment and culture has been exciting and very positive. Even successful grants veterans have bought into this concept. The following quote from Dr. William Wiener, professor and former vice provost for research at Marquette University, attests to the positive impact the quality circle concept has when implemented and reinforced from an institution's grants/research office.

> Marquette University has more than doubled its external funding since Bauer and Associates have assisted us with our Research Development Program. This is due in part to the growing use of quality circle reviews where faculty provide a small group of interested people with a draft of their proposal for critical analysis. Quality circles have greatly enhanced the quality of the proposals that we submit to funding agencies. Quality circle reviews provide the faculty with feedback on their draft proposals which results in stronger applications.

Consistently funded grantees have traditionally taken advantage of a presubmission review of their proposals by a colleague or two. While this technique is positive, its value depends on how knowledgeable those reviewing your proposal are of the field and how much they know about the actual peer-review system that will be used by the reviewers. For example, while a four-hour review of your proposal by one of your colleagues will be quite detailed, it may actually be counterproductive in its suggestions if the real reviewer is going to spend just one hour reviewing it. The secret to improving your federal proposal is to conduct a mock review that emulates the actual review system as closely as possible. Of course, the *first* step is to be proactive and to make sure you have enough time to take advantage of this most valuable technique. The *second* step is to get the relevant information on the reviewers and the scoring process.

Proactive grantseekers initiate proposal development early in the federal grant cycle and therefore have sufficient time to have their proposals reviewed by their peers before submission. You will improve your proposal and significantly increase your chances for success by asking several colleagues or members of your grants advisory committee to voluntarily role-play being the review team that will ultimately pass judgment on your proposal. This pre-submission review process is really a test run or mock review, and the group conducting it acts as your quality circle, as described in William Edwards Deming's work on total quality management (TQM).[1]

If you follow the TQM model, you will not pay your quality circle participants to take part in the activity. They should be motivated by their desire to help you improve your proposal, increase its probability of excellence, and, thus, enhance the image of your organization. It is to everyone's advantage to position your institution in the most favorable manner. In many institutions, the grants office will help you set up this improvement exercise and, when necessary, may even pay for refreshments or lunch. In some instances, course release time is also offered as an incentive for leading mock reviews.

The following quote from Dr. Amy Henderson-Harr, director of the Office of Research and Sponsored Programs at SUNY Cortland, further bears out the impact that quality circle reviews can have on an entire institution.

At SUNY Cortland, we are able to use the quality circle concept of peer review and the skills acquired to not only improve our grant success rates, but apply the teachings to improving other aspects of academic work, including curriculum proposals, program assessments and interdisciplinary collaborations to improve what we do. The quality circle process has brought seasoned faculty together with novice grant seekers to jointly enrich and advance scholarship. Most importantly, the quality circle seminars have changed the way we see ourselves, in that we have higher standards and know that we can do better by changing the way that we approach grants through the application of quality circles. We're much more apt to think strategically in pre-planning, developing thematic connections throughout the text, relying upon each other for areas we need help on, and accept[ing] feedback. Most of all, we're learning from each other and respecting what we all bring to the process as members of our institution. It's enlightening and transformative. Perhaps the best of all!

As previously mentioned, the most significant factor in the success of this improvement exercise is how closely each aspect of the mock review resembles the actual federal or state review. The benefits you can derive from this technique are directly related to your ability to create the scenario in which the actual reviewers will find themselves.

To arrange a quality circle that is similar to what the actual review will be like, secure pertinent information on the background of last year's reviewers, a copy of the scoring system that will be used, and an outline of the actual process. Through preproposal contact (see chapter 12), you should have already collected information about the setting in which your proposal will be reviewed.

To make this exercise as valuable as possible, provide your mock review group or grants quality circle with data on the following:

- The training each reviewer receives.
- The setting in which proposals are reviewed (the federal agency, the reviewer's home, both sites, and so on).
- The review process: Does one reviewer defend the proposal while others try to locate flaws or weaknesses?
- The scoring system: Are scores averaged? Are the highest and lowest scores eliminated and the remainder averaged?
- The amount of time spent reviewing each proposal.

Your quality circle participants should also be provided with a copy of the *CFDA* and/or the program application guidelines, as well as information on past grantees and results of preproposal contact with grantor staff. Providing copies of funded proposals at the meeting as references is valuable. However, they need not be considered required reading.

It is essential that you instruct the members of your grants quality circle to spend only the same amount of time reviewing your proposal as the actual reviewers will. Some of your mock reviewers may mistakenly think they will be helping you by taking an inordinate amount of time to read your proposal carefully. However, if actual reviewers will skim parts of the proposal, then our mock reviewers should do the same. Remind your quality circle participants that they should be trying to *mirror* the actual reviews, not do a better job than them! If the actual reviewers will invest over sixty minutes reviewing and scoring each proposal, consider distributing your draft proposal to the members of your grants quality circle before they come together. Ask them to bring the proposal to the meeting with the positive areas highlighted. They should also bring their scores for each section and suggestions on the areas to be improved.

The proposal sequence to be followed should mirror that which the actual review will undergo. One exception is in the evaluation of the title and abstract/summary. The participants should read and score the title and the abstract/summary, and discuss the impact they (the title and abstract/summary) had on their expectations of what the project was about. They should also discuss the impression the title and the abstract/summary gave them concerning the organization of the proposal.

Four or five reviewers/participants should be selected to participate in the mock review/quality circle. The Sample Letter/E-Mail Inviting an Individual to Participate in a Grants Quality Circle (exhibit 14.1) and the Federal/State Grants Quality Circle Worksheet (exhibit 14.2) will help you carry out this valuable exercise.

Exhibit 14.3 outlines the roles that each person on the quality circle will play. The greatest difficulty in conducting the quality circle falls on the

EXHIBIT 14.1
Sample Letter/E-mail Inviting an Individual to Participate in a Grants Quality Circle

Date

Name
Address

Dear _____:

I would like to take this opportunity to request your input in helping our [organization, group, team] submit the very best grant proposal possible. We are asking that you review the enclosed proposal from the point of view of the federal reviewer. The attached materials will help you role-play the actual manner in which the proposal will be evaluated.

Please read the information on the reviewers' backgrounds and the scoring system and limit the time you spend reading the proposal to the time constraints that the real reviewers will observe. A grants quality circle worksheet has been provided to assist you in recording your scores and comments.

A meeting of all mock reviewers comprising our quality circle has been scheduled for [date]. Please bring your grants quality circle worksheet with you to this meeting. The meeting will last less than one hour. Its purpose is to analyze the scores and brainstorm suggestions to improve this proposal.

Sincerely,

Name
Phone Number

EXHIBIT 14.2
Federal/State Grants Quality Circle Worksheet

The following information is designed to help you develop the proper focus for the review of the attached proposal.

1. The Review Panelists

   Proposals are read by review panelists with the following degrees and backgrounds:

   Degrees: _____

   Backgrounds (Age, Viewpoints, Biases, and so on):_____

   _____

   _____

2. The Time Element and Setting

   Number of proposals read by each reviewer:_____

   Average length of time spent reading each proposal: _____

   Proposals are read at the:

   ___ reviewer's home ___ reviewer's work ___ funder's location ___ other site

3. The Scoring System

   a. The scoring system that will be employed is based on a scale of: _____

   b. The areas to be scored are (list or include attachment):

Area	Total Possible Points	Your Score

   c. According to the total points per area, how many points represent an outstanding, superior, adequate, weak, or poor score? For example, if the total points possible for one area are 25, 0–8 = poor, 9–12 = weak, 13–19 = adequate, 20–23 = superior, and 24–25 = outstanding.

   _____

   _____

   d. After recording your scores, list the positive points of the proposal that may appeal to the actual reviewer. Also list those areas that seem weak and may cost valuable points. List suggestions for improvement.

   _____

   _____

   _____

EXHIBIT 14.3
Roles for Conducting a Quality Circle Review

Group Facilitator
The group leader/facilitator is responsible for keeping the group on task, having the group focus on the proposal's positive aspects before moving on to its negative ones, and reinforcing a constructive learning atmosphere. The facilitator may engage in reading and scoring the sections as well, but should reserve his or her comments and scores till last. The group leader may decide to facilitate discussion only if that is his or her desire.

The facilitator will request the scores for each section or part of the proposal before asking for the positive areas and areas to be improved. The facilitator is advised to rotate the request for comments to start each section among the participants, and to encourage everyone to participate. The facilitator will set a constructive tone and learning focus by asking *each* participant for his or her *positive* comments *first*, and will interrupt any participant who moves to the areas to be improved before each participant has presented his or her comments. After all positive comments have been presented the focus will turn to the areas that need to be improved in order to raise the score for each section.

Proposal Initiator(s)/Writer(s)
The creator(s) of the proposal under review may choose to either attend the quality circle meeting, or not be present and just receive the results. If present, they should not be allowed to interrupt the process, defend the proposal, or provide any additional information. However, they may ask questions to clarify points at the conclusion of the discussion on each of the sections to be reviewed. A short introduction including information learned through preproposal contact or from successful grantees or past reviewers may be included to help prepare the participants.

Quality Circle Participants
The exercise participants are expected to adhere to the suggestions on reading time frames, development of helpful comments, and the scoring of each section. They are allowed to raise questions, but asking questions of the proposal initiator(s) should be kept to a minimum and allowed only when necessary to promote a realistic review.

facilitator. The facilitator's main job is to keep the process of review, evaluation, and discussion positive. The purpose is to role-play how the reviewer will see this proposal and to put the most positive and productive foot forward. The instructions are quite clear. Ask each quality circle participant for the positive comments before moving to the areas to improve. In order to avoid quality circle participants giving their own opinions, the facilitator will use the actual scoring system and the criteria that the actual reviewers will employ to evaluate, rank, and score the proposal.

This is not a critique, nor a defense of a dissertation. To succeed and become a practice that proposal developers want to be involved in, it must be a positive experience. Learning what may be missing or could be improved is beneficial and constructive for the proposal developer if the experience is handled correctly.

In some cases it is not feasible to assemble a group of volunteers for a quality circle. There may be too few colleagues in your organization to conduct a role-playing activity such as this, confidentiality may be an issue, personality problems may exist, or competition in the field could rule out the possibility of such an activity occurring. One option in these instances would be to ask one or two individuals whom you trust from outside your organization or off campus to review your proposal. Provide them with the same data and worksheets discussed above, and, if necessary, offer them an honorarium for their efforts ($200 is common). You could request that they sign a nondisclosure agreement. Most university grant offices have these agreement forms and will be happy to share a copy with you. This way you can tailor the agreement to your project with minimal effort. Seldom are these extraordinary security measures necessary with colleagues, but this is an option you may want to consider to ensure that no one steals your idea.

A look at a few selected scoring systems and criteria reveals the importance of knowing how your proposal will be reviewed and how important it is to share this information with your mock reviewers. Please note that by the time this book is published, the scoring rubrics and criteria presented here may have changed. Therefore it is important that you validate the evaluation system to be used on your proposal and procure information on the most current one.

The first example from the Office of Educational Research and Improvement is characterized by a specific point system, heavily weighted toward national significance and project design.

Example 1

National significance	30 points
Quality of project design	30 points
Quality of potential contribution of personnel	15 points
Adequacy of resources	15 points
Quality of management plan	10 points
Total	100 points

Examples 2 and 3, the National Institute on Aging (example 2) and the National Science Foundation (example 3), do not use evaluation systems based on a total of 100 points. They use a rating system more than a point system. In situations like these, the grantseeker must ask more questions of the grantor

so that he or she can ascertain what looks "good" under each criterion. After all, to play the game you need to know *all* the rules!
Example 2

- Scientific, technical, or medical significance
- Appropriateness and adequacy of research
- Qualifications of principal investigator/staff
- Availability of resource
- Appropriateness of budget
- Adequacy of plans to include both genders and minorities
- Protection of human subjects

Example 3

- Criterion 1: What is the intellectual merit of the proposed activity?
- Criterion 2: What are the broader impacts of the proposed activity?

Exhibit 14.4 shows NIH's grant application scoring system. This scoring system uses a 9-point rating scale from 1, which equals exceptional, to 9, which equals poor, for the overall impact/priority score as well as the individual review criteria. Ratings are provided only in whole numbers, not decimals.

Few techniques suggested in this book will have a more dramatic effect on the quality of your proposals than the grants quality circle. Support for this activity will be rewarded through the promotion of a better image with reviewers and federal staff, as well as an increase in quality proposals from staff members participating in this activity. After the suggestions from your quality circle have been incorporated into your final proposal, you are ready to move on to submission.

Use the action steps' chart shown in figure 14.1 to plan ahead for incorporating the use of a quality circle review into your plan.

Note

1. Gary Fellers, *The Deming Vision: SPC/TQM for Administrators* (Milwaukee: ASQC Quality Press, 1992).

EXHIBIT 14.4
The NIH Grant Application Scoring System

Impact	Score	Descriptor	Additional Guidance on Strengths/Weaknesses
High	1	Exceptional	Exceptionally strong with essentially no weaknesses
High	2	Outstanding	Extremely strong with negligible weaknesses
High	3	Excellent	Very strong with only some minor weaknesses
Medium	4	Very Good	Strong but with numerous minor weaknesses
Medium	5	Good	Strong but with a least one moderate weakness
Medium	6	Satisfactory	Some strengths but also some moderate weaknesses
Low	7	Fair	Some strengths but with at least one major weakness
Low	8	Marginal	A few strengths and a few major weaknesses
Low	9	Poor	Very few strengths and numerous major weaknesses

Minor Weakness: An easily addressable weakness that does not substantially lessen impact
Moderate Weakness: A weakness that lessens impact
Major Weakness: A weakness that severely limits impact

Non-numeric score options: NR = Not Recommended for Further Consideration, DF = Deferred, AB = Abstention, CF = Conflict, NP = Not Present, ND = Not Discussed

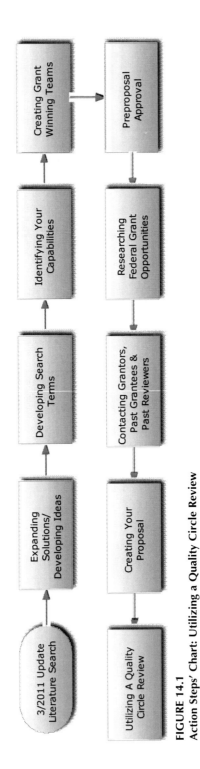

FIGURE 14.1
Action Steps' Chart: Utilizing a Quality Circle Review

15

Submission

What to Do and What Not to Do

A LTHOUGH THIS CHAPTER addresses the federal grants area, much of the information it contains can also be applied to other government funding sources such as state, county, and city. Irrespective of which type of public funding source you are submitting your proposal to, you do not want to do anything at this late stage that may have a negative impact on your submitted proposal's outcome.

What to Do

Submit your proposal a day or two before the deadline. A week before is even better. Do not position yourself as a last-minute applicant who beats the deadline by a few minutes. After all your hard work you do not want to position yourself as a loser. Grantors have told me that they worry about funding last-minute Herculean proposal developers because they are likely to experience problems with their expenditure rates (that is, having leftover money that ends up as a grant continuation or extension), late or missing reports and evaluations, and a host of other maladies that could make the grantor's program look bad to Congress.

Follow all instructions and every rule. Do not wait until your proposal has been written, has undergone a mock review, and is ready to be sent out before you read the submission guidelines prescribed by Grants.gov. Review the submittal requirements early to make sure you have enough time to comply with them. Do not jeopardize your chances for success by failing to show funders that you have read and complied with their rules for submission.

Unfortunately, many grantseekers read the requirements too late and find that they cannot meet the grantor's deadlines. They then include a note with their proposal saying that they will forward the necessary documents at a later date. This is a red flag to grantors and alerts them that this applicant may be a problem. This may even get your proposal automatically rejected.

Even with extensive application guidelines and instructions, grantseekers make mistakes in obtaining appropriate or authorized signatures and following specific requirements regarding page length, number of pages, assurances, and so on. In fact, it would be too time consuming to list all of the problems federal grantors have in gaining compliance with their rules. Review and follow the submittal procedures contained in your application package carefully.

Grants.gov is the primary means for applying for federal grants, and its submittal procedures must be followed precisely. The process can be timely, and problems are bound to occur if you attempt it at the last minute. In fact, it can take longer to submit your proposal electronically than it did with the old hardcopy system that Grants.gov has replaced. If you wish to apply for a grant through Grants.gov, you and your organization must complete the Grants .gov registration process. To register, your organization will need to provide its Data Universal Number System (DUNS) number. If your organization does not know its DUNS number or needs to register for one, visit Dun & Bradstreet at fedgov.dnb.com/webform/displayHomePage.do. You should receive your DUNS number information online the same day you register. Your organization must also be registered with the Central Contractor Registration (CCR). Ask the grant administrator, chief financial officer, or authorizing official of your organization if your organization has registered with the CCR. If your organization is not registered, you can apply online by going to www.ccr .gov. If your organization already has an Employment Identification Number (EIN) or Taxpayer Identification Number (TIN), then you should allow one to three business days to complete the entire CCR registration. If your organization does not have an EIN or TIN, then you should allow two weeks for obtaining the information from the IRS when requesting the EIN or TIN via phone or Internet. In addition, your organization needs to renew its CCR registration once a year. This step may take up to five business days. When your organization registers with CCR, you must designate an E-Business Point of Contact (E-Biz POC). This person will identify a special password. The password gives the E-Biz POC authority to designate which staff member(s) from your organization are allowed to submit applications electronically through Grants.gov. Staff members from your organization designated to submit applications are called Authorized Organization Representatives (AORs). Before you can submit proposals online via Grants.gov your E-Biz POC has to approve AORs to submit applications on behalf of your organization, and the

AORs must have completed profiles with Grants.gov to create their username and password. All of these steps should be completed fairly quickly. However, registration problems can arise at one stage or another. Therefore, start early so you do not miss any deadlines due to nonregistration.

The workload at Grants.gov has increased tremendously since Congress has mandated a move to a paperless grants system. Federal applications submitted via Grants.gov increased 50 percent from 2008 to 2009 to over three hundred thousand submissions. The federal economic stimulus funds have pushed this number much higher. The accompanying increase in workload can result in problems. So again, start early and submit early.

The date and time of submittal will be recorded with your proposal. Keep this in mind when submitting your proposal. Especially since a program officer once confided in me that her office used the date and time record as one way to break ties when proposals were scored equally.

What Not to Do

It is recommended that you limit the use of elected representatives in the grants process, especially at submittal time. Your institution may have rules governing who can contact elected officials. Between the time it takes to get permission and the controversy over the earmarking of federal grant funds, I recommend you avoid congresspeople and senators. Federal bureaucrats view the use of congresspeople and their aides as potentially unethical and possibly illegal. Elected officials want to be viewed by you, the voter and grant applicant, as ready to help in any way, but their assistance should be enlisted only when your own efforts have failed in preproposal contact and information gathering about past grants and federal program priorities.

Do not ask program officers for extra time or a later submittal date, and do not ask to send in any parts of the proposal after the deadline. Do not contact program officers after submission. This is viewed as an attempt to influence the grantor's review process and decision. On a rare occasion, advancements in the field could dramatically affect a proposal you have already submitted. In this instance, you should alert the program officer of the ramifications of the advancements and how they will affect your proposal's protocol or budget. Send the program officer an e-mail explaining the situation and ask him to pass the information on to the reviewers if he or she feels it is appropriate to do so. For example, a piece of equipment or software that could reduce the length of your grant period or result in significant savings could impact your selection as a grantee. Therefore, it would be optimum if the program officer passed this information on to the review group. However, it is solely at the discretion of the program officer to send the new information to the reviewers.

Other Submission Techniques

- Check to see what your proposal looks like when received by electronic submission. What happens to graphics and to the layout and design? A little care may pay off dramatically.
- Double-check with your institution's grants office to see when it needs your proposal in order to do its job and who the Authorized Organization Representative (AOR) is to make the transmittal official.
- Check with your grants office to see if you (or it) could send a copy of your proposal abstract or summary to your congressperson's office. Advise the congressperson that you do not want or expect any intervention at this point, but let him or her know the approximate or anticipated date of the notice award (usually several months away). In most cases, federal granting officials will inform the congressperson of awards before they notify the grantee. Therefore, it is important to alert your congressperson that you have submitted a proposal and that you will contact him or her again closer to the notification date. Let your congressperson know that you would appreciate it if he or she would contact you immediately if he or she receives notice of your award first so that you can prepare a joint public relations release. Remind your congressperson that you are not requesting an earmark or for him or her to contact a program officer.

Place the submittal date for your federal application on your action steps' chart (see figure 15.1).

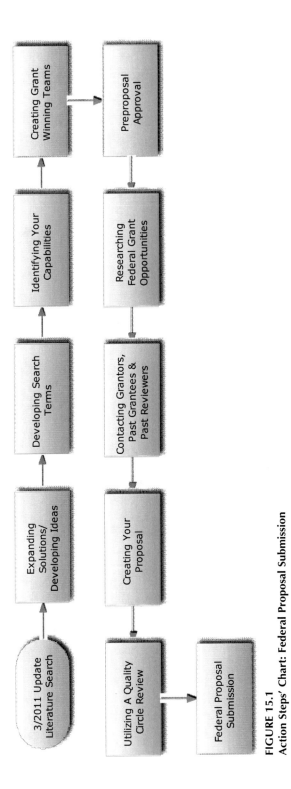

FIGURE 15.1
Action Steps' Chart: Federal Proposal Submission

16

Federal Grant Requirements

Many nonprofit agencies exhibit great fear and trepidation over the many rules regarding federal grant moneys. These fears are basically unwarranted and should be of concern only to nonprofit organizations that do not have adequate fiscal rules and regulations. The restrictions governing usage of federal funds are understandable and in many case reasonable. Yes, there are instances of disallowed expenditures two or three years after a grant has been completed, but they are avoidable. Most people remember the exception rather than the rule. Over $500 billion in federal grant funds were awarded last year and only a small fraction of grantees will have their expenditures disallowed or experience a problem with an audit. Most likely, your existing personnel, accounting, and purchasing procedures will be adequate. If you must make changes in your system to ensure the adequate handling of federal funds, however, do so. Such changes will increase the credibility of your system.

With the increase in consortia grants and grants with several coprincipal investigators who may be with different nonprofit organizations, you will be required to list one partner as the official fiscal agent for the funds. All partners must comply with relevant Office of Management and Budget (OMB) circulars for each organization. If your nonprofit is not experienced in federal grants management, include a college or university partner in your consortia and ask it to be the fiscal agent. Colleges and universities have experience in this area and have the software systems in place to comply with the guidelines.

The Federal Grants Requirement Worksheet (exhibit 16.1) will help you comply with most federal grant requirements. If your institution has a grants

EXHIBIT 16.1
Federal Grants Requirement Worksheet

Project Title: _____

Project Director: _____

Federal Account Identification Number: _____

Agency Staff: _____

Agency Phone Number: _____ Agency Fax Number: _____ Agency Email: _____

Notification of Award Received on (Date): _____

Start Date of Project: _____ End Date of Project: _____

Dates Reports Are Due: _____

Final Report Due On (Date): _____

Number of Years Funding Can Be Applied For: _____

Matching or In-Kind Requirements: _____% $_____

Where Matching or In-Kind Records Will Be Kept:_____

Who Will Be Responsible for Keeping Them: _____

Federal Rules Governing This Grant

OMB Circulars/Guidelines Governing Grant Expenditures:

_____

_____

Location of OMB Circulars/Guidelines Governing Grant Expenditures:

_____

_____

Special Rules and Federal Management Circulars (List from Assurances Section
   of Proposal):

_____

_____

Location of Special Rules and Federal Management Circulars:

_____

_____

Federal Rules and Your Organization's Policy On

Copyrights: _____

_____

Patents: _____

_____

Drug Usage and Counseling: _____

(*continued*)

EXHIBIT 16.1
(*Continued*)

Fair and Equal Employment: _____
_____

Institutional Review Boards (Include Person Responsible for Compliance
and Approval)

Human Subjects:
_____
_____

Animal Subjects:
_____
_____

Recombinant DNA:
_____
_____

Radioactive Material:
_____
_____

Research Misconduct:
_____
_____

Other:
_____
_____

administration office, this worksheet may not be necessary, but you, the project director, still need to know the facts so that you can help in the overall administration of your grant.

Federal Grants Requirement Worksheet

The Federal Grants Requirement Worksheet will help you familiarize yourself with and keep abreast of the basic obligations your nonprofit organization agrees to fulfill by accepting federal grant funds.

1. Complete the first section of the worksheet when you receive notice of funding. Include the federal account identification number and all other information you can supply. It is critical that you record the actual start date or date funded so that you do not charge any grant expenditures before the grant's official award date. Review your project planner and record the dates on which you must supply progress indicators/milestones/progress reports.
2. List the OMB circulars that will govern your grant expenditures (see exhibit 16.3 at the end of the chapter) and where the circulars are located.
3. Record any information about the number of years of funding that can be applied for.
4. Indicate the percentage and dollar total of the cost-sharing/matching fund requirements, where the records will be kept, and who will be responsible for keeping them.
5. Acceptance of federal funds requires that your organization have a policy regarding drug use and counseling of employees.
6. If your grant calls for the creation of unique materials, make note of the rules regarding copyrights, patents, ownership, and use. Noting these in advance reduces problems later.
7. The fair and equal employment rules are reasonable and should pose no problems for most nonprofit organizations.
8. List the office or person responsible for approval of projects that involve copyrights or patents, or the use of human and animal subjects, recombinant DNA, or radioactive material. If you work for an organization that already has institutional review boards, be sure to check with those groups. If your organization does not have institutional review boards or committees, do not initiate them. Instead, involve a university- or college-related individual on your grants advisory committee, and ask him or her to use his or her institution's review board.

Even though your proposal may not call for the performance of hard-core research, the federal government is very broad in its interpretation of what activities pose a potential danger to humans. In fact, federal officials require human subjects' approval for most needs assessment surveys, model projects, and demonstration grants.

Raising and Documenting Matching Funds

One of the more confusing areas of federal grants is the requirement of matching funds or in-kind contributions (also known as cost sharing). An organization can be asked to supply cash, services, or facilities to match a percentage of the grant. This requirement may change over the years that federal funds support the project. For example, year 1 may require a 20 percent match, year 2 a 40 percent match, and year 3 a 50 percent match.

In some cases, the federal instructions state that a match is not required but encouraged. If you have inquired into this matter, discovered that a match will help you get funded, and have designated a specific amount in your budget for a match or in-kind contribution, be aware that this match must be documented and will be subject to an audit to verify the amount. It is always wise to document and list the efforts and costs that will be provided by your organization and partners. Review your project planner for any personnel, consultants, contract services, supplies, equipment, or materials that will be contributed to your project. Remember not to list anything that is being supplied to this grant that was provided under any other federal program.

The Worksheet on Sources of Matching Funds (exhibit 16.2) can help you plan a successful matching funds campaign before you approach federal agencies. The worksheet contains several standard methods for cost sharing and provides an evaluation system for each method. (This worksheet can also be useful when working with foundations and corporations that request matching support.)

Federal Grants Management Circulars

The highly regulated, detailed rules about grants management are probably the most imposing characteristic of federal grants. These rules may specify allowable costs, indirect cost rates, accounting requirements, and the like. Before getting involved in government grants, you and your accounting department should review the appropriate grants management circulars. Such a review usually diminishes fears about your organization's ability to comply with federal grant requirements. In most cases you will find that your organization has safeguards in effect that meet the requirements.

The Office of Management and Budget produces circulars outlining uniform standards for financial dealings with government granting agencies. These circulars can be accessed online at www.whitehouse.gov/omb/circulars/. To obtain circulars that are not available online, call the Office of Management and Budget's information line at (202) 395-3080.

The following section is a broad description of OMB Circular A-110.

OMB Circular A-110

OMB Circular A-110 is entitled "Uniform Administrative Requirements for Grants and Agreements with Institutions of Higher Education, Hospitals and

EXHIBIT 16.2
Worksheet on Sources of Matching Funds

Project Title: _____

Total Project Cost:$_____

Match Required: _____% $_____

Review each of the following sources of matching funds. Check with federal officials to ensure that your match is in compliance with their rules and will be accepted. Make sure that nothing listed under your match has been provided from federal funds.

1. Personnel—List the percentage of time and effort of each individual who will be contributing to the match. Include salaries, wages, and fringe benefits.

   Options:
   Include the time and effort of volunteers, consultants, and/or corporate sponsors if allowable by the grantor.

   If the project calls for staff training or development, will your organization be required to increase salaries? If so, check with the grantor to see whether this can be listed as a match.

2. Equipment—List any equipment that will be purchased primarily to carry out this project. Include the cost of each piece and the total equipment cost.

3. Facilities—List the location, square footage, and cost per foot for each facility and the total facilities (space) cost.

4. Foundation/Corporate Grantors—What other grantors could you approach for a grant to match this grant?

   Foundations:

   Corporations:

5. Fund-raising Activities—In some cases you may have to resort to fund-raising activities to develop your matching portion. List the activities and the net return expected from each.

   Special Events (Dance, Raffle, etc.):

   Sales of Products:

   Other:

Other Non-Profit Organizations." This circular is a guide to the rules regarding federal grants. The circular is divided into the following four subparts:

- Subpart A—General
- Subpart B—Pre-Award Requirements
- Subpart C—Post-Award Requirements
  Financial and Program Management
  Property Standards
  Procurement Standards
  Reports and Records
  Termination and Enforcement
- Subpart D—After-the-Award Requirements

OMB Circular A-110 also includes an appendix that addresses contract provisions.

Other Grants Management OMB Circulars

Colleges and universities will also be interested in OMB Circular A-21, which defines cost principles for federal research and development grants to educational institutions. All nonprofit organizations should familiarize themselves with OMB Circular A-122, "Cost Principles for Non-Profit Organizations," and state and local governments must also review OMB Circular A-87, "Cost Principles for State, Local and Indian Tribal Governments," and OMB Circular A-102, "Grants and Cooperative Agreements with State and Local Governments." Please be advised that you should always refer to the most current circular of the specific rules and regulations in your area.

Exhibit 16.3 lists all of the grants management OMB circulars in numerical sequence. Fears concerning the expenditure of federal grant funds are reduced when you request the appropriate OMB circulars for your type of organization and review the rules with your fiscal staff. From purchasing to personnel, your organization will most likely already have the necessary safeguards in place. Those areas that look as if they will pose a problem can be addressed in a general manner for all federal grants, or handled separately case by case to avoid any difficulties.

EXHIBIT 16.3
Grants Management OMB Circulars

Cost Principles
   A-21   Educational Institutions
   A-87   State and Local Governments
   A-122 Non-Profit Organizations

Administrative Requirements
   A-102 State and Local Governments
   A-110 Institutions of Higher Education, Hospitals, and Other Non-Profit
       Organizations

Audit Requirements
   A-133 States, Local Governments, and Non-Profit Organizations

17

Dealing with the Decision
of Public Funding Sources

THE FEDERAL GOVERNMENT has continued to make improvements in the entire grants process. This includes making award determinations that are
understandable and consistent across all of its agencies and one thousand
granting programs. Instead of making determinations that left grantseekers
confused (such as "supportable but not fundable") most federal granting
agencies now use the following determinations:

- Accepted as written and at the requested amount of funding.
- Accepted with modifications (usually budget modifications, which will
  affect some activities.
- Rejected with reviewer's comments (the proposal did not reach the level
  or score required for funding, but comments have been included, possibly to encourage resubmittal).
- Rejected without reviewers' comments (the proposal did not reach the
  level required to invest the time necessary to respond to the proposal in
  detail, no comments were included, and thus the grantseeker has no idea
  whether to resubmit).

Accepted

If your proposal is accepted as constructed and at the requested amount, consider taking the following steps:

1. Thank the grantor. Whether you are notified by phone, letter, or e-mail, send the program or project officer a thank-you letter expressing your appreciation for the time and effort staff and reviewers expended on your proposal.
2. Request the reviewers' comments, and include your e-mail address.
3. Ask the federal official for insight into what you could have done better. Yes, you can even improve a funded proposal. Learn how.
4. Invite the program or project officer for a site visit.
5. Ask the official what mistakes other grantees often make in carrying out their funded grant so you can be sure to avoid those errors.
6. Review the reporting requirements. What does the grantor require (milestones, progress indicators, budget documentation, changes in budget categories, and so on) and when?

Accepted with Budget Modifications

Should your proposal receive this response, do the following:

1. Send the funding source a thank-you letter.
2. E-mail or call the funding source and suggest that the program officer refer to your project planner to negotiate the budget terms.
3. Discuss the option of reducing some of the project's methods or activities to arrive at the amount the funding source has in mind or was recommended by the reviewers.
4. If several activities must be eliminated, consider dropping the accomplishment of an objective or reducing the expected degree of change.
5. If you are forced to negotiate away the supporting structure necessary to achieve your objectives or prove or disapprove your hypothesis, be prepared to turn down the funds. After all, you do not want to enter into an agreement that will cause you to lose credibility later.

Rejected with Comments

If your proposal is rejected but reviewer suggestions and comments are provided, review them. Are there comments or suggestions common to several of the reviewers? Do the comments point to a basic problem with the approach or protocol or with the importance of dealing with the problem in general? Do the reviewers suggest changes that you could entertain in a resubmittal without dramatically altering your grants approach? Do the comments suggest resubmittal?

If you get the sense from the reviewers' comments that resubmittal with the suggested changes is a good idea, consider the following:

1. Sending the funding official a thank-you letter or e-mail in appreciation for his or her time and effort as well as that of the reviewers and staff. Let the funding official know that although you were aware of the risk of failure before you invested your time in applying, you would appreciate assistance in changing your proposal and reapplying.
2. Asking the funding official for more suggestions.
3. Finding out whether your proposal could possibly be funded as a pilot project, as a needs assessment, or in some other way.
4. Asking whether there are any ways the funding source could assist you in getting ready for the next submission cycle, such as conducting a preliminary review.
5. Asking whether it would be wise for you to reapply. What are your chances and what would you have to change? (Reapply if the program officer is even the slightest bit optimistic.)
6. Asking whether you could become a reviewer to learn more about the review process and how to improve your proposal.

By examining the reviewers' comments, you may find that some reviewers scored a section of your proposal outstanding, while others gave the same section a low score. This situation can create a dilemma. Changing your proposal to reflect one reviewer's comments may negate another reviewer's comments, and your changes could result in resubmission scores that are just average. Ask the grantor what you can do about this situation. Also, ask an outside expert to review your proposal; even if you must pay someone to review the proposal, you need insight into what is causing this discrepancy.

Your resubmittal application should take the reviewers' comments to heart and the changes you make in your proposal should reflect them. You may even mention that the changes made in your resubmittal were suggested by the original reviewers. Sending the same proposal in hopes of different reviewers and a better outcome is not viewed positively. Some reapplications will require you to address the changes between the revised proposal and your initial attempt in a separate section of the proposal.

Rejected without Comments

Agency reviewing procedures call for a process that eliminates proposals with a low likelihood of funding from a thorough review. Some grantors even require that 25 to 50 percent of the applications they receive are given this brief and expedited review and then returned to the applicants without reviewer comments. Many of the rejected applications that are not read thoroughly or evaluated and scored are believed to be of low quality and not likely to produce the intended outcomes. Often, they are also cited for errors in the application itself or for nonallowable costs or inappropriate ideas.

If your proposal is rejected outright and you do not receive comments, or if you receive a notice stating that there were many more credible proposals than funding available, it may be necessary to develop a different approach and not even consider resubmitting the same proposal. It does no good to defend your proposal or to write a nasty response. When rejected, I like to think that I may be ahead of my time and more visionary than the reviewers. Discuss options with your advisory group and brainstorm a different approach to solving the problem.

In addition, write or e-mail the program officer to thank him or her for the opportunity and ask if you could

- be a reviewer to learn how to prepare a better proposal and
- meet with him or her to discuss a new approach.

No matter what the determination (accepted, accepted with modifications, rejected with comments, or rejected without comments), or the degree to which your proposal was reviewed, your response to your grant application's outcome must be positive. Whether you are jubilant or depressed, thank the grantor and demonstrate your willingness to learn from the experience and, if possible, the funding source's feedback.

Be sure to put a reminder to deal with the funder's decision on your action steps' chart so you do not forget to send a thank-you (see figure 17.1).

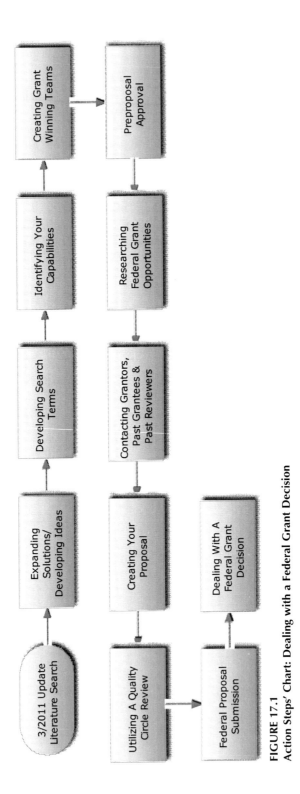

FIGURE 17.1
Action Steps' Chart: Dealing with a Federal Grant Decision

18

Follow-Up with Government Funding Sources

THE OBJECTIVE OF FOLLOW-UP is to position yourself as an asset to funding sources and not a pest. You want to develop professional relationships and maintain contact with funding sources throughout the grants process, not just at submittal and award time. In addition to advising funders of your willingness to serve as a reviewer, consider

- sending them copies of your accepted articles,
- forwarding notes on special articles or books in your area to them,
- inviting them to visit your organization,
- asking whether they would like to speak at your professional group or association's conference, or at a special grants conference,
- asking them what meeting or conferences they will be attending so that you can look them up, or
- requesting information about what you can do to have an impact on legislation affecting their funding levels or allocations.

By remaining on grantors' mailing lists and reviewing their agency publications (that is, *NSF Guide, NIH Bulletin*) or the *Federal Register*, you will gain knowledge of the next funding opportunity. Do not wait until next year's deadline to begin thinking about your ensuing application. Start to plan for next year right after funding decisions are made for the current year.

The best way to learn what is going on is to visit the funding source personally. Keep in touch. Watch for meeting announcements in the *Federal Register*. Testify at committee hearings that will affect the agency and its funding level.

Send the agency blind copies of your efforts to have an impact on legislation for the program. By doing so, you are helping to ensure that its program receives continued appropriations. It ensures that they have a job, and that you continue to have a funding source. Use your association memberships and legislative committees to push for changes that benefit the particular agency, and write to Senate and House appropriations committees to increase funding. Attend professional meetings and sessions that program officers are speaking at, and ask questions.

Developing Continued Grant Support

Although federal officials may change jobs and positions, they seem to reappear again and again. A systematic approach to recording research on funding sources and officials will prove useful as you come across old friends and make new ones. By maintaining your relationships, whether you have received funding or not, you demonstrate to funding sources that you plan to be around for a while and that you will not forget them as soon as you receive their checks. Unfortunately, changes in staffing at government agencies make maintaining contacts more difficult. Just when things are going great, the program officers you have been working with will move on. But take heart; they may appear again somewhere down the grants road, so keep on their good side!

If you have used the concepts presented in this manual to develop a proactive grants process, you have a system that alerts you to changes in program rules, deadlines, and the like through the *Federal Register*, mailing lists, personal contacts, and established links. The key to continued success is to repeat these steps that have brought you to this point.

Part 3

PRIVATE/FOUNDATION FUNDING OPPORTUNITIES

19

Understanding the
Private Foundation Marketplace

THE FOUNDATION GRANTS MARKETPLACE is dynamic, fascinating, and very lucrative for the astute grants person. However, the zeal to go after foundation grants must be tempered by the fact that this sector of the grants marketplace has fallen by 8.9 percent in recent years. Foundation assets are generally in the stock market and because of this the majority of foundations have been hit hard by losses. Nonetheless, even with its recent decline of $3.8 billion, there is still $38.44 billion to consider for your projects.

Foundations grant funds to many of the projects and research that government grantors will not. They provide a unique source of funds for nonprofits that are seeking funds for nontraditional, but much-needed, projects. And they are a great source of grants to develop the needs documentation and preliminary data that federal grantors will not support.

While I cannot say I have researched all foundations relative to their grant recipients, I can say that I have yet to come across a foundation that provides support for personal debt reduction, the paying off of mortgages, or personal gifts. So forget those mass-marketed e-mail alerts about using the private foundation marketplace to get rich personally. They are all scams. But, for your nonprofit organization, this marketplace can be a gold mine.

In addition to greater funding flexibility and variety, 99 percent of foundations require an abbreviated proposal that is typically less than two to three pages in length, and some may require only a one-page letter of intent. While this may sound great, the brevity of the process can encourage grantseekers to simply locate the name and address of twenty or thirty foundations and send the same letter proposal to each of them. This "dear occupant, please send foundation money" approach is a fatal mistake, resulting in rejection and negative positioning. In addition, the foundations receiving these massive amounts of inappropriate proposals are totally overwhelmed. As Martin Teitel, a foundation director, writes in his book *"Thank You for Submitting Your Proposal,"* "People find or buy lists of funders, plug them into their database, and send out what must be immense numbers of generic proposals. These misplaced proposals waste the effort of busy grantmakers, and clog up the funder screening system."[1]

In order to develop an appreciation of the dilemma caused by hundreds of thousands of misplaced proposals, you must look at the facts. In 2009 foundation grant making represented 13 percent of the $303 billion in philanthropic giving in the United States. This equates to roughly $38 billion for which approximately 1,500,000 nonprofit organizations competed. This $38 billion was granted by approximately 110,000 501(c)(3) private-grant-making foundations. A study of the 10,000 largest independent foundations conducted by the Foundation Center and the Urban Institute in collaboration with Philanthropic Research reported that nearly three-quarters of the independent foundations surveyed did not have *any* paid staff. A 2006 Foundation Center survey of 20,891 foundations with at least $1 million in assets, or making grants of $100,000 or more, substantiated this dismal statistic—only 16.8 percent or 3,532 of the 20,891 foundations surveyed reported having staff. A 2009 study by the Foundation Center surveyed 11,617 foundations including the top 1,000 foundations based on total giving. The survey showed that of the 11,617 foundations, 3,178 or 27.4 percent reported having staff. Even though this is an increase over the 2006 figures, the number of foundations with staff positions is still much lower in comparison to federal grantors. *Every* federal granting agency has an office and staff.

Because of the lack of staff, foundation board members are generally the ones who review all submitted proposals and make the granting decisions. Few foundations use professional reviewers or experts in the field to review proposals. If there is a support person, he or she is normally responsible for just logging in proposals and perhaps for an initial screening of them to see if they contain anything close to what the foundation values. Many foundations even share directors and support staff in an effort to reduce costs.

You might think that of the 110,000 private-grant-making foundations most would have a website. A 2009 survey conducted by the Foundation Center of 11,617 of the larger foundations indicated that only 26.1 percent or 3,035 maintained a website. While the federal government has moved to electronic submittal, only a few hundred of the foundations with websites provide an interactive application form that allows for electronic preparation and submission of proposals. While the number of foundations with websites and electronic application processes will certainly increase, change is slow and most foundations lack the motivation to make submittal easier—a move that would make their workload greater!

To fully understand private foundations you need to think like the wealthy individuals who create them and serve on their boards. Let us assume you have created a foundation to move vast sums of your wealth into a tax-deductible entity that will allow you, your family, and your friends to fund projects and organizations that further your values, beliefs, and life's work. According to IRS rules, you must give away at least 5 percent of the market value of your foundation's assets each year to the nonprofit groups your bylaws designate as recipients or the IRS will penalize your foundation and levy a tax. However, the costs related to the administration of your foundation (that is, staffing, office space, equipment, travel, board salaries, and so forth) are included in this 5 percent. For instance, if the market value of your foundation's assets is $10 million, and you decide to disburse the minimum required amount of 5 percent or $500,000, you can subtract from this the cost of your director, support staff, office, and overhead, which could easily reach $250,000, leaving you only $250,000 to give away in the form of grants. So what can you do to reduce your administrative costs and increase the portion of the 5 percent you distribute through the grants process? You can decide not to hire a director or create an office, or have a staff. After all, you do not need a staff or reviewers. You know what you want to fund; thus, you want to make as much money as possible available for grants. Now you are thinking like the creator of a foundation.

The desire of foundations to support nonprofit organizations is evidenced by a study conducted by the Foundation Source (*Chronicle of Philanthropy*, July 15, 2010). The study showed that small and medium foundations exceeded the IRS's 5 percent asset requirement. This is a very positive sign, especially during a time when overall foundation grants have declined.

To be a successful foundation grantseeker, you must discover what your prospective foundation funding source values, seek to understand how it looks at the world, and present your project in such a way that to reject it would actually conflict with the foundation's values, stated beliefs, and past giving patterns. Review chapter 1 and the concept of values-based grantseeking to increase your understanding of private foundations and what motivates the individuals who create them. To further assist you in this research process, read the following brief descriptions of the basic types of foundations and then review the Grantseekers' Private Foundation Decision Matrix (table 19.1) to help you select which of the four basic types of private foundations is right for your project—national general purpose, special purpose, community, or family.

TABLE 19.1
Grantseekers' Private Foundation Decision Matrix

Type of Foundation	Geographic Need	Type of Project	Grant Award Size for Field of Interest	Image	Credentials of P.I./P.D.	Preproposal Contact	Application	Review System	Grants Admin. (Rules)
National General Purpose	National need—local regional population	Model, Innovative	Large, Medium	National image	National	Write, phone, email	Short concept paper— longer form if interested	Staff and some peer review	Few audits and rules
Special Purpose	Need in area of interest	Model, Innovative, Research	Large to small	Image not as critical as solution	Strong image in field of interest	Write, phone, email	Short concept paper— longer form if interested	Board review (some staff)	Few audits and rules

Community	Local need	Operation, Replication, Building/ Equipment	Small	Local image	Respected locally	Write, phone, email, go see	Short letter proposal	Board review	Few audits and rules
Family	Varies—but geographic concern for need	Innovative, Replication, Building/ Equipment, Some Research	Medium, Small	Regional image	Local, Regional	Write, phone, email	Short letter proposal	Board review	Very few audits and rules
Nonprofits, Service Clubs, etc.	Local	Replication, Building/ Equipment, Scholarship	Small	Local image and member involvement	Local	Write, phone, email, present to committee or member	Short letter proposal	Committee review and/or member vote	Few audits and rules

National General Purpose Foundations

To be designated as a national general purpose foundation, a foundation does not need to fit a hard-and-fast definition. *National general purpose* refers to the foundation's scope and type of granting pattern. Foundations in this group have a philanthropic interest in several subject areas and make grants for proposals that will have a broad-scale impact across the United States and the world. They prefer model, creative, innovative projects that other groups can replicate to solve the same or similar problems. Since national general purpose foundations like to promote change, they do not usually fund deficits, operating income, or the many necessary but not highly visible or creative functions of organizations. Recently a growing number have been funding operating costs because the nonprofit organizations they depend on to do the work they value may not be around to apply if they (the nonprofits) cannot make payroll.

National general purpose foundations have staff and, in some instances, use professional consultants as reviewers. Their applications are usually longer than those of the other types of foundations, and they often have more rules and regulations. They expect those they fund to have major players and experts on staff and in consortia, and their grant size is larger than those of other foundations. In addition, they are likely to have websites.

Of the 110,000 private-grant-making foundations, there are probably less than 300 national general purpose foundations. Even though there are so few, most people have no trouble naming one, such as the Rockefeller or Ford Foundation. This is because they get a lot of attention for the size of the awards they make and the initiatives they launch. Unfortunately, the public image of these well-known foundations is what leads many grantseekers into thinking that the foundation marketplace in general makes more and bigger grants than it actually does.

Special Purpose Foundations

Often confused with national general purpose foundations because some are very large and financed by unusually large asset bases, special purpose foundations are different in that they define their area of concern quite specifically. For example, the Robert Wood Johnson Foundation is a special purpose foundation in the health field, and the Exxon Education Foundation and the Carnegie Foundation for the Advancement of Teaching are special purpose foundations focusing on education. While grant sizes can be considerable, special purpose foundations put the applicant's likelihood of making a contribution, or a breakthrough, in their area of concern foremost and *may* put less importance on staff prestige, publishing, and so forth.

There are probably only a few hundred of these dedicated special purpose foundations, and the key to success in this marketplace is to match your project with the foundation's specific area of interest and to demonstrate how your project will impact it.

Community Foundations

According to the Foundation Center, there were 717 community foundations in the United States in 2009. Although they use a variety of geographic parameters to define *community*, community foundations are easy to identify because their name denotes the area they serve (for example, San Diego Foundation, Cleveland Foundation, North Dakota Foundation, and Oregon Foundation).

Some think that community foundations are family foundations that restrict their granting to a particular state, city, or zip code. This is not the case. Community foundations fund projects and programs that no other type of foundation would consider supporting. From program deficits, to operating funds, to seed money for a needs assessment that might lead to a larger state or federal grant, community foundations exist to deal with local needs. They do not care if prospective grantees have national stature in their field. They just want to make sure that the funds they grant will be used to make a difference in the communities they serve. In general, community foundations are concerned with what works and are more interested in supporting the replication of successful projects than in taking chances with experimental approaches or research.

Many community foundations have special programs that help smaller, family foundations by administering their investments and assisting them in soliciting applications, selecting grantees, and meeting their IRS reporting requirements. The community foundation may sponsor a grants forum or focus meeting for these smaller, local foundations, but most of these grantors actually fall under the family foundation category.

Family Foundations

There were approximately 35,693 grant-making family foundations in 2006. These foundations represented more than one-half of all independent foundations and accounted for $16 billion in grants. Because their granting patterns represent the values of the family members whose interests have been memorialized by the creation of the foundations, granting patterns of family foundations vary widely from foundation to foundation and change frequently. Therefore, you must research them thoroughly to keep abreast of changes in interests and commitment.

Sixty percent of family foundations reported less than $1 million in assets in 2006, and most fund locally and in small amounts. In fact, 48 percent gave less than $50,000 in 2006. However, if they value what you propose, and you are in the right locale, you should consider them when developing your grants plan.

Nonprofit Organizations, Membership Groups, Professional Societies, and Service Clubs

In addition to the four basic types of private foundations, many nonprofit organizations, membership groups, professional societies, and service clubs award grants, and many even have foundations attached to them. The awards made through these groups are usually small and limited to a special field of interest. For example, a Kiwanis group may choose to provide support only for the purpose of improving business education in local schools.

The application forms used by these groups are typically short and easy to complete, and they will often provide funding for things that the four basic types of foundations would not consider supporting. While they have been known to provide matching funds for government grants, support for travel to conferences and meetings, and honorariums for experts and guest lecturers, they are particularly interested in funding things that will improve their image and the image of their members in the community.

Types of Grants Made by Private Foundations

The major vehicle of support by private foundations is a cash grant or award. The majority of foundations do not make grants to individuals except in the form of scholarships, and even those may be made through educational institutions. Most private foundations prefer that the third-party 501(c)(3) tax-exempt organization affiliated with the grantee handle and disburse the award.

Program-related investments (PRIs) are an alternative to cash grants and awards, and foundations that make them do so as a supplement to their existing grant programs. In the PRI vehicle your organization applies to a foundation for a low-interest loan, venture capital, or an investment in a charitable-use property. Foundations made $310.5 million in program-related investments to nonprofits in 2006. While this is only a small percentage of the billions in total foundation giving, PRIs should be considered as a potential component of your grants plan. However, if you are interested in seeking a PRI you must do careful research on the foundation first to ensure that this is the type of work the foundation is interested in.

PRIs are often made to organizations with an established relationship with the grant maker. A large portion of PRI dollars support affordable housing and community development. PRI support has also been provided for a variety of capital projects such as preserving historical buildings, repairing churches, emergency loans to social service agencies, and protecting and preserving open space and wildlife habitats.

Another type of foundation that is a financial force in many local communities is the private-grant-making health foundation created from the conversion of nonprofit hospitals and health maintenance organizations to for-profit status. Federal law requires that proceeds from the sale of assets of tax-exempt entities go to charity. One way this requirement can be met is to establish a foundation to benefit the community previously served by the nonprofit. Most of the private grants making health foundations are dedicated to funding health-related projects, although some define health broadly and do provide funding for a variety of community purposes. It is uncertain how the newly passed health care legislation will affect these foundations. However, since the legislation currently utilizes private health care and corporations, they may do well.

Grantseekers' Private Foundation Decision Matrix

The Grantseekers' Private Foundation Decision Matrix (see table 19.1) summarizes the principal types of private foundation funding sources, their major funding characteristics and preferences, and their similarities and differences. Familiarizing yourself with this information will help you create a prioritized list of the best foundations to approach and to determine the appropriate amount of funding to request from each.

Keep in mind that the size of the majority of foundation grant awards is smaller than grantseekers think. Instead of making the mistake of asking for an inappropriate amount of funding from one foundation, consider breaking your proposal into fundable parts with each part appealing to the values and grant award sizes of a different type of foundation funder.

Column 1 of the matrix lists the major foundation funding source types. Columns 2 through 10 provide information on variables such as geographic area, need, type of project, and award size. Please note that the matrix is meant to point you in the right direction only. Follow-up research will allow the proactive grantseeker to further estimate the funder's interest, the appropriateness of the project, and the proper grant size to request before proposal preparation and submission.

To achieve grants success you must be vigilant in attempting to consider all aspects of your proposal from the grantor's point of view. It should be increasingly evident that the "one proposal fits all" method of grantseeking will not meet with a positive response from such a diverse group of private grantors.

Who and What Private Foundations Fund

Most foundations award the majority of their funding in the states where they are located, and unfortunately, there is a great disparity in the number of foundations from state to state. In fact in 2007, 46 percent of the 50 largest foundations by total giving were located in just three of the fifty states (California, New York, and New Jersey).

If you are located in one of the other forty-seven states, remember that even nonprofit organizations in states with none of the 50 largest foundations still attract some grants from foundations located in other states. For example, North Dakota is a state with none of the largest foundations. Yet, in a national sample of all grants of $10,000 or more awarded by more than 1,000 of the larger U.S. foundations, North Dakota was still able to attract 247 grants totaling $21,652,707.

In 2009 the majority of the $38 billion awarded in foundations grants was awarded in grants of less than $10,000. However, the Foundation Center's database includes individual grant records of $10,000 or more awarded by a national sample of 1,490 larger U.S. foundations. The data culminating from this analysis provide valuable insight into what foundations prefer to fund. Grantseekers willing to review this information and use it in a creative manner will be paid well for their efforts.

Instead of spending time rationalizing that your project fits into a grantor's funding priorities, spend your time considering the areas in which foundations concentrate their support and how you can redefine your project to fit into those areas with the greatest percentage of foundation grants. Table 19.2 illustrates foundation grants by recipient category. A quick review of this table demonstrates that health receives the greatest percentage of foundation grants at 22.9 percent, with education a close second at 21.8 percent.

Within each recipient category you should examine the subcategories to determine which get the largest part of the money. Table 19.3 breaks education into several subcategories and shows that of the grants given to education, higher education received the greatest percentage, followed by elementary and secondary. With this in mind, if elementary education is your project's original focus and you redefine it to include a higher education component by partnering with a college or university, you could substantially increase your chances of receiving a grant from a foundation. While I do not

TABLE 19.2
Foundation Grants by Recipient Category

Recipient Category	Percentage of Foundation Grants
Education	21.8
Human Services	12.5
Health	22.9
Arts/Culture	12.5
Public/Society Benefit	10.0
Environment/Animals	8.6
Science/Technology	2.6
International	5.7
Religion	2.2
Social Science	1.2

Source: Giving USA 2010: The Annual Report on Philanthropy for Year 2009

want you to become a sheep in wolf's clothing by making your project look like something it is not, review how you can redefine your project (chapter 5) and think of how a consortium or a different lead partner would provide a much better match to foundation interests and granting patterns.

Also review the *type* of support you are searching for (that is, building and renovation, program development, research, and so on), and ask yourself if you could change your focus slightly (redefine it) to appeal to more grantors because of their preferences for certain types of support. Table 19.4 shows types of support by percentage of dollar value of grants. Based on this information, if you were seeking a grant to fund computer equipment and software you would not expect to attract a foundation grant since computer systems/technology accounts for only .4 percent of the total awarded by percentage of dollar value. Further research on the Foundation Center's

TABLE 19.3
Percent of Foundation Grants by Education Subcategory

Education Subcategories	Percent of Education Grants by Subcategory
Policy Management	0.2
Elementary/Secondary	6.7
Vocational/Technical	0.1
Higher Education	9.4
Graduate/Professional	2.6
Adult/Continuing	0.1
Library Science/Libraries	0.9
Student Services	0.5
Education Services	1.3
Total Percent of Foundation Grants to Education	21.8

Source: Giving USA 2010: The Annual Report on Philanthropy for Year 2009

TABLE 19.4
Types of Support Awarded by Percentage of Dollar Value of Grants

Type of Support	Percentage of Dollar Value of Grants
General Support	19.2
Capital Support	15.8
Capital Campaigns	3.0
Building/Renovation	8.0
Computer Systems/Technology	0.4
Equipment	1.1
Land Acquisition	0.5
Endowments	2.2
Debt Reduction	0.1
Collections Acquisition	0.6
Program Support	51.0
Program Development	41.5
Conferences/Seminars	0.9
Faculty/Staff Development	1.5
Curriculum Development	1.0
Electronic Media/Online Services	1.6
Collections Management	1.1
All Other	3.3
Research	13.6
Student Aid Funds	3.5
Other	2.3
Not Specified	18.1

Source: Giving USA 2010: The Annual Report on Philanthropy for Year 2009

website reveals, in a sample of over 1,000 larger foundations, that this area attracted only 1,110 grants of the 232,228 awarded.

By redefining how the computer equipment and software was going to be used and by whom, you could refocus on a type of support that would increase your chances for funding. For example, if you could demonstrate that it was to be used in conjunction with program development you would dramatically increase your chances since program development received 41.5 percent of the total awarded by percentage of dollar value. When redefining your project you should also take into consideration the average dollar value of grants. For instance, the average dollar value for a computer systems/equipment grant is $92,093, while the average size for a program development grant is $200,672.

Many colleges and universities have rules about who can contact foundations. While I applaud the idea of coordination and control to protect the grantseeker's image, a review of table 19.4 documents how absurd it is to keep the tight control over access to foundation grants in order to keep the development officer's interest in capital campaigns as a priority, especially since capital campaigns represent only 3 percent of the percentage of dollar value of foundation grants!

The private foundation grants marketplace is misunderstood not only by individual grantseekers, but also by entire institutions that have added to the confusion by arbitrarily deciding that government grant applications and contracts should go through a university grants office and that foundation grant proposals should be handled by an institution's development office. One reason in support of this decision is that the development office in most universities is tied to a university foundation—the 501(c)(3) entity required to submit proposals. However, the problem lies in the fact than many development offices limit the access that faculty members have to private foundations so that they (the development offices) can use the foundation marketplace to attempt to fund administrative priorities, such as capital campaigns and endowments. This problem is compounded by the fact that only a small percentage of foundation dollars is actually awarded to fund these types of capital support projects. For example, a quick review of table 19.4 (types of support) demonstrates clearly that foundations prefer to fund the types of projects that emanate from faculty, such as program and research grants (over 50 percent).

While some universities have dealt with this issue by developing two separate 501(c) tax-exempt entities, one for the university's overall grants effort and another for its development effort, one thing is critical for the grantseeker to understand. The quest for a private foundation grant needs to be coordinated within your institution or organization so that you can make sure you do not approach a foundation that is already being approached by several of your colleagues. Not only is this embarrassing, but it presents the prospective grantor with a negative image of you and your institution.

Many foundations allow only one proposal from one institution at one time and will immediately disallow all of the proposals submitted by the institution if they receive multiple applications. To avoid this type of problem, use one or more of the research tools presented in chapter 20 to locate the foundation most suited to fund your project, and then develop a profile of what it funds. Take this profile to your grants or development office (or any other pertinent office) to gain approval to make preproposal contact. This will provide your institution with the heads-up it needs to ensure its integrity with prospective funding sources and to move you one step closer to grants success.

Note

1. Martin Teitel, *"Thank You for Submitting Your Proposal": A Foundation Director Reveals What Happens Next* (Medfield, MA: Emerson & Church Publishers, 2006), 28–29.

20

Researching Potential
Private Foundation Grantors

How to Find the Foundation That
Is Best Suited to Fund Your Project

A KEY TO SUCCESSFUL GRANTSEEKING with foundations is to gather the most complete and accurate information possible on funding sources before you approach them. The Foundation Research Form (exhibit 20.1) will help you do this. Review exhibit 20.1 carefully so you know what to look for and how to use this information. Complete one worksheet for each foundation you research. Seldom will you uncover all the data requested in exhibit 20.1, but try to complete as much information on the form as possible, and remember that even a partially completed worksheet will help you make a more intelligent decision on whether you should solicit grant support from a particular foundation funding source.

For each foundation your research uncovers, look first at its areas of interest, activities funded, organizations funded, and geographic funding preferences. Do not even bother recording the foundation's name and address on the worksheet (exhibit 20.1) unless it funds what you want where you are. You should think of yourself as a broker that is seeking to match the interests of each partner. If there is a match, move right to the money. Although foundations can grant more than the minimum 5 percent of their assets required by the IRS, many follow the 5 percent guideline. Therefore, uncovering financial information such as the amount of their asset bases can be very insightful.

In addition to the research you conduct on grant-making foundations, you should also uncover and record as much information as possible on the decision makers in those foundations. The Funding Executive Research Worksheet (exhibit 20.2) is designed to help you do this.

EXHIBIT 20.1
Foundation Research Form

The following form outlines the data you need to collect in order to make a decision to seek funding from this grant source. Your attempts to collect as much of this information as possible will prove rewarding. (When feasible, record the source of the information and the date it was recorded.)

1. Name of Foundation: _____
   Address: _____
   Phone: _____ Fax: _____ E-mail: _____
   Website: _____

2. Contact Person: _____
   Title: _____
   Any Links from Our Organization to Contact Person: _____
   _____

3. Foundation's Areas of Interests: _____
   _____
   _____

4. Eligibility Requirements/Restrictions:

   a. Activities Funded/Restricted: _____
      _____
      _____

   b. Organizations Funded/Restricted: _____
      _____
      _____

   c. Geographic Funding Preferences/Restrictions: _____
      _____
      _____

   d. Other Requirements/Restrictions:
      Application Information _____
      Proposal Length/Restrictions _____
      Application Submittal _____
      Deadline Date(s)_____
      Submittal Rules_____

5. *Information Available*   *In Possession Of*
   IRS 990-PF Tax Return (Year)   _____
   Guidelines   _____
   Newsletters   _____
   Annual Report   _____
   _____   _____
   _____   _____

(*continued*)

EXHIBIT 20.1
(*Continued*)

6.
   a. Board Members:

   _____

   _____

   _____

   b. Staff   Full-Time   Part-Time

     _____   _____   _____

     _____   _____   _____

     _____   _____   _____

7. Deadline: _____
   Application Process/Requirements/Submission:

   _____

   _____

   _____

8. Financial Information
   Asset Base:$_____
   Are there current gifts to build the asset base? Yes _____ No _____
   If yes, how much? $_____
   Total number of grants awarded in 20__: _____
   Total amount of grants awarded in 20__: $_____
   High Grant: $_____
   Low Grant: $_____
   Average Grant: $_____
   In our interest area there were _____ grants, totaling $_____
   High grant in our interest area: $_____
   Low grant in our interest area: $_____
   Average grant in our interest area: $_____
9. Grants Received versus Grants Funded
   Number of proposals received in 20__: _____
   Number of proposals funded in 20__: _____
10. Sample Grants in Our Area of Interest:
   Recipient Organization   *Amount*

   _____   _____

   _____   _____

   _____   _____

   _____   _____

EXHIBIT 20.2
Funding Executive Research Worksheet

1. Funding Source Name: _____

2. Name of Contact Person/Contributions Officer: _____

3. Title: _____

4. Business Address: _____
   _____

5. Education
   College: _____
   Post Graduate: _____

6. Military Service: _____

7. Clubs/Affiliations: _____
   _____

8. Corporate Board Memberships: _____
   _____

9. Business History (Promotions, Other Firms, etc.): _____

10. Other Philanthropic Activities: _____
    _____

11. Newspaper/Magazine Clipping(s) Attached: Yes _____   No _____

12. Contacts/Linkages in our Organizations: _____
    _____

13. Recent Articles/Publications: _____

14. Awards/Honors: _____

Naturally, you do not have to have information on a foundation's executives (that is, directors, trustees, board members, contributions officers, and so forth) in order to consider submitting a proposal, but the more you know about the decision makers, the greater your chances of success. The information you collect and record on your Funding Executive Research Worksheet will help you in three major ways:

- It will allow you to determine, in advance, likely preferences and biases you will encounter if you are lucky enough to arrange an in-person meeting.
- It will make it easier to locate links between your organization and a funding source.
- It will assist you in structuring your proposal and in presenting the problem and the solution in a way that will attract the attention of the decision makers.

Recording accurate research on foundation decision makers will raise your chances of success. In addition, your ability to attract future funding will increase as you develop a history and file on each of the grantors in which you are interested. Enlist volunteers to ferret out the information you need. Let your research guide your solicitation strategy and proposal development process. Talk to your public library's librarian or a college or university librarian after you read this chapter to see what additional resources and techniques they suggest.

Foundation Funding Research Tools

Basic research tools for developing our list of potential foundation grantors can be accessed at little or no charge on the Internet and usually within a short distance from your workplace. The whole point of your research effort is to focus on the sources most likely to fund your proposal. Even if you are a novice grantseeker, do not be tempted to send letter proposals to any and all foundations that are even remotely related to your project area. If preproposal contact is allowed or a proposal format is provided or suggested, take every opportunity to develop an individualized, tailored proposal for each of your best prospects.

The Foundation Directory

The Foundation Directory is the major source of information on the largest U.S. foundations. Available in hardcopy and through a variety of online subscription options, the 2010 edition provides information on the top ten thousand U.S. foundations by total giving. The *Directory* contains key facts on fields of interest, contact information, financial data, names of decision makers, and sixty thousand sample grants. In addition there are several indexes to help in your search for potential funding sources.

One technique that will add a whole new dimension to your foundation grants effort is to become adept at using the index to donors, officers, and trustees, which contains approximately seventy-three thousand names. When your organization's friends provide you with their links, pay special attention to those people who list board memberships or friends on foundation boards. In most cases, your friends will be willing to discuss your project with fellow board members or with friends who serve on other boards.

The Foundation Directory Part 2 is also available for your use. The 2010 edition of this directory includes the next ten thousand largest foundations by total giving and features over forty thousand sample grants.

You may also access *The Foundation Directory Supplement*, which provides the latest facts on thousands of foundations in *The Foundation Directory* and *The Foundation Directory Part 2*. Changes in foundation status, officers and trustees, contact information, and giving interests are highlighted in new entries.

The directories described above and the supplements are published by the Foundation Center, 79 Fifth Avenue, New York, NY, 10003-3076. To order one of these products or for more information on *Foundation Directory Online* subscription plans, call the Foundation Center's customer service line at (800) 424-9836 or visit the Foundation Center's website at www.foundation center.org/marketplace.

Using *The Foundation Directory*

The most productive approach to using the *Directory* is to first review chapter 5 on redefining your project idea. After identifying key words and fields of interest (for example, environment, health education curriculum development, and folk arts for children), you can use the *Directory's* subject index to determine which foundations have an active interest in the area for which you are seeking grant support. Another approach is to use the types of support index to identify foundations interested in your type of project (for example, conferences/seminars, building/renovation, equipment, program development, and matching or challenge grants).

Before you rush into reviewing the actual foundation entries, remember that a significant portion of foundations possess a geographic homing device. In other words, they give only where they live. The *Directory's* geographic index will point you in the direction of those foundations that may be interested in your project because of its location.

The best match will be a foundation that funds your subject area, type of project, and geographic area. Do not despair if the use of the geographic index produces limited prospects. Many foundations have a national and even an international interest in certain areas. While these foundations may not have granted funds in your state or community before, they may do so if approached properly.

As you do your research, be sure to record the name of the foundation, the state, and the directory entry number for each foundation you are interested in. Recording this information will help you refer to the foundation quickly.

The sample *Foundation Directory* entry provided in exhibit 20.3 shows the contents or data elements found in most of the *Directory's* entries. For a complete listing of data elements, review the "How to Use the *Foundation Directory*" section in the publication's introduction. Please note that the sample shown in exhibit 20.3 was taken directly off of the Foundation Center's website and that you would have to refer to the actual entry to view the information for the Community Foundation of Greater Birmingham in its entirety. However, for the purpose of explanation, assume that the grantseeker is interested in securing a grant for a project aimed at introducing low-income

EXHIBIT 20.3
Foundation Directory **Entry**

Sample Entry

Entry number	25
	The Community Foundation of Greater Birmingham ▼
Street address	(formerly The Greater Birmingham Foundation)
	2100 First Ave. N., Ste. 700
	Birmingham, AL 35203 (205) 328-8641
Person to whom inquiries should be addressed	*Contact:* Kate Nielsen, Pres.
	FAX: (205) 328-6576;
	E-mail: info@foundationbirmingham.org; → E-mail and URL
	URL: http://www.foundationbirmingham.org

Establishment data — Established in 1959 in AL by resolution and declaration of trust; corporate side established in 1997.

→ Year-end date of accounting period

Foundation type: Community
Financial data (yr. ended 12/31/02): Assets, $118,000,000 (M); gifts received, $13,100,000; expenditures, $12,500,000; giving activities include $11,700,000 for 1,200 grants (high: $125,000; low: $75).

→ Assets at market value (M) or ledger value (L)

→ Total expenditures figure

Purpose and activities: To make life better in the greater Birmingham, Alabama, area, by connecting caring people and key resources with community needs, today and tomorrow.

Areas of foundation giving

Fields of interest: Arts; Education; Environment; Health care; Human services; Neighborhood centers; Community development; Public affairs.

→ Amount and number of grants paid

Types of grants and other types of support

Types of support: Capital campaigns; Building/renovation; Equipment; Program development; Publication; Seed money; Curriculum development; Matching/challenge support.

→ Separate information on amount and number of employee matching gifts, grants to individuals, or loans

Specific limitations on foundation giving by geographic area, subject focus, or types of support

Limitations: Giving from unrestricted and field-of-interest funds limited to Blount, Jefferson, Shelby, St. Clair, and Walker counties of AL. No support for religious or political purposes from unrestricted and field-of-interest funds. No grants to individuals or for scholarships, endowment funds, operating budgets, deficit reduction, national fundraising drives, conference or seminar expenses, benefits tickets, or replacement of government funding cuts.

Publications: Application guidelines, Annual report, Financial statement, Grants list, Informational brochure, Newsletter.

→ Printed material available from the foundation

Application information: Please see foundation's Web site for application instructions. Agencies new to the foundation must attend an overview session prior to submitting a grant proposal. Application form not required.

Application information

Initial approach: Letter
Copies of proposal: 3
Deadline(s): Check foundation's Web site; currently, Mar. 15 and Sept. 15
Board meeting date(s): Biannually (May and Nov.) for distribution of unrestricted funds; other meetings as needed
Final notification: June and Dec.

Officers: Cameron M. Vowell, Ph.D., Chair.; Jeffrey H. Cohn, M.D., Vice-Chair.; Kate Nielsen, Pres.

→ Officers and Trustees or other governing bodies

Directors: Kirkwood R. Bolton; Ralph D. Cook; Edward M. Friend III; Susan N. Haskell; Ted C. Kennedy; Thomas H. Lowder; Margaret M. Porter; Van L. Richey; Carole W. Samuelson, M.D.; William E. Smith, Jr.; Odessa Woolfolk.
Number of staff: 8 full-time professional; 3 part-time professional; 1 full-time support; 1 part-time support.
EIN: 636019864

→ IRS Identification Number

Selected grants

Selected grants: The following grants were reported in 2002.
$1,000,000 to University of Alabama, Birmingham, AL, For construction of the interdisciplinary Biomedical Research Building, payable over 5 years.

For a complete listing of data elements, see "How to Use *The Foundation Directory*" in the Introduction.
Please refer to the actual entry to view the information for this foundation in its entirety.

Symbols

▼ Identifies foundations for which in-depth descriptions have been prepared for inclusion in the Foundation Center's *Foundation 1000.*
❖ Indicates entries prepared or updated by Center staff from public records.
☆ Indicates foundations that did not appear in previous edition.

‡ Indicates individual is deceased.
(L) Ledger value of assets.
(M) Market value of assets.
• Officer is also a trustee or director.
+ indicates an unspecified number of grants.

children in Birmingham to theater. The Community Foundation of Greater Birmingham may be a good choice for the prospective grantee to examine further because the grantseeker's project falls within one of the foundation's stated fields of interest—the arts—and will take place in one of the foundation's preferred geographic funding areas—Jefferson County, Alabama. The prospective grantee will have to conduct more in-depth research to discover how much money the Community Foundation of Greater Birmingham has actually awarded to similar projects and to determine the high, low, and average size grants awarded in the arts area.

Internal Revenue Service Tax Returns

Form 990-PF is the annual tax return that U.S. private foundations must file with the IRS. Federal law requires that all foundations provide their tax returns for public information purposes. A foundation's 990-PF return gives fiscal details on receipts and expenditures, compensation of officers, capital gains or losses, and other financial matters and provides the foundation's application guidelines, the names of its board members/officer/trustees, and a complete list of the grants it has paid.

While the *Foundation Directories* are useful reference tools, they are basically compilations of information from many sources, and there is no guarantee as to the accuracy of the information provided. The Internal Revenue Service, however, deals in specifics. By reviewing the returns of private foundations you believe to be your best funding prospects, you can find valuable information such as the actual amount of assets, new gifts received, total grants paid out, and so on. Most important, you can view a list of all the grants they have paid, including grants for less than $10,000.

Larger foundations often issue annual reports or have websites that contain a listing of their grants. But the IRS form 990-PF may be the only source where you can find a complete grants list for smaller and midsized foundations.

Exhibit 20.4 is a sample of parts of form 990-PF. Taken off of the Foundation Center's website, this sample demonstrates that finding the information you need on a 990-PF is relatively easy.

- Page 1, top section and line 25 provide date, name, address, assets, and grants paid.
- Page 6, part VIII, line 1 provides the list of officers, directors, trustees, and foundation managers.
- Page 10, part XV, line 2 a, b, c, d provides application information.
- Page 11, part XV, line 3 provides grants and contributions paid during the year or approved for future payment (which gives you some indication of how involved the funding source is in awarding multiple-year grants).

For more information on what forms 900 and 990-PF are and where you can find them visit foundationcenter.org/getstarted/faqs/html/990pf.html.

Copies of tax returns for the past three years for all foundations can be viewed for free at the Foundation Center's reference collections in New York City and Washington, D.C. The Atlanta, Cleveland, and San Francisco offices of the Foundation Center contain IRS form 990-PF returns for the Southeastern, Midwestern, and Western states, respectively.

You can also access foundation tax returns on the web in PDF format at the following sites:

- foundationcenter.org/findfunders/990finder/
- www.guidestar.org

Please note that the tax returns you will be able to access will typically be one to two years old. In addition, if you cannot find a particular organization's 990-PF, it may be because the organization you are looking for files a 990 instead. In general, churches, hospitals, schools, and publicly supported organizations file 990s.

The Foundation Center

Incorporated as a nonprofit organization in 1953, the Foundation Center was formed by a foundation as an independent national service center. Part of the Foundation Center's mission is to provide accurate information on philanthropy with special emphasis on foundation grant making. The center covers its operating expenses through grants from foundations and corporations, the sale of publications, and fee-based subscriber services. The center operates five reference collections, located in New York City, Washington, D.C., Cleveland, San Francisco, and Atlanta. Each of these is staffed by Foundation Center employees. There are also many Foundation Center Cooperating Collections operated by libraries, community foundations, and other nonprofit agencies throughout the United States.

Locate the collection nearest you by visiting foundationcenter.org/ collections. In addition to having a core collection of the Foundation Center's publications, many Cooperating Collections have IRS tax returns for their state and perhaps neighboring states. The collections will also have several other valuable grants resource materials, including

- computer-generated printouts or guides that list grants by subject area,
- state foundation directories,

EXHIBIT 20.4
IRS Foundation Annual Return Form 990-PF

Form 990-PF — Return of Private Foundation or Section 4947(a)(1) Nonexempt Charitable Trust Treated as a Private Foundation, 2009

(continued)

EXHIBIT 20.4
(Continued)

Part XIV Private Operating Foundations (see page 27 of the instructions and Part VII-A, question 9)

1a If the foundation has received a ruling or determination letter that it is a private operating foundation, and the ruling is effective for 2006, enter the date of the ruling . . . . .

b Check box to indicate whether the foundation is a private operating foundation described in section ☐ 4942(j)(3) or ☐ 4942(j)(5)

2a Enter the lesser of the adjusted net income from Part I or the minimum investment return from Part X for each year listed

	Tax year		Prior 3 years		(e) Total
	(a) 2006	(b) 2005	(c) 2004	(d) 2003	
b 85% of line 2a					
c Qualifying distributions from Part XII, line 4 for each year listed					
d Amounts included in line 2c not used directly for active conduct of exempt activities					
e Qualifying distributions made directly for active conduct of exempt activities. Subtract line 2d from line 2c . .					

3 Complete 3a, b, or c for the alternative test relied upon:

a "Assets" alternative test—enter:
  (1) Value of all assets
  (2) Value of assets qualifying under section 4942(j)(3)(B)(i)

b "Endowment" alternative test—enter ⅔ of minimum investment return shown in Part X, line 6 for each year listed . .

c "Support" alternative test—enter:
  (1) Total support other than gross investment income (interest, dividends, rents, payments on securities loans (section 512(a)(5)), or royalties)
  (2) Support from general public and 5 or more exempt organizations as provided in section 4942(j)(3)(B)(iii)
  (3) Largest amount of support from an exempt organization
  (4) Gross investment income . .

Part XV Supplementary Information (Complete this part only if the foundation had $5,000 or more in assets at any time during the year—see page 27 of the instructions.)

1 Information Regarding Foundation Managers:
a List any managers of the foundation who have contributed more than 2% of the total contributions received by the foundation before the close of any tax year (but only if they have contributed more than $5,000). (See section 507(d)(2).)

b List any managers of the foundation who own 10% or more of the stock of a corporation (or an equally large portion of the ownership of a partnership or other entity) of which the foundation has a 10% or greater interest.

2 Information Regarding Contribution, Grant, Gift, Loan, Scholarship, etc., Programs:
Check here ▶ ☐ if the foundation only makes contributions to preselected charitable organizations and does not accept unsolicited requests for funds. If the foundation makes gifts, grants, etc. (see page 28 of the instructions) to individuals or organizations under other conditions, complete items 2a, b, c, and d.

a The name, address, and telephone number of the person to whom applications should be addressed:

APPLICATION
INFORMATION

b The form in which applications should be submitted and information and materials they should include:

c Any submission deadlines:

d Any restrictions or limitations on awards, such as by geographical areas, charitable fields, kinds of institutions, or other factors:

Form **990-PF** (2006)

Part XV Supplementary Information (continued)

3 Grants and Contributions Paid During the Year or Approved for Future Payment

Recipient		If recipient is an individual, show any relationship to any foundation manager or substantial contributor	Foundation status of recipient	Purpose of grant or contribution	Amount
Name and address (home or business)					

a Paid during the year

GRANTS PAID

Total . . . . ▶ 3a

b Approved for future payment

FUTURE GRANTS

Total . . . . ▶ 3b

Form **990-PF** (2006)

- other publications from the Foundation Center (see the list of resources for more detail), and
- searchable foundation grant-related databases.

Electronic Retrieval and Database Searches

The Foundation Center offers *Foundation Directory Online (FDO)*. This online resource contains information on nearly one hundred thousand U.S. foundations and corporate donors, over two million grants, and over five hundred thousand key decision makers. It has five plan levels with monthly, annual, and two-year subscription options. It offers up to nine comprehensive databases of grant makers, companies, grants, and 990s, plus five databases covering RFPs, philanthropy news, foundation-sponsored publications, nonprofit literature, and jobs. In addition, it has up to fifty-four search fields including keyword searching—even across all recent IRS 990s. See fdonline.foundationcenter.org.

Many public libraries, university libraries, and higher education grants offices are able to perform free electronic searches of *The Foundation Directory Online* and other resources containing foundation grants information. Explore the possibility of computer search and retrieval by contacting an established grants office near you. Many large nonprofits, colleges, and universities already subscribe to searching tools and enlisting their services can save you money.

There are several other electronic funding databases available that are accessible by subscription only but offer current and in-depth information and vary in price.

- *GrantSelect*, an online database compiled and edited by Schoolhouse Partners, contains approximately 13,000 funding opportunities provided by more than 5,800 sponsoring organizations. See www.grantselect.com.
- *The Chronicle of Philanthropy's Guide to Grants* database presents all corporate and foundation grants listed in the *Chronicle* since 2001. See www.philanthropy.com/grants.

Foundation Websites and the Internet

The use of the Internet to research private grantors and to apply online is limited, but growing. In a 2000 survey of 18,323 foundations including the top one thousand foundations, only 4.6 percent maintained websites. By 2009 this figure had grown to 26.1 percent. While this is a dramatic increase, there are still many foundations without websites. There are a variety of reasons why more foundations do not have websites, including lack of staff and limited geographic giving interests. Many foundations give only locally and do not want the unsolicited worldwide proposals that having a website may bring. Some private grantors, particularly those that are technology based, do allow Internet submittal of proposals, but that number is also surprisingly small.

Through portals such as the Foundation Center's Foundation Finder (foundationcenter.org/findfunders/foundfinder/), grantseekers can find links to the websites of a few thousand foundations, corporate grant makers, grant-making public charities, and community foundations. In addition, the Council on Foundations (www.cof.org) offers links to over two thousand of its members' websites, and Philanthropy News Network Online (www .pnnonline.org) provides links to many private foundations, corporations, and community foundations.

Exhibit 20.5 is a sample of a foundation's website and the type of information you can sometimes gather online. In this example, you can obtain the Jean and Louis Dreyfus Foundation's guidelines, application procedure, grants list, and roster of trustees and staff from its website. (Note that the Dreyfus Foundation is presently only accepting letters of inquiry from organizations that have a prior relationship with the foundation.) However, for the majority of grant makers you will still need to use alternative research methods for obtaining this information.

Several nonprofit organizations have developed websites with grantor information. There are also bulletin boards and chat boxes that focus on foundation and corporate grantors. Check with your membership groups and your peers to see what is available, or perform your own Internet search.

Conducting research to locate your most likely foundation grantors need not be labor intensive or costly. Using electronic databases and websites in your search will save you time, but the actual information you will find is identical to that in the print form. The key is to locate the data that will enable you to estimate your chances for success before you invest any more time in seeking a foundation grant.

Since you are already armed with knowledge on the foundation marketplace (see chapter 19) and now know how to research potential private foundation grantors, when will you integrate this activity into your action steps' chart? In some cases you may need to address the foundation grants process before your federal grant aspirations because you need preliminary data or because you need to finish a publication first. Refer to figure 20.1 and configure your plan.

EXHIBIT 20.5
Sample Foundation Website

THE
JEAN & LOUIS DREYFUS
FOUNDATION, INC.

Grant Guidelines

Application
Procedure

Grants List

Trustees and Staff

Web site design and
hosting by:
THE
FOUNDATION
CENTER

315 Madison Avenue
Suite 900
New York, NY 10017
Tel: 212-599-1931
Fax: 212-599-2956
E-mail: info@jldreyfus.org

HOME

Grant
Guidelines

Application
Procedure

Grants List

Trustees
and Staff

GRANT GUIDELINES

THE
JEAN & LOUIS DREYFUS
FOUNDATION, INC.

The Jean and Louis Dreyfus Foundation was established in 1979 from the estate of Louis Dreyfus, a music publisher, and that of his wife, Jean. The mission of the Foundation is to enhance the quality of life of New Yorkers, particularly the aging and disadvantaged. The Foundation disburses grants mainly within the five boroughs of New York City and primarily in fields supportive of aging, arts, education, and social services.

The Foundation is committed to funding direct service organizations and those projects which will produce systemic change. To this end the Foundation favors programs which can eventually be replicated or which have the potential to be funded by independent or government sources in the future. Occasionally organizations will be awarded grants to strengthen their infrastructure or for general operating support. The Foundation encourages matching funds from other charitable organizations, public financial drives, individuals, and government bodies.

Grants are made only to organizations whose tax exempt status has been recognized by the IRS. Grants are never made to individuals.

(*continued*)

EXHIBIT 20.5
(*Continued*)

HOME

Grant
Guidelines

Application
Procedure

Grants List

Trustees
and Staff

APPLICATION
PROCEDURE

THE
JEAN & LOUIS DREYFUS
FOUNDATION, INC.

PLEASE NOTE: The Foundation's deadlines for letters of
inquiry have changed: they are now July 15th and January 15th
for Fall and Spring cycles respectively.

Until further notice, the Foundation will be accepting
letters of inquiry only from organizations that have a prior
relationship with the Foundation. We ask that all other
grant seekers refrain from sending letters at this time.

Initial inquiries should consist of a one to two page letter
describing the grantee organization and outlining the project in
question. Letters should be sent by mail to:

Ms. Edmée de M. Firth
Executive Director
Jean and Louis Dreyfus Foundation, Inc.
315 Madison Avenue
Suite 900
New York, NY 10017

Letters of inquiry are due no later than January 15th and July
15th for the Spring and Fall board meetings respectively. All
such inquiries will be acknowledged with a letter of receipt,
and further communication will follow if a full proposal is
being requested. Letters received later than the established
deadlines will be automatically held until the next review
cycle. Any discussion or indications of interest concerning a
grant application should not be construed as a commitment by
the Foundation. All requests will be approved or rejected in
writing.

Any questions about the Foundation and its application
procedure should be directed to Jessica Keuskamp, Program
Director (contact information below):

Jessica Keuskamp
Program Director
Jean and Louis Dreyfus Foundation, Inc.
Tel: 212-599-1931
Fax: 212-599-2956
E-mail: info@jldreyfus.org

EXHIBIT 20.5
(*Continued*)

HOME

Grant
Guidelines

Application
Procedure

Grants List

Trustees
and Staff

GRANTS LIST

THE
JEAN & LOUIS DREYFUS
FOUNDATION, INC.

Total Grants for 2008 — $1,191,500

Aging | Arts | Education | Social Service

GRANTS FOR AGING — 2008

Bowery Residents Committee $15,000
Delancey Street Senior Center

Casita Maria $10,000
Homebound Peer Visitors Program

City Bar Justice Center $15,000
Economic Justice Initiative for Seniors

Encore Community Services $15,000
Encore 49 Residence

Food Bank for New York City $10,000
Senior Food Programs

Grand Street Settlement $15,000
Baruch Elders Services Team (BEST)

Medicare Rights Center $20,000
Expansion of the Medicare/Medicaid Assistance
Project

Montefiore Medical Center $25,000
Elder Abuse Project

Mount Sinai Medical Center $15,000
Caregivers and Professionals Partnership
Program

New York Foundaton for Senior Citizens $15,000
Long Term Care Ombudsman Program

One Stop Senior Services $10,000
One Stop Senior Support Program

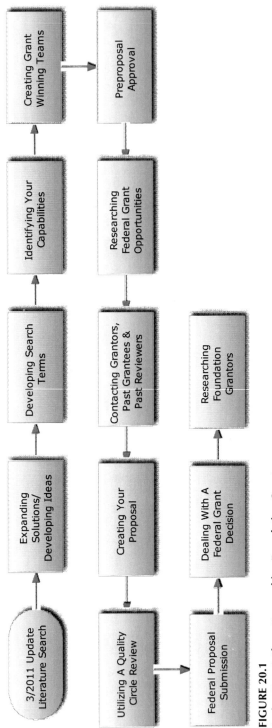

FIGURE 20.1
Action Steps' Chart: Researching Foundation Grantors

21

Contacting a Private Foundation before Submission

CONTACTING THE PRIVATE FOUNDATION before you write your proposal will help you validate your research and gather additional information about the grantor's priorities and interests. Most importantly, preproposal contact will allow you to tailor your proposal according to the particular approach or method that each private foundation will find interesting and provide you with the information needed to determine the appropriate amount to request. You can also use this contact to explore the grantor's feelings about funding only a portion of the total amount your project requires. The purpose of this contact is not to convince the grantor to fund your proposal but to ensure that your approach will meet the grantor's needs. By contacting the foundation funding source before you submit, you increase your chances of success over five times. Do not miss out on this tremendous opportunity if you have a contact person or you have a linkage to help you get in the door.

How to Contact Private Foundation Grantors

Now that you realize how important preproposal contact is, here is the bad news. Most private foundations are understaffed, and as many as ninety thousand have no staff. Therefore, making contact with them is very difficult. Many private foundation application instructions state "no contact except by letter," and your research will show that many addresses for private funding sources are actually addresses for trust departments of banks, accountants' offices, websites, or post office boxes.

Naturally, you do not want to talk to a trust officer at a bank, but speaking with a foundation board member would be a big help. With so few foundations occupying their own offices, the chances of talking to a foundation's director or staff are limited to the largest foundations. What is significant, however, is that each foundation usually has eight to ten board members. This means that there are approximately 1,100,000 board members serving the 110,000 foundations, and you may be surprised at how many your advocates know! These board members are the actual decision makers, and they can be contacted effectively through your webbing system.

One foundation director underscored the importance of using links to board members when she told me that

- one-third of her foundation's grants will be awarded to her board members' favorite nonprofit organizations,
- one-third will go to her board members' friends' favorite nonprofits, and
- one-third will be up for grabs to those who write creative, persuasive proposals that match the interests and values of her foundation.

At this point your research should already include the names of your best foundation prospects' decision makers and board members. Ask the leaders of your organization whether they know any of these people and, if so, whether they would help you by using this informal means of contact. Perhaps your link can set up lunch or a conference call. If you do not uncover a link, your plan should be to follow the grantor's guidelines as outlined in the various resource publications (see chapter 7 for more information on webbing and links).

If there is an office and contact is not ruled out or discouraged, you should

- write a letter requesting a visit,
- telephone to set up a visit or phone interview, and/or
- make a personal visit to the grantor.

Contact by Letter

Be very selective when sending a letter requesting an appointment and information on a grantor's program. Since very few private foundations have the staff resources necessary to respond to written requests, do not be surprised if you receive a proposal rejection notice even though you asked only for application guidelines or an appointment.

Exhibit 21.1 provides a sample letter to a foundation requesting information. (This letter could be sent as an e-mail, but not all foundations provide

EXHIBIT 21.1
Sample Letter to a Private Foundation Requesting Information

Date

Name
Title
Address

Dear _____:

I am developing a project which deals with _____ and provides benefits to [or in] _____. My research indicates that this area is an important concern of the [name of foundation].

Please use the enclosed e-mail address or label to send me information on your desired format for proposals or other guidelines. I would also appreciate it if you could add us to your mailing list so that we could receive your annual reports, newsletters, and any other materials you think might be useful to us as we work on this and related projects.

Thank you for your cooperation.

Sincerely,

Name/Title
Organization
Address
E-mail Address

---

e-mail addresses for correspondence purposes.) This letter may be the only way to receive an application form from the hundreds of foundations that do not have a website and state that you must send for their application. Please note that this is not a letter proposal or letter of inquiry. These types of proposals will be described in chapter 22.

Contact by Telephone

Telephone contact with a private foundation may take the place of face-to-face contact or may be used to set up a visit. When you are successful at telephoning a private foundation, you can be sure you have contacted one that falls within the small percentage of those having an office and a paid staff. Even if you are telephoning the grantor in hopes of setting up a visit, be ready to discuss your project. Many grantors use the telephone very effectively for quickly assessing projects and determining their interest in them before agreeing to discuss the project face-to-face or inviting you to make a written application. After all, it is much easier to tell a grantseeker that they are not really interested in a project over the telephone than it is in person, or to have to read about an idea that is not going to make it.

If the grantor wants to discuss your project before giving you an appointment, ask whether you could fax, e-mail, or mail a one- or two-page letter of inquiry or a concept paper and call back when he or she has your outline in hand and has had time to review it.

If he or she agrees to a visit, set the date. Do not offer any more information at this time, but do ask what he or she recommends that you bring. Also ask about

- presenting a laptop-driven PowerPoint presentation or full motion video;
- the number of staff to be present so that you can bring the appropriate number of copies of information about your organization;
- the possibility of him or her making a visit to your location; and
- his or her travel plans, whether he or she will be near you, or whether he or she will be attending any conferences or meetings you will attend or where you will be presenting.

If a personal visit is not possible, you will be forced to discuss your project over the telephone. The questions you ask over the phone will actually be the same as those you would ask if you were to make a personal visit. Therefore, review the following section on the visit and designate the questions to ask a funding source.

The Visit

Visiting in person is the best way to get to know the foundation, but visits are difficult to arrange since most foundations have no office and are not heavily staffed. If you are fortunate enough to get a visit, use your time wisely.

Who Should Go

Your credibility will be higher if you take a nonstaff representative with you. An articulate, impressive volunteer, advocate, advisory committee member, or board member is an excellent choice. Two people are the maximum. You do not want to overpower the grantor by sending three or more people. Use the information you collected from your webbing and linkages to choose a partner that provides a close match to the funding source. Use age, education, club affiliation, and other personal characteristics as the basis for your choice.

On several occasions I have had a past grantee help me make preproposal contact. In one instance, the past grantee arranged lunch for all of us when the grantor made a site visit to her program.

Dress according to the information you have about the funding source. Dress in the foundation world is generally conservative, and usually it is better to be overdressed than underdressed. Dress codes differ in the East, the West, the South, and the Midwest, so be aware of geographic influences. The best person to ask about the appropriate dress for a particular funding source may be a past grantee.

Materials to Bring

The materials you will need to bring are those you have already gathered and organized in your proposal development workbook (Swiss cheese book). You may also want to bring sample audiovisual aids that document the need in a more interesting or vivid manner and help show the funding source how important it is to meet the need *now*. If you do use audiovisual aids, make sure they are in balance with your request. A three- to five-minute DVD that documents the problem and your organization's selected uniquenesses would be appropriate if you are making a large request ($250,000), but inappropriate for a smaller ($5,000) request. At this point it is still proper to have several possible approaches to meeting the need. Therefore, you should have the cost and benefits and pros and cons of each approach outlined and ready for presentation. You want to learn which approach the prospective funding source likes best; you are not trying to convince the grantor that you have "the one and only way to solve the problem." Your Cost-Benefit Analysis Worksheet from chapter 4 will usually elicit more than enough response to begin a conversation.

Be ready to use the various parts of your Swiss cheese book for answers to questions like "Why should we give the money to you instead of some other organization?" Refer to your section on the uniquenesses of your organization (personnel, mission, and so on).

Questions to Ask a Foundation Funding Source

Review these questions to determine which would be the most appropriate to ask based on your current knowledge of the funding source. You may want to assign specific questions to each of the two individuals going to the meeting and prepare for the visit by role-playing various answers.

1. We have developed several feasible approaches. Would you please look at them and comment on which one looks the most interesting to you (or would look the most interesting to the board)?
2. Last year, your foundation awarded $_____ to our kind of project and the average size of the award was $_____. Will this remain consistent?
3. Our research indicates that your deadlines last year were _____ and _____. Will they be the same this year?
4. Does it help if proposals are submitted early? Do proposals that are submitted early receive more favorable treatment?
5. How are proposals reviewed by your foundation? Who performs the review? Outside experts? Board members? Staff? Is there a scoring system or checklist they use that you could share with us?
6. Are there more current granting priorities? (Give them a copy of your research sheet to determine whether your research accurately reflects their priorities.)
7. What do you think of submitting more than one proposal in a funding cycle?
8. Is the amount we are requesting realistic in light of your current goals?
9. Have you ever provided grant support jointly with another funding source and, if so, is that approach appropriate here?

The following two questions should be asked only when the grantor seems very encouraging.

10. Would you look over our proposal before our formal submission if we finished it early?
11. May I see a proposal that you have funded that you think is well written, or would you recommend one and I will contact the grantee to make the request? This would provide us with a model for style and format.

Ask question 12 only if the grantor is not very encouraging.

12. Can you suggest any other funders who may be appropriate for this project?

Private Foundation Report Form

Each time a member of your staff contacts a funder in person, over the phone, or through e-mail, he or she should complete and file a Private Foundation

EXHIBIT 21.2
Private Foundation Report Form

Complete one of these forms after each contact with a private foundation.

Funding Source: _____

Funding Source Address: _____

_____

Funding Source Contact Person: _____

Telephone Number: _____ Fax: _____ E-mail: _____

Contacted On (Date): _____

Contacted By (Name): _____

Type of Contact: Phone _____ Visit _____ Other (Explain) _____

Objective of Contact: _____

_____

_____

_____

Results of Contact: _____

_____

_____

_____

Follow-up: _____

_____

Report Form (see exhibit 21.2). This simple procedure has a number of important benefits. It will keep you from damaging your credibility by repeating the same questions or having the funder say, "I gave that information to _____ from your organization. Don't you people ever talk to each other?" Also, it will allow another person from your organization to pick up where you leave off when you take that next promotion.

Successful grantees recognize the importance of contacting the funding source before writing the proposal. The purpose of the contact is not to make small talk but to validate research and gather data needed to address the grantor's hidden agenda. Using the techniques in this chapter to contact and record contact with private grantors will be an essential part of your grant-seeking strategy.

While this action step is critical to your success, contacting a foundation before submission may not always be possible. However, if your research uncovers a way to contact the prospective grantor, go to figure 21.1 and place this step in your plan.

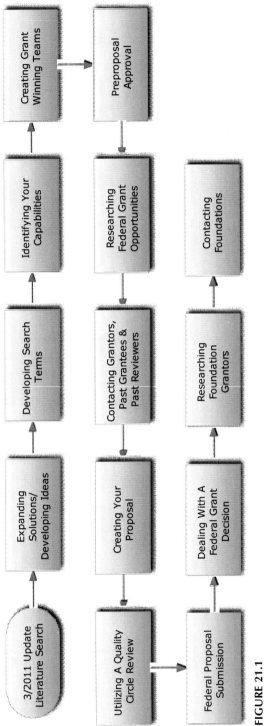

FIGURE 21.1
Action Steps' Chart: Contacting Foundations

The flowchart contains the following steps:

- 3/2011 Update Literature Search → Expanding Solutions/Developing Ideas → Developing Search Terms → Identifying Your Capabilities → Creating Grant Winning Teams → Preproposal Approval → Researching Federal Grant Opportunities → Contacting Grantors, Past Grantees & Past Reviewers → Creating Your Proposal → Utilizing A Quality Circle Review → Federal Proposal Submission → Dealing With A Federal Grant Decision → Researching Foundation Grantors → Contacting Foundations

22

Applying for Private Foundation Funds
Letter of Inquiry and Letter Proposal

Creating a Winning Letter of Inquiry

WHILE THIS MAY SOUND LIKE an exercise in semantics, a letter of inquiry (LOI) is really just a very condensed proposal. It is a one- to two-page miniproposal aimed at interesting the foundation enough to invite you to submit a full proposal. Basically, the LOI should describe the grantee organization and outline the project in question. It is qualitatively different from a letter proposal in that it lacks the specifics and details. However, it still must include and, indeed, highlight the components of your project or program that will motivate the grantor to request more information. You do not have to explain how you will do everything, but you must establish that you have a plan and that you will provide more information in the full proposal.

The natural tendency when faced with the challenge of writing a one-page letter of inquiry is to focus intently on what it is *you* want to accomplish and how you want to do it. In contrast, most prospective grantors are self-focused and intent on what *they* and *their* organization value and think is in their best interests.

If you look at this process from the grantors' point of view, they skim through hundreds to thousands of proposals in search for those that reflect and reinforce their values. They want to know how the goals/objectives of *your* program relate to *their* mission and how the results will satisfy *their* goals. They are generally adverse to risks (unless your research shows otherwise). They do not want to invest their grant funds in uncertain or unproven projects/research. They are understaffed, and few have experts in the field to refer to for scientific or programmatic evaluations. If they have staff members who perform initial screening and logging of proposals, these staff members may have little professional training and usually base their initial screenings on a general description of the areas in which the foundation board is interested. Therefore, it is imperative that your LOI immediately focuses on the grantor and provides a clear picture or summary within the first few sentences of what your project seeks to create. You will be able to do this if you have done a good job researching your foundation prospect and have reviewed its most recent 990-PF tax return (see chapter 20).

Letters of inquiry are more difficult to create than other types of proposals that allow more words. With a LOI you must weigh each word and spend hours, not minutes, on each paragraph. After all, you have only a few words to hook the reader. You must write from the foundation's vocabulary, values glasses, and point of view, and avoid terms, acronyms, and buzzwords that shift the focus to you.

Your LOI should be on your best stationery, preferably with a list of your board members' names in the left margin. Board members provide credibility. If you have formed a special advisory committee for your project, you might want to consider having their names in the margin, especially if some of them are nationally or even locally known.

Almost all proposals, whether they are letters of inquiry or letter proposals, should start with the name or title of the proposed project. The title is a necessary handle on which the grantor will rely to log your proposal into his or her database and to refer to your proposal when, and if, it comes up for discussion by the board. Your title should not be too lengthy, but like the rest of your proposal it should focus on what will be changed, how it will be changed, and who will benefit. Foundation grantors see their funds as impacting a problem, changing a target population, or furthering a favorite solution or protocol. Your LOI, and its title, should focus on the problem to be solved and the difference that will be made.

Foundation board members make assumptions based on titles. They assume they understand what the project proposes to accomplish based on the words used in the title. Unfortunately, there may be a disjuncture here, and the proposal may not deal with their expectations at all. To make sure this does not happen to you, read your title to several individuals who know nothing about your project, and ask them what they think the proposal that follows is all about. You will probably be amazed at the misconceptions and find yourself creating a new, clearer title aimed at steering the reader in the right direction.

Follow the title with a short paragraph (two to three sentences) summarizing the project. Use positive action words and a few well-chosen facts.

The next paragraph should focus on the issue that the project will seek to reduce or solve. Your research should provide some insight into other projects and approaches the foundation has funded. Yours should not be identical, but you can pick up a theme or preference by looking at what they have granted in the past. It is not "We hope to change this situation." It is "Together we *will* change this situation."

Follow this with a paragraph on how you will impact the problem or issue. Include a few sentences on how and why your organization or consortium is particularly well suited to bring about the change you suggest. Most foundations will require some idea of the budget and cost. Usually in an LOI the budget can be in paragraph form. But be sure to be clear on what the total cost will be and if there are any other funders (already committed or to be approached) and any in-kind or matching commitment from your organization or consortium.

The secret to a successful letter of inquiry is to follow the foundation's specifications and to create a miniproposal that is motivating and compelling. The goal is to have the funding source request a full proposal that meets its needs and interests. But many grantseekers have been surprised when their brief LOI resulted in a check without the need to submit a longer proposal!

Some foundations have specific guidelines for LOIs. For example, the Park Foundation requests that applicants submit (a) a cover letter that includes a summary of the project and (b) an inquiry cover sheet that is downloadable from its website. As is always the case, make sure you know the guidelines for the foundation you are interested in.

If you have submitted a letter of inquiry that has won you the opportunity to submit a full proposal, or the grantor's guidelines request that you submit a full or longer proposal, the following format will assist you. Remember, even a full proposal is usually thought of as a letter, not as a lengthy treatise on the topic. Many grantseekers have reported that they like to prepare the slightly longer letter proposal described in this chapter and then edit it to a shorter letter of inquiry making sure that they are keenly aware of what they must cut out and thus what they choose not to say.

The Letter Proposal

Historically, private foundations have used the letter proposal format as the primary component of their application process. Now federal and state granting programs are showing a shift in this direction, and some are requesting a short three- to five-page preproposal document that is similar to creating a letter proposal. Public funding sources may call the letter proposal a white paper, a preproposal paper, or a concept paper. Foundations may call it a letter proposal or just a short, brief proposal that, in most cases, is limited to two pages. In some cases grantors will not send a prospective grantee an application package unless they like the approach outlined in the letter proposal or concept paper. Although this preproposal screening may sound negative at first, it really is not such a bad idea because it prevents grantseekers from completing a more lengthy application for a project that the prospective grantor has little interest in funding or reviewing.

Foundations use the letter proposal format simply because they do not have the time or staff to read long, tedious proposals. They want short, concise letters and grant billions of dollars each year based on two to three pages of content. Some larger foundations may send out a request for proposals. They will specify details such as length, but most are less than five pages and many request that they be double-spaced.

Letter proposals are often read by board members during relatively brief meetings. A survey of foundations revealed that most foundations meet one to three times a year for an average of one to three hours each time. Within this short time frame, they must read an overwhelming number of letter proposals; therefore, it is imperative that your proposal attract and retain their interest.

In an effort to save time, some groups of grant makers have adopted a common grant application format to allow grant applicants to produce a single proposal for a specific community of funders. Go to foundationcenter .org/findfunders/cga.html for a list of participating groups. However, before applying to any funder that accepts a common application form, be sure to check that your project matches the funder's stated interests and ascertain whether the funder would prefer a letter of inquiry in advance of receiving the application.

If your research provides you with an application format to follow, use it exactly as outlined. For instance, the Herbert B. Jones Foundation provides guidelines for the application format as well as the program budget and unequivocally states that applicants must adhere strictly to the format presented. Some foundations, like the Smith Richardson Foundation in Connecticut, even provide a concept paper template to follow. Some of the foundations that have a website provide an application form that can be printed off-line in lieu of a letter proposal. For example, the Jones Foundation in Washington, D.C., will only accept proposals that are completed on its grant application form, which is accessible by downloading it from the foundation's website or by calling the foundation to have one sent to you. Keep in mind that online application forms often are not interactive. Therefore, you usually cannot change the amount of space allotted to each section. Whatever the case may be, follow all guidelines exactly, but look for opportunities where you can incorporate all or any of the main components of the letter proposal suggested here into the prospective funding source's required format.

Constructing a Letter Proposal

In general, when writing a letter proposal, use more white space, bullets, and short, inviting paragraphs. Never use small fonts in an effort to include more. Board members are usually older and small font will make your proposal less likely to be read. If font is not specified, use 12 to 13 characters per inch. Double-space when required, and read and heed all application guidelines.

The main components of a letter proposal are as follows:

- an introductory paragraph stating the reason for writing,
- a section explaining why this grantor was selected,
- a needs section that presents the problem you will solve,
- a solution section that states what you will do and how,
- a uniqueness paragraph that shows why your organization is the best choice for implementing the solution,
- a request for funds section that asks for money and summarizes your budget,
- a closing paragraph that provides a contact for more information if needed,
- signatures of your highest-ranking officials and partners, and
- attachments, if allowed.

Introductory Paragraph

Begin by stating your reason for writing to the funding source, and mention who your link to the grantor is, when possible. In some cases your link may prefer to remain anonymous and endorse your proposal at a board meeting. In other instances your link may actually instruct you to refer to him or her in your proposal. If so, you could say something such as the following:

Katie Macrino [your link, a past board member, trustee, or staff member of the foundation] and I have discussed the mutual concerns of the Kleineste Foundation [funding source] and [your organization] in meeting the nutritional needs of the elderly [subject area or problem].

If you cannot mention a link, begin your letter proposal with the next most important factor—why the grantor was selected for solicitation or how you knew the grantor would be interested in your proposal.

Why the Grantor Was Selected

Foremost in the reader's mind is why he or she should be reading your proposal. This is your opportunity to position yourself and your organization as winners that do their homework. You want the prospective funding source to know you are not blanketing the foundation world with a "one proposal fits all" approach. What you need to make clear in this paragraph is that, based on what you have discovered through your research, you believe the funding source is very likely to find your proposal interesting. This means saying, for example, "Our research indicates that your foundation is committed to the support of health care for the indigent. In the last three years you have dedicated over $4 million to this important area." In this example, you would also refer to the percentage of the funding source's total grant dollars that went to supporting health care for the indigent or mention a major or significant accomplishment made in this area through a previously awarded grant.

This paragraph need not be long. You want to demonstrate that you have taken the time to research the funding source's interests and that your proposal will address an issue that has been a concern of the grantor. By doing so, your proposal will command the respect of the reader and warrant the investment of time he or she will take to review it. At this point, it is obvious that this proposal is tailored to this foundation.

Again, you are following Festinger's theory of cognitive dissonance. To keep the reader interested in your proposal, you are going to have to present a proposal that reinforces his or her values and feelings of worth and importance. Seek to align your organization with the values of the grantor by adding something such as, "It is with our mutual concern for (or commitment to) the welfare of the indigent that we come to you with this exciting proposal."

Needs Section

While this may be referred to as your vision or statement of purpose, there must be an underlying situation or problem that must be remedied or changed by your action and the foundation's support. You do the work, and the grantor supplies the necessary ingredient—the money.

If you have constructed a proposal development workbook as suggested in chapter 3, you already have gathered statistics, case studies, quotes, and articles to document a compelling statement of need for action. The main difference between stating the need in a letter proposal to a foundation and stating it in a federal grant application is that you have the opportunity to incorporate the human element in your appeal to the private grantor. While your letter proposal must be based on fact, you can help the foundation board members motivate themselves by presenting the more human side of the problem. The challenge is to portray compelling needs without overusing either the facts (by quoting too many research articles) or the human-interest aspects of the problem.

Select the component of the need that will most likely convince the grantor that the gap between what is and what ought to be must be closed *immediately*. To accomplish this you must have done research on the values and perspective of the grantor. Use what you have learned to describe the gap in a manner that is tailored to each particular funding source. With today's technology you could even scan a picture into your needs paragraph that may be worth a thousand words.

In a few paragraphs, your letter proposal must

- include a few well-chosen statistics,
- exhibit sensitivity to the geographic perspective of the grantor, and
- portray the human side of the problem.

Whether your proposal is for a model project, research, or a service model, your statement of need must be more compelling than your competitor's to keep the reader interested. Readers must want to read the rest of your proposal to discover what you are going to do about closing the gap you have so eloquently and succinctly documented. Many novice grantseekers overlook or underestimate the importance of the needs section of their letter proposal; they assume readers must already know about the need since they have granted funds to this area in the past. This assumption is a mistake. Grantors do know about the need, but they expect you to command their respect by proving *your* expertise in the field by documenting the problem as in the following example.

> The need for cancer prevention and treatment in the United States continues to grow—but not equally for all races. If you were diagnosed with cancer in 1950, you would have a slightly higher survival rate if you were black. Today, however, the statistics are dramatically reversed. In a study by Stotts, Glynn, and Baquet, African Americans were ranked first among U.S. ethnic groups with the lowest cancer survival rate and first with the highest age-adjusted rates of cancer incidence and mortality. What happened to reverse this rate of survival and what can be done about it?

The importance of documenting the gap between what exists now and what could be, should be, or will be done with your foundation partner's investment is the basis for your accountability. If you can provide a visual and dramatic picture of the problem and document the incidence and severity of it and how it affects your target population, you can then tell the grantor how the situation will change and how the change will be measured in the solution section of your letter proposal. It is not a canceled check that the grantor wants; it is a changed situation, and the achievement of your project's objectives and goals.

Solution Section

What will you do to close the gap you have just documented? The solution section of your proposal calls for a brief description of the approach you propose to use to solve the problem. In most cases your approach will not totally eliminate the problem, but you must describe how much of the gap you will close (your objective). While describing how you will close the gap, include the measurement indicator you will use to evaluate the success of your approach. Foundations do not want elaborate evaluation designs here. However, you do need to give them an idea of how much will change as a result of your proposed solution. Review the section in chapter 13 on writing objectives.

Depending on the number of total pages allowed, one entire page of your proposal may be dedicated to this section, or you may have to limit this section to one or two paragraphs of five to seven lines each. While you need to have a legitimate plan, you must guard against making the methodology too elaborate. Since you are the content expert, you may have difficulty viewing your proposal from the reader's point of view. Ask yourself the following questions:

- How much does the reader really need to know about the proposed solution?
- Will the reader understand my plan?
- Will the words used in the description of my solution be familiar to the reader?
- Is all the information included critical to convincing the funder that I have a sound, worthwhile plan, or am I including some of it just for myself?

Remember, while you are concerned with how you will solve the problem, grantors are concerned with what will be different after their money is spent. If possible, use this section to summarize your approach and objectives and refer the funder to your project planner for more information as in the following example:

What can we do in Smithville to promote the sharing of responsibility for education among schools, parents, and children? At Smithville Elementary School we have developed a program aimed at increasing responsible behavior and encouraging parental involvement in the classroom and at home. Teachers will actually work with parents and students to develop tailored, individual contracts to produce increases in all levels of education and the quality of course work. The attached project planner outlines each objective and the activities that will foster the changes we desire. Through the education and involvement of parents in their children's responsible use of out-of-school time, our program will provide the catalyst for decreasing time spent on computer games, texting friends, and television viewing by students. The goal is to increase the completion of homework assignments, improve test scores, and promote physical activities that will improve the health of our youth.

Uniqueness Section

This part of your letter proposal could also be called the "why we are capable and qualified" section. In the uniqueness section, you want to assure the grantor that your organization is the best choice for implementing the solution. Assuming you have held the reader's interest up to this point, he or she knows

- why you have selected the funding source,
- that there is a compelling need, and
- that you have a plan to address this need.

The key question in the grantor's mind at this critical moment is whether your organization is the right one to address the problem.

If you have completed the uniqueness exercise in chapter 6, you already have a list of your organization's strengths and positive qualities and, if appropriate, the unique advantages of your consortia members. Select items from the list to include in this section of your letter proposal. Choose credibility builders that will convince the grantor that you have the commitment, staff, skill, buildings, and equipment to do the job. For example, you could say something like,

> Serving the elderly has been the sole mission of Rock of Ages Home for over fifty years. Since our inception we have continually received superior ratings from the state board. Our staff members represent over three hundred years of experience, and their commitment to doing more than their call of duty is exhibited by their willingness to *volunteer* time to develop this model approach for serving Alzheimer's patients.

Request for Funds Section

You must make a precise request for money. If you want to demonstrate that you have done your homework, refer to the fact that your request is (or is close to) the grantor's average-size award for your area of interest.

If your request from this grantor does not cover the entire cost of the project, reference those other sources that have already given support, list the others you will be approaching, or mention that such a list is available upon request.

You can summarize the budget categories that make up your total request, or you can provide prospective grantors with the portion of the budget that you would like them to fund. Since you are working under a severe space limitation, your budget summary should be arranged in paragraph form or in several short columns. If you submit your project planner with your proposal, you can refer to the column subtotals in your planner. For example, "The salary and wages, including fringe benefits, total $24,000. The work of the project director and other employees called for in this proposal is documented on page 3 in columns G, H, and I of the project planner."

To keep the focus on the value of the project and the results that you are seeking, you may want to divide the cost of the project by the number of people who will benefit from it. Consider the effect your project may have over several years, and calculate a cost per person served or affected by the project. For example, "In the next five years the equipment that you provide under this grant will touch the lives of approximately five thousand students by helping them to read on grade level for the first time, and at a cost of only $5.63 per person served."

This section should also make reference to how you expect to sustain the project/program after its creation. Foundations do not want to look bad because a program they started ultimately left its recipients in the lurch or out in the cold.

Before constructing this component of your letter proposal, review the foundation's guidelines once again. Some foundations have very specific budget guidelines that must be strictly adhered to.

Closing Paragraph

Many grantseekers close their letter proposals with a statement reflecting their willingness to meet with the prospective grantor to discuss their proposals. While a visit is highly unlikely unless the prospective grantor is a large foundation with a staff, I have had a foundation grantor make a visit to my organization before making the funding decision. However, references to such a meeting are usually futile. Instead, use the closing of your proposal to underscore your willingness to provide any further documentation or information the funding source may desire.

This brings up the question of who from your organization will be the best person to communicate with the prospective grantor. While you, the proposal developer, may have written the proposal, you probably will not be the individual to sign it. Therefore, in your closing paragraph request that your prospective grantor contact you (or the individual responsible for the project) for more information or to answer any questions. For example, "I encourage you to telephone me at my office or to call Ms. Connors directly at _____ to respond to technical questions or for additional information." Be sure to include a telephone number and extension, and test the line that will be used for this purpose to be certain that it is answered by a courteous and knowledgeable representative of your organization. You could also refer the grantor to your organization's website for more information or for answers to frequently asked questions. Your contact person's e-mail address should be included as well.

Signatures

Even though you are submitting what seems to be a letter, it is a grant application and constitutes an agreement between your organization and the grantor if it is accepted. Therefore, as is standard in agreements, the administrator or officer who holds the appropriate rank and responsibility to enter into these types of arrangements should sign it. If the link to the grantor is not your chief operating officer or chief executive officer, there is no reason why two individuals cannot sign the proposal—the link and the administrator or your consortia partner.

Because the board is legally responsible for the consequences of your organization's actions, including a board member's signature along with the chief executive officer's may impress the grantor. Just remember that the purpose of the signature is to provide the proposal with legal commitment and credibility.

Attachments

Most foundations require the inclusion of certain attachments such as a

- list of current board of directors, trustees, and officers showing names and professional affiliations,
- copy of 501(c)(3) IRS determination letter of tax-exempt status,
- audited financial statement for the most recent fiscal year,
- operating budget for the organization as a whole,
- project budget,
- collection of recent publications,
- organizational background including history and mission, and
- curricula vitae for the project's senior staff.

Most foundations do not encourage prospective grantees to submit any additional materials with their proposal. This includes other attachments as well as DVDs, CDs, videotapes, and so on. You could, however, consider including your project planner as a page in your proposal rather than as an attachment, and be sure to always refer to it by page number. In general, your proposal should give the impression that you have more information you are willing to give the prospective grantor if desired. Including too much with the proposal, however, may reduce the likelihood that it will be read and funded.

As you can now see, the letter proposal follows an orderly progression that focuses on the needs and interests of the funding source. As you gain insight into your prospective grantor, you will develop the ability to write grant-winning foundation proposals. A sample letter proposal to a foundation (see exhibit 22.1) is included for your review.

EXHIBIT 22.1
Sample Letter Proposal to a Foundation

Nikhil Allen, Executive Director
A.O. Smith Foundation
1409 East Oxford Pkwy
Henderson, NV 89400

Dear Mr. Allen:

While working with creative programs to reduce dropout rates in Nevada's K–12 schools our staff provided pilot program training to your funded project in the Clark County School District. Dr. Jean Sanchez from *Drop In to Win* found our session and materials extremely helpful. He encouraged our non-profit organization, *Nevada Read by 3*, to explore a grant opportunity with the A.O. Smith Foundation. Your record of supporting twenty-six innovative programs with over $3 million in grant funding, documents your concern and passion for young people and aligns perfectly with our case statement and mission (see www.readby3.com).

Nevada's dropout rate continues to increase with every survey. Currently Clark County has the fifth worse graduation rate in the country at 44.5 percent (*Las Vegas Sun*, January 2, 2009). The current recession and Nevada's 15 percent unemployment rate has resulted in a 25 percent cut in education and a leading gubernatorial candidate who pledges to eliminate one in five current teaching positions.

K–12 teachers in Nevada are facing pay cuts, decreasing benefits, and increasing class sizes. To make matters worse, there are no funds for in-service education or materials to help the classroom leader who has already been struggling and is now faced with increasing numbers of educationally disadvantaged students.

EXHIBIT 22.1
(*Continued*)

Research by Dr. Timin Brown on evaluating model projects on dropout reduction in Virginia and Ohio has documented a direct correlation between reading skills in third grade and dropout rates. Dr. Brown has developed an intervention program titled *Read by 3*, which has been designed to dramatically reduce dropout rates and problematic classroom behavior. Essentially, students in the program are not promoted to fourth grade unless they reach the corresponding reading level. Dr. Brown's evaluation of similar programs in other states has documented success when the schools, teachers, and parents buy into the concept.

Once in the program, the K–3 classroom leader will receive training, materials, and mentoring to set up the reading success that the program relies on. Participating teachers will receive a "Read by 3 Tool Box" and support to put the program in place.

Over the next ten years this proactive program will dramatically reduce dropout rates and increase high school completion. Of course there will still be a need for programs like Dr. Sanchez's *Drop In to Win* while these new readers work their way up the educational staircase. But ours is a solution that will change the situation in the long run.

We have letters of commitment from eleven urban and rural school districts to join the program. A.O. Smith Foundation's support of $250,000 in year 1 will enable five of these districts to initiate the program. Our research indicates that the A.O. Smith Foundation understands the value of multi-year funding, and after evaluation we expect year 2 and year 3 of your Foundation's support to be matched by 10 and 20 percent respectively. Our goal is to have year 4 paid by state funding.

Your support is catalytic to making these changes in the face of what are difficult days for the classroom leader who is feeling abandoned and unappreciated. We stand ready to supply you and your board with any additional information you may need to make your decision. We also invite you to visit our office and to meet with our key personnel. Please direct all questions and correspondence to our project director, Dr. Brown at [telephone number] or [email address].

Sincerely,

Dr. Thomas Watkins, Director
Nevada Read by 3

If you have made the decision to use the foundation grants marketplace, it is time to commit to writing the proposal. Be sure you know the foundation's deadline for submittal and then move to your action steps' chart (see figure 22.1). Log the deadline date(s) and the name of the foundation(s) you will write your proposal for in your plan.

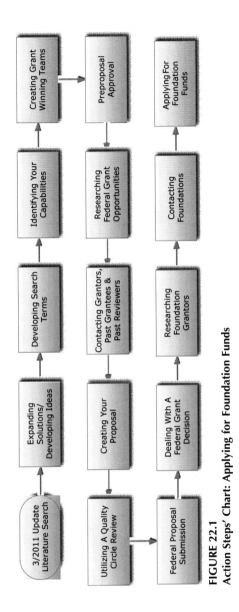

FIGURE 22.1
Action Steps' Chart: Applying for Foundation Funds

23

Proposal Submission, the Decision, and Follow-Up

Private Foundation Funding Sources

Foundation Quality Circle/Proposal Review Committee

BEFORE SUBMISSION you want to ensure that your proposal is of the highest quality. Just as with government grant proposals, you should put your foundation proposal through a quality circle or proposal review committee critique. This process is much easier than it is with federal proposals since foundations seldom have a scoring system or peer review. But the lack of information on what foundation board members are looking for and how they evaluate proposals is disconcerting to the serious foundation grantseeker. The best suggestion I can provide is to invite a group of four to six people whose backgrounds most closely resemble those of the foundation board's to come together for one hour to review your proposal. This exercise works well when you provide breakfast or lunch.

You can find a list of the foundation's board members on the foundation's tax return (990-PF), and then you could also look up each member in *Who's Who in America* (see list of resources), which can be found in your public library. However, you cannot go wrong if you assume they are educated and wealthy and want to carry out projects that reflect similar values as those of the past projects they have supported. Their values and interests change very slowly.

Provide quality circle participants with any background data on the foundation decision makers that you can uncover. Ask the group members to read your proposal rapidly, and designate those areas they think the foundation's board would like with a plus symbol (+) and those areas they think could be improved with a minus symbol (−). Ask them for their suggestions on improvement and how they think you can incorporate the revisions into your final proposal. Rewrite your proposal accordingly. Thank your mock review/quality circle participants and tell them you will let them know the outcome. Send them an e-mail or handwritten thank-you note a week after the exercise. In some cases, I have attached a copy of the improved proposal, highlighting the improvement made due to the feedback given by the quality circle participant.

Submittal

The submittal deadlines set by private foundation funding sources must be taken just as seriously as those of the government. If you cannot meet a deadline, you will appear to be a poor steward of funds, so try to be prompt, or, better yet, early. Private foundations, unlike the government, have been known to give a few extra days' "grace" period when the prospective grantee has a good explanation for the delay and the benefit of personal contact. However, it still does not look good when you need extra time, especially when the deadline has usually been published for a year or more, or worse yet, has been the same date for many years.

When you are submitting your request to a large foundation, you can

- deliver it in person,
- have an advocate or board member deliver it for you,
- send it in by the United States Postal Service or private carrier, or
- submit it electronically via the Internet if available.

When sending in your proposal, always request a return receipt. Obtain delivery confirmation whether you use the United States Postal Service (USPS), the United Parcel Service (UPS), or FedEx. This way you will have proof that your proposal arrived on time, along with a signature that could prove useful in follow-up.

It is expected that an increasing number of foundations will develop websites and offer online proposal submittal. If your prospective funding source has a website, be sure to check if this method of submittal is available to you. Even if you submit your proposal electronically, print it off and make sure that electronic submittal did not somehow affect its visual attractiveness. In several of my online submittals I have asked the grantors if I could supply a duplicate print copy. Note on each copy that a duplicate has been provided, and be sure to get both copies (the electronic and the print version) in before the deadline. As a courtesy, you can also offer to provide the grantor with a copy of the proposal for each of its board members.

Make note of the following:

- Send the contacts/links you discovered through the webbing and linkage process a copy of your letter proposal.
- Ask these friends to push for your proposal at the board meeting or to contact their friends or other board members to encourage a favorable decision.
- Minimize personal contact once you have submitted your proposal to avoid appearing pushy.

The Decision and Follow-Up

Private foundation grantors are generally more prompt than government funders at letting you know their decision about your proposal. They will give you a simple yes shortly after the board's scheduled meeting. If the answer is yes, you should do the following immediately:

- Send both a handwritten and an e-mail thank-you letter to the funding source. One foundation trustee told me that one of the only records that her foundation keeps on grantees is whether or not they thank the foundation. She said, "If an organization that receives a grant doesn't thank us, they do not receive another grant from us."
- Find out the payment procedures. Usually the acceptance letter comes with a check. If a check is not enclosed, the letter will at least inform you of when you will receive payment. Due to staff shortages, small foundations will usually grant the entire amount requested in one lump sum. Large foundations with staff may make partial or quarterly payments based on your cash forecast.
- Check on any reporting procedures that the funding source may have. Most small foundations consider the canceled check a completion report. However, I suggest you send the funding source a more formal completion report as a courtesy.
- Ask the funding source when you might visit to report on the grant, and invite funders to visit you when traveling in your area.
- Ask, or have your link ask, the funding source what was best about your proposal and what could have been better. Although most grantors will not comment on your proposal, it cannot hurt to ask.

Most funding sources feel neglected once they have given away their money. You can get on their list of good grantees by following up. Your follow-up checklist should include

- putting funding sources on your public relations mailing list so that they will receive news or press releases,
- keeping your funding source files updated and having a volunteer maintain current lists of grants funded by each of your grantors, and
- writing to funding sources two years after they have funded you to let them know how successful you are and to thank them again for their farsightedness in dealing with the problem.

Since you are now aware of the critical staff shortage in foundations, you should not be surprised that most foundations do not even send out rejection notices. Hopefully, this will be less the case as more foundations use e-mail. A woman in one of my seminars remarked that she was still waiting to hear about a foundation proposal she submitted two years prior. I assured her that it was rejected. With foundation grants, no news is bad news. In either case, rejection or no news, I suggest you do the following:

- Send a thank-you letter to the funding source. Express your appreciation for the time and effort spent on reviewing your proposal.
- Remind the funder what an important source of funds it is.
- Ask for helpful comments on your proposal and whether the funding source would look favorably on resubmission with certain changes.
- Ask whether the funder could suggest any other funding sources that may be interested in your project.

If the foundation has no staff and you have no links, you may not find answers to your questions. Try again. Successful grantseekers are persistent! However, you should also be aware that you may not hear *anything* from the funding source.

The steps suggested in part 3 of this book follow the book's unifying principle: that is, look at everything you do from the perspective of the grantor. From preproposal contact, to writing your thank-you letter, to follow-up, consider how you would want to be appreciated and recognized for your contribution now and in the future.

Part 4

PRIVATE/CORPORATE FUNDING OPPORTUNITIES

24

Understanding the Corporate Marketplace

THE CORPORATE PHILANTHROPIC MARKETPLACE has undergone major financial/ market pressures and significant shifts in its priorities. According to Giving USA, corporate giving rose 5.5 percent in 2009. While any increase in the grants marketplace should be viewed as positive, there are some factors to be considered when attempting to understand this increase in this important source of grant funds. Much of the 2009 increase can be attributed to company in-kind donations, which are less affected by recessions. This was particularly true in the case of increased in-kind gifts from pharmaceutical firms in the form of pharmaceutical drugs to individuals in need. In actuality, cash contributions from corporate foundations dropped about 3 percent from 2008 to the end of 2009 with corporate foundation grants accounting for only 31 percent of total corporate support. Cash and in-kind contributions from company budgets accounted for 69 percent of the total corporate figure of $14.1 billion. Even with the increase of 5.5 percent, this $14.1 billion in total corporate giving is far from the 2005 peak. In any event, the recovery shown by the 5.5 percent increase is heartening when you consider that the Standard & Poor's 500 Index (a generally agreed upon barometer of corporate strength) lost 48.3 percent of its value from March of 2007 to February of 2009 and that the 2008 drop in corporate philanthropy was almost 10 percent in itself.

To understand the present corporate marketplace and to make any predictions concerning its future, it is useful to look at corporate grants and corporate philanthropy from a historical perspective.

The concept of corporate self-interest as the guiding principle of corporate philanthropy actually has its basis in law. The Internal Revenue Act of 1935 made it legal for corporations to deduct 5 percent of their pretax revenues for charitable donations. The general consensus was that these gifts (which many still view as the purview of the stockholders and not the corporation) were to be used for purposes that directly benefited the corporation's business or interests. It took eighteen years for this concept to be challenged.

In 1953 in *A.P. Smith Manufacturing Co. v. Barlow et al.,* the New Jersey Supreme Court ruled that corporate contributions for purposes other than a direct benefit to the business were indeed legal. The case involved a contested gift of $1,500 made by the A.P. Smith Manufacturing Company's board of directors to Princeton University for general maintenance. Until that time, the company's corporate practice had been to sponsor only educational research projects that related to the company's business. The stockholders charged that the gift was a misappropriation of corporate funds, but the Supreme Court ruled otherwise. This ruling has been referred to as the "Magna Carta" of corporate philanthropy, and it ultimately changed the ground rules for corporate contributions forever.

The year 2011 will mark the fifty-eighth anniversary of this ruling, which made it legal for a corporation to award gifts and grants that do not directly benefit its business. Still, corporate giving is primarily motivated by corporate self-interest. Corporate giving is usually a "this-for-that" exchange. Even when the grant may not be directly related to the corporation's business/ products, the corporation still receives public relations value in the community or marketplace. As a corporate grantseeker you must view their proposed investment in your organization (the grant) through their values glasses.

Historically, education has received the largest portion of the corporate philanthropic dollar. As you ponder your ability to attract corporate support for your college, university, school, or educationally related nonprofit group, you need to consider the following. Traditionally, higher education has been industry's subcategory of choice. Corporations figured out long ago that without the raw ingredient of a trained workforce they could not produce salable products or services. Today, they realize that they need higher education graduates to maintain a competitive place in an increasingly global marketplace. However, higher education cannot assume that it will always receive the largest share of the corporate education dollar. A considerable challenge has been successfully mounted by secondary education, elementary education, and even preschool education.

While education has historically attracted the most *cash* share of corporate philanthropy, human services and health receive a greater percentage of total corporate contributions when you consider all forms of support (cash and noncash). One reason for this may be the escalating costs of health care and the fact that health and human services programs, projects, and research may provide direct benefits to employees, which decreases the need for services and, hence, lowers the corporation's employee health costs.

While one could argue that support for education, human services, civic and community affairs, and health makes a company look good and enhances the general community, how would you explain a corporation's interest in arts and culture? As a past board member and grantseeker for a museum, I once asked a corporate contributions' committee member how I could make my museum proposal more attractive to the committee. I was told I should document certain overriding factors, such as

- the use of the museum by current corporate employees, their families, and their friends;
- the number of corporate employees and/or their family members who volunteer at the museum;
- how the museum interfaces with the local chamber of commerce and how its presence promotes tourism and visitors to the area; and
- the existence of programs designed to provide family tours and so forth to those whom the corporation is seeking to recruit.

As a result of our conversation, we developed a community introduction program that matched our board members with prospective employees that the corporation was seeking to hire and relocate to our area. This moved us from a grant to support the museum to a contract to provide an introduction service, but it was undesignated cash that we could use as we saw fit.

Whether a corporation supports education, human services, civic and community affairs, health, or arts and culture, you can be sure that its expenditures, be they philanthropic dollars or noncash gifts, are related to its enlightened corporate self-interests. The bottom line is that as you develop your corporate grants strategy, you must review your institution's or organization's ability to provide corporations with what they value.

As the global marketplace expands and the multinationals merge and make hostile takeovers, corporate philanthropic activities become even more difficult to track and predict. U.S. companies purchased by foreign-based corporations have a very different sense of and experience with philanthropy. And international giving has become a growing category of corporate philanthropy as more and more companies have developed a worldwide presence.

Before you begin to refine your approach, consider the varied mechanisms that companies employ to make their corporate investments.

Corporate Investment Mechanisms

Corporations use four basic mechanisms for investing in and making grants to nonprofit organizations.

Corporate Contributions Programs

Corporate contributions programs are the mechanism of choice in corporate philanthropy. Usually high-ranking corporate officials decide what portion of the corporation's net earnings before taxes (NEBT; the bottom line of profits after manufacturing, sales, and marketing costs have been deducted) will be made available as gifts and grants. This money is then deducted from the corporate taxes due the government and directed to a corporate contributions committee to disperse to colleges, universities, and other nonprofit organizations that the corporation values. Interests vary from company to company but generally fall within the categories discussed above (education, human services, civic and community affairs, health, and arts and culture). Committee members may be corporate executives and representatives of employee groups or unions. Since many of the existing corporations are relatively small, with only a few employees, it can be surmised that the larger the company, the more likely it is to have a corporate contributions program and to engage in this mechanism of corporate philanthropy.

The latest IRS rules allow corporations to donate up to 10 percent of their pretax income (NEBT) in gifts and grants to nonprofit organizations as a tax deduction. However, the practice of donating a *set* percentage annually is not widespread. In fact, estimates are that only 35 percent of all of the corporations in the United States dedicate *any* funds to nonprofit organizations.

At the beginning of the twenty-first century, the Bush administration backed a change in legislation to increase the corporate profits write-off from 10 percent to 20 percent. Even if this had passed, the current upper limit of 10 percent of deductions has never been approached, and allowing 20 percent would likely have had little impact on increasing the percentage of giving. For example, when the limit was 5 percent, the average pretax profits donated were just over 2 percent. When the limit was raised to 10 percent, the average declined to around 1 percent and has remained there. Irrespective of the percentage donated, corporate profits are currently at record levels and, therefore, the corporate contributions marketplace warrants your investigation and consideration.

It is interesting to note that corporate philanthropic contributions are not required to be reported to stockholders in an itemized format. Stockholders are not entitled to a list of recipient organizations and the associated amounts of grants support. Only the IRS receives such a list with the corporate tax return and it is not at liberty to share it with anyone.

Because corporate tax returns are not publicly available, it is difficult to ascertain the funding priorities of corporate contributions programs. Historically, health and human services are the biggest recipients of corporate contributions programs, followed by international support, and then education. It is no surprise that international support is one of the main recipients of corporate contributions programs. Contributions made by corporations usually benefit the corporation, its employees, or the community in which it operates, and since we are rapidly becoming a global economy, the "community" is changing to an international one. However, the funding priorities of corporate contributions programs are somewhat different than those of the next group—corporate foundation grants.

Corporate Foundation Grants

In this grants mechanism, companies designate a portion of their entitled write-off of pretax profits to be transferred to a foundation (usually named after the corporation) from which grants are paid. The main reason for initiating a corporate foundation is to stabilize a corporation's philanthropy program. Corporate foundations lead to a more uniform and stable approach to corporate social philanthropy than giving programs that rely solely on a percentage of company profits each year. Programs tied to company profits are subject to the seesaw effect, because profits can vary widely from year to year. Funds from the corporate foundation corpus can be moved to grants in lean profit years.

Many corporations maintain both a corporate contributions program and a corporate foundation. This allows the company some flexibility in making grants. For example, if profits are down one year, the corporate contributions program can be supported by expending some of the assets that have built up in the foundation. The corporation can level out the highs and lows of its corporate contributions over periods of high, low, and no profits and still maintain some level of support for its favorite nonprofit organizations. While all foundations are required to pay out a minimum of 5 percent of their assets, corporate foundations have historically paid out a much higher percentage, especially in the years marked by recession or low corporate profits.

Like the other types of foundations discussed in chapter 19, corporate foundations must list the benefactors of their grants and make their tax returns available for public viewing. This requirement can become a problem for corporations when their stockholders object to the types of organizations or specific projects that the corporate foundation supports. In addition, the public scrutiny to which the corporate foundation is subject allows for social activists and leaders of particular causes to research the foundation's giving pattern and arrange for demonstrations at stockholder meetings that could result in negative public relations. To avoid such problems, many corporations make only noncontroversial grants (for example, a grant to the United Way) through their foundation; they make all other grants through their corporate contributions program that does not require public disclosure.

Since corporate foundations are an extension of a profit-making company they tend to view the world and your proposal as any corporation would. They must see a benefit in all of the projects they fund. Many of these corporate foundations fund grants only in communities where their parent corporations have employees or a special interest. Table 24.1 shows the largest recipients of corporate foundation grants by percentage of grant dollars. Proposals related to education are the top recipient of corporate foundation grants (23 percent), followed by human services (20 percent). Note that while international support is historically the second highest recipient of *corporate contributions programs*, it falls to seventh place in *corporate foundation support* (3 percent).

Corporate Marketing

While it is estimated that 25 percent of corporate support to nonprofits comes in the form of donated products, this figure is probably deceptively low. Corporate support in the form of products is likely to be far greater than the reported levels, but data on this marketing mechanism are difficult to collect and analyze. Much is simply not reported and thus is impossible to track.

Many corporate contributions of products may not be recorded as gifts per se because they are being used to position the products in the user population to gain future sales. In essence, these product gifts could be questioned

TABLE 24.1
Corporate Foundation Grants by Recipient Category

Recipient Category	Percentage of Grant Dollars
Education	23.0
Human Services	20.0
Public Affairs/Society Benefit	19.0
Health	14.0
Arts/Culture	13.0
Environment/Animals	4.0
International Affairs, Development, and Peace	3.0
Science/Technology	3.0
Other	1.0

by the IRS because they do not qualify as true gifts; some quid pro quo (or this-for-that) is involved in these transactions, but the company writes off the associated costs before net earnings are ever calculated to avoid any problems.

Corporate Research, Contributions, and Grants

Corporations have traditionally supported colleges, universities, and non-profit organizations' attempts to apply science to further the development of new technologies, patents, and breakthroughs in their fields of interest. Some corporations also contribute to nonprofit organizations based on the nonprofit's ability to contribute to the testing, improvement, or creation of a new product. The litmus test as to whether the support provided is really a grant is whether the nonprofit that is the recipient of the corporate support is acting as a free agent or is a captive contractor for the corporate sponsor of the proposed work.

To be considered a true corporate grant, the results of the research must be published and shared for the "greater good" of the field. If the work is to be prescribed by the corporation, or the freedom to publish the resulting data is restricted, and any patents derived are the sole ownership of the corporation, the corporation's support will not be viewed by the IRS as a grant but rather as a fee for services rendered or a corporate contract. If the support is viewed as a corporate contract, it is not allowed to be written off as a charitable contribution. However, it could be considered as a research or marketing cost and as such could be deducted before the company arrives at its net earnings before taxes.

While you do not need to be concerned with how the company deducts these costs from its balance sheet, it is crucial to both you and your institution/organization to clarify the intellectual property rights (copyrights, patents, and so forth) before entering into any research-related agreement.

Review your proposed project and consider how it provides your prospective corporate grantor with what it values. Then, based on these variables, determine which corporate grant-making mechanism best fits your project (see exhibit 24.1). Compare the corporate self-interest variables in the column on the left of the exhibit to the four basic mechanisms for corporate support presented in the top row of the exhibit.

Corporate Funding and Ethical Issues

Most researchers are aware of the traditional hierarchy of grant support. By tradition, government, peer-reviewed grants have been viewed as the most pres-

EXHIBIT 24.1
Corporate Grants Support Worksheet

Corporate Self-Interest	Corporate Contributions Program Gifts and Grants	Corporate Foundation Grants	Corporate Marketing Contributions and Grants	Corporate Research Program Contributions and Grants
Ability to Attract High-Quality Personnel				
Benefits Workers and/or Their Families				
Benefits Overall Community Where Parent Corporation Has Factory or Special Interests				
Positions Product in Such a Way That It Results in Future Sales				
Product Development—Tests, Improves, or Creates a New Product				
Research—Furthers Knowledge in Corporation's Field of Interest				
Other				

tigious, followed by foundation grants (not always peer reviewed and subject to foundation board bias), and finally, corporate grants (reviewed by a biased corporate grants committee looking for a return on its investment). However, the traditional ways of looking at corporate grants have changed dramatically over the last decade. One reason for this change has to do with the government's cuts in research. The cuts have encouraged, if not forced, universities to partner with the corporate world to collaborate, transfer technology, and develop intellectual property. Sheldon Krimsky, in his book *Science in the Private Interest: Has the Lure of Profits Corrupted the Virtue of Biomedical Research?*, questions whether universities should be turned into instruments of wealth rather than protected enclaves whose primary roles are as sources of enlightenment.[1] The traditional assumption that research findings that come from the ivory tower of higher education are true and not biased or corrupt has been challenged by science selling findings to the highest bidder.

There exists a tremendous pressure to trade off the values of higher education as the costs for supporting research soar and the government cuts its funding for peer-reviewed research and continues to support earmarked noncompetitive grants. Not only has Congress pushed the bounds of ethical standards related to research but it also has left the university and the researcher little choice but to surround themselves with corporations that have never been the bastion of ethical standards.

The big question now is how much financial gain the researcher will get by proving what the company wants. In fact, the incentives given by companies in stock and whether the company is owned by the researcher have now become the operant questions from which to judge the research findings.

Corporate support for research presents problems all across the nonprofit sector because the profits from potential products are so high. How far can this corporate interest in research take us? Several universities have auctioned off exclusive rights to their intellectual resources and their reputations to corporate bidders as a result of budget cuts. They pledge to maintain scientific ethics, but would they really do research that questioned their corporate partners' products? The lines are so blurred that some universities have actually warned their researchers that they could be sued if their research costs their corporate sponsors to lose profits.

The bottom line is that researchers must be very careful when dealing with corporate grantors. They come at a price. Being forewarned is being forearmed.

Note

1. Sheldon Krimsky, *Science in the Private Interest: Has the Lure of Profits Corrupted the Virtue of Biomedical Research?* (Lanham, MD: Rowman & Littlefield, 2004), 2.

25

Researching Potential Corporate Grantors

How to Find the Corporate Funding Source That Is Best Suited to Fund Your Project

T O BE A SUCCESSFUL CORPORATE GRANTSEEKER, you will need to gather accurate information on your prospective corporate grantors before you approach them. The Corporate Research Form (exhibit 25.1) outlines what information you will need to collect. The biggest mistake you can make with this marketplace is to send the same proposal to all the companies in your area. Your research will result in your ability to create targeted, tailored, winning proposals.

How you research the corporate marketplace depends on many factors, including the type of corporate grants mechanism you are pursuing. You must ask why a corporation would value your proposal. If your project is related to products, product positioning, produce development, or research, you can cast a wide corporate net. In fact, you can move beyond local boundaries and look all across the country for the corporations best suited to fund your project.

To do so, you must first determine which major corporations could possibly be affected by your project. Develop a list of the products and services (the key words) that could be related to your project, and then access the *US NAICS (North American Industry Classification System—United States) Manual* at your university or public library. By searching the *US NAICS Manual*, using your key words, you can discover the names of the corporations that might be interested in your project. For example, if your project uses innovative ways to educate people with visual impairments, you might use the *US NAICS Manual* to locate companies that manufacture equipment for the blind or the latest telecommunications equipment that could be used in your solution.

EXHIBIT 25.1
Corporate Research Form

The following form outlines the data you need to collect in order to make a decision to seek funding from this grant source. Your attempts to collect as much of this information as possible will prove rewarding. (When feasible, record the source of the information and the date it was recorded.)

Name of Corporation: _____

Name of Corporate Foundation: _____

Name of Corporate Contributions Program: _____

Address: _____

Phone: _____ Fax: _____ E-mail: _____

Website: _____

Contact Person: _____

Title: _____

Any Links from Our Organization to Contact Person: _____
_____
_____

Corporation's Areas of Interests: _____
_____
_____
_____

Eligibility Requirements/Restrictions:

a. Activities Funded/Restricted: _____
_____
_____

b. Organizations Funded/Restricted: _____
_____

c. Geographic Funding Preferences/Restrictions: _____
_____
_____

d. Other Requirements/Restrictions: _____
_____
_____
_____
_____

(*continued*)

EXHIBIT 25.1
(Continued)

Information Available   *In Possession Of*

IRS 990-PF Tax Return (Year)   _____ (Corporate Foundation Only)
Guidelines   _____
Newsletters   _____
Annual Report   _____
Previously Funded Proposals   _____
Reviewer Information   _____
Evaluation Criteria   _____

Contributions Committee Members/Board of Directors/ Foundation Officers:
_____
_____
_____
_____

Deadline(s):_____

Application Process/Requirements:
_____
_____
_____

Financial Information

Fiscal Year: _____
Corporate Sales:$_____
Parent Company:_____
Corporate Sites: _____
# of Employees: _____
Credit Rating: _____ Source: _____
Private or Publicly Held: _____
If Publicly Held: Stock Price $_____ Dividend: $_____
Products Produced/Distributed: _____
_____
_____

For Corporate Foundations:

Asset Base: $_____
Are there current gifts to build the asset base? Yes _____ No _____
If yes, how much? $_____

EXHIBIT 25.1
(*Continued*)

Total number of grants awarded in ____: _____
Total amount of grants awarded in ____: $_____

High Grant: $_____
Low Grant: $_____
Average Grant: $_____

In our interest area there were: _____ grants, totaling $_____
High grant in our interest area: $_____
Low grant in our interest area: $_____
Average grant in our interest area: $_____

Grants Received versus Grants Funded
Number of proposals received in ____: _____
Number of proposals funded in ____: _____

Sample Grants in Our Area of Interest:

Recipient Organization   *Amount*
_____   _____
_____   _____
_____   _____
_____   _____

Please note that while the North American Industry Classification System (NAICS) has replaced the U.S. Standard Industrial Classification (SIC) for statistical purposes, you will find that some publications still refer to SIC codes. Like the NAICS, the SIC is a system for classifying establishments by type of economic activity. Although the principles of the systems are the same, NAICS codes may vary considerably from the SIC codes.

You will also want to find out if there are major industry-specific associations or membership groups that fund research or projects in your field. For instance, the Society of Manufacturing Engineers funds beneficial research in its field, and there are many more like it.

While you should look outside of your local area for corporate grantors when your project is related to research and product development, remember that most corporations give where they live. Therefore, you may find that targeting corporations that are hundreds or thousands of miles away is not productive unless they have a vested interest in your project or research.

Checking with your grant office and development office is always recommended when dealing with corporations, and it is absolutely essential when contacting companies close to home. Corporate people assume that anyone who submits a proposal or contacts them has the approval of the institution or organization he or she represents, and you risk negative positioning if the right hand does not know what the left is doing. This does not mean that you should not consider local corporations, but do your research and make a case to your organization as to why you and your project should be allowed to proceed to submittal with each target corporation.

There are several great sources of information on corporate support. The Foundation Center, in particular, is a good source for information on corporate foundation grants. Its publication, the *National Directory of Corporate Giving*, provides information on 2,800-plus company-sponsored foundations and an additional 1,200 corporate-giving programs. It is available in print. The online version, *Corporate Giving Online*, contains more than 3,500 company profiles; over 40,000 grant makers, including foundation and corporate giving programs; and descriptions of approximately 350,000 recently awarded grants. It also offers three ways to search—by company, by grant maker, and by grants. The *Corporate Giving Directory*, published by Information Today, Inc., is another good source. It provides profiles on 1,000 of the largest corporate foundations and corporate direct-giving programs in the United States. (See the list of resources for ordering information.) In addition, the annual 990-PF tax returns for corporate foundations can be accessed through the Foundation Center's regional and cooperating collections and on the web (see chapter 20).

Corporate funders can also be found through the Internet, especially since many companies now maintain a presence on the web. There are several helpful portal sites available, including

- foundationcenter.org/findfunders/ (the Foundation Center's website),
- www.cafonline.org (Charities Aid Foundation), and
- www.fundsnetservices.com/ (Fundsnet Services Online).

While it makes sense to check out these websites and the corporate grant resource books available in your local public library and at the Foundation Center's regional collections, another important source for data is your local chamber of commerce. Your chamber of commerce can provide you with a list of local corporations and information on number of employees, total value of payroll, and products and services provided. You can obtain this list by visiting or phoning your chamber, and in some instances the information is available on its website.

This list is most valuable as you begin to target your local grantors and develop your strategy on why they should be interested in your proposal. For example, when I was an associate professor at the University of Alabama, Birmingham, I asked for and received a list of the area's largest employers from the local chamber of commerce (see exhibit 25.2). By reviewing the information on the list, I discovered the following facts:

- The university I was employed by was the area's largest employer.
- Of the top ten largest employers, only three were profit-making corporate prospects.
- Seventy percent of the ten largest employers were nonprofit organizations and in competition with me for corporate support.
- Seventy percent of the next group (ten to twenty largest employers) were profit making but had only 19,890 employees in total compared to the nonprofits' 87,556 employees.

In addition to having to deal with the harsh reality of these facts, I also had to come to terms with the fact that hundreds of local nonprofits were targeting this corporate group, that the rest of my university had designs on the same local corporations that I did, and that I would have to plead my case for approval to submit a proposal to a development team comprising representatives from colleges and departments other than mine.

If your institution or organization is not in a large metropolitan area, and there is no chamber of commerce, contact your nearest economic development agency, industrial park headquarters, or business incubator. One of

EXHIBIT 25.2
Chamber of Commerce List: Top Employers—Birmingham/Hoover Metropolitan Area

Company	Employees
1. University of Alabama at Birmingham	18,750
2. BellSouth	5,485
3. Baptist Health System, Inc.	5,000+
4. Birmingham Board of Education	5,000
5. City of Birmingham	4,989
6. Jefferson County Board of Education	4,800
7. Jefferson County Commission	3,875
8. AmSouth Bancorporation	3,785
9. Bruno's Supermarkets, Inc.	3,477
10. Children's Health System	3,200
11. Wachovia	3,094
12. Alabama Power Company	3,000
13. Blue Cross-Blue Shield of Alabama	3,000
14. Drummond Company, Inc.	2,900
15. Brasfield & Gorrie, L.L.C.	2,800
16. St. Vincent's Hospital	2,800
17. United States Postal Service	2,800
18. Compass Bancshares	2,696
19. Brookwood Medical Center	2,600
20. American Cast Iron Pipe Company	2,400

these groups should have the data you need to uncover the corporations in your geographic area.

Once you have identified your distant and nearby potential corporate funding sources, the Internet and your public library or local college library will have several resources to help you gather more information to determine your best prospects for funding.

The following websites are a good place to start researching corporate information. In general, they will provide basic information about the company itself such as areas of company operations, products and services, corporate officers, and fiscal data:

- www.sec.gov/edgar/searchedgar/webusers.htm (EDGAR database that contains information on companies whose stocks are traded publicly);
- biz.yahoo.com/i (Yahoo! Finance Company and Fund Index, a searchable database with information on over 9,000 public companies in the United States);
- www.hoovers.com (Hoover's Online, a comprehensive subscription-based site that provides information on public and private companies in the United States and abroad); and
- www.lambresearch.com/CorpsExecs.htm (the Companies and Executives section of David Lamb's Prospect Research Page).

Several of the Dun & Bradstreet or Standard & Poor's products and publications will provide the basic information you will need on profitability, board members, and so on.

The *D&B Million Dollar Database* is the online equivalent to the well-known *Million Dollar Directory*. It is a subscription-based database that provides basic data on U.S. companies, such as addresses, ticker symbols, key officers, number of employees, sales, and so on. It also provides brief, searchable executive biographies and titles, listings of international offices of U.S. companies, and the ability to download lists of companies. It covers companies with at least $9 million in sales or 180-plus employees. The database is updated monthly, with company data updated every sixty days. Also available online, on a subscription basis, is the *D&B North American Million Dollar Database* that provides information on U.S. and Canadian leading public and private businesses, and the *D&B International Million Dollar Database* that provides information on international companies. (See the list of resources for ordering information.)

Exhibit 25.3 has been taken directly from Dun & Bradstreet's website (www.dnbmdd.com/mddi/sample.aspx) and is an example of what an entry in the *D&B Million Dollar Database* looks like.

Standard & Poor's Register—Corporate (File 527) is a database that provides information on over 100,000 public and private corporations worldwide,

EXHIBIT 25.3
Sample Entry from the *D&B Million Dollar Database*

Gorman Manufacturing Company

Marked for Output	[]
D&B D-U-N-S Number	80-480-0217
Company Name(s)	Gorman Manufacturing Company
Trade Styles	
Street Address	492 Koller St.
City	San Francisco
State/Province	CA
Zip Code	94110
County	San Francisco
Phone Number	(415) 555-0000
Sales	$10,600,000
Employees Here	100
Employees Total	105
Location Type	SINGLE LOCATION
Line of Business	COMMERCIAL PRINTING
Primary SICs	27520000 COMMERCIAL PRINTING, LITHOGRAPHIC
Secondary SICs	
Primary NAICS	
Secondary NAICS	
Ownership/Control Date	1965
Metropolitan Area	SAN FRANCISCO–OAKLAND, CA
State of Incorporation	CA
Import/Export	IMPORTER
Public/Private	PRIVATE
Ticker Symbol	
Bank	FIRST SECURITY NAT BANK OF NEV
Accountant	ABC ACCOUNTING
CEO	Leslie Smith, President
Executives	Mr. Kevin J Hunt, Sec-Treas
Other Officers	Robert F Woods
Executive Biographies	

LESLIE SMITH YEAR OF BIRTH: 1926 Graduated from the University of California, Los Angeles, in June 1947 with a BS in Business Management. 1947–1965 general manager with Raymor Printing Co., San Francisco, CA. 1956 formed subject with Kevin Hunt.

KEVIN J HUNT YEAR OF BIRTH: 1925 Graduated from Northwestern University, Evanston, IL in June 1946. 1946–1965 general manager for Raymor Printing Co., San Francisco, CA. In 1965 formed subject with Leslie Smith.

including current address, financial and marketing information, and a listing of officers and directors with positions and departments. Most of the companies covered have sales in excess of $1 million per year. The database's print counterpart is *Standard & Poor's Register of Corporations, Directors, and Executives, Volume 1*. Additional information on officers and directors is included in *Standard & Poor's Register of Corporations, Directors, and Executives, Volume 2*. Further information on companies can be found in another S&P database, *Standard & Poor's Corporate Descriptions* plus *News (File 133)*. Both of the S&P databases are available online through Dialog, a service of the Dialog Corporation (see the list of resources for ordering information). In addition, some university and public libraries will have access to these Dialog databases for a fee, and some will have hardcopies of the *S&P Registers* for free use. Exhibit 25.4 has been taken from Dialog's website and is a sample record from *Standard & Poor's Register—Corporate Database*.

The biographical information provided in *Standard & Poor's Register of Corporations, Directors, and Executives, Volume 2* includes the age, the educational background, and the residence of the corporate executive, as well as his or her other corporate affiliations and activities. This biographical information is very valuable in that it can be used with your grants advisory committee to uncover links and expand corporate relationships.

In addition to these references, your library should also have *Who's Who in America* and other books on outstanding individuals in your geographic area. The more you know about the people you will be approaching for a grant, the more prepared you will be to create a powerful appeal that motivates the grantor to award you funds. Corporate leaders have much more written about them than federal bureaucrats, and your local librarian can show you how to use free resource tools to learn more about corporate grant prospects. Check the list of resources in the back of this book for commercially available materials that you will find helpful in your search for corporate funding sources.

Profits are the bottom line in corporate philanthropy. If there are no profits there is little incentive to donate money to reduce taxes. Since corporate contributions depend on a company's profitability, your corporate research should include information on revenue. There are several ways to obtain accurate data on profitability. You can

- access a corporation's website to learn about its new products and plans.
- track a corporation's stock prices on the DOW, NASDAQ, or AMEX.
- include a stockbroker on your advisory group to help you monitor corporate profits.
- involve a corporate executive on your advisory group who subscribes to Dun & Bradstreet's financial services and ask him or her to request a Dun

EXHIBIT 25.4
Sample Record *Standard & Poor's Register—Corporate Database*

Dialog (R) File 527: S&P Register – Corp.
(c) 2003 McGraw-Hill Companies Inc. All rts. reserved

0018401

Company	CHEMDESIGN CORP.
Parent Company	(Subsidiary of Bayer AG)
Street Address	310 Authority Dr.
City, State, Zip Code	Fitchburg, MA 01420
Telephone	(978)345-9999
Business	Manufacturing, Manufactures, devel. & sells fine chemicals on a custom basis
NAICS codes	325998; 325110
NAICS descriptions	All Other Miscellaneous Chemical Product Manufacturing; Petrochemical Manufacturing
Year Started	1982
Sales	$61.00 Mil
Employee Total	395
Market Territory	NATIONAL, INTERNATIONAL
Special Feature	THIS IS A SUBSIDIARY A PUBLIC COMPANY
Stock Exchange	NYS
Ticker Symbol	XYZ
Accounting Firm	Deloitte & Touche Boston MA
Bank	Citibank
Law Firm	Miles & Stockbridge

EXECUTIVES AND DIRECTORS

Chrm, Pres & Chief Exec Officer	Archibald, Nolan D.
Exec V-P	Stevens, William E.
Exec V-P (Worldwide Inf Serv)	Barcus, James F., Jr.
Sr. V-P (Power Tools Group)	Sherman, George M.
Sr V-P (Household Products Group)	Heiner, Dennis G.

OTHER DIRECTORS:

Battle, William C.	Bolton, John E.
Decker, Alonzo G., Jr.	Franklin, Barbara H.
Krikorian, Robert V.	Muncaster, J. D.
Pugh, Lawrence R.	Storrs, Thomas I.
Voell, Richard A.	Watkins, Judy

& Bradstreet report on your prospective corporate grantor. This report will rate the fiscal stability of the company and give you a sense of the company's ability to support your proposal. (A corporate person will understand the values of corporations and may have linkages to companies you are interested in pursuing for grant support.)

* purchase a few shares of stock in each publicly held company in your area. If you receive a dividend check, you will know the company made money! Using this technique you will also receive corporate reports, proxy statements, and up-to-date information on top corporate administrators and board member changes. You might even make some money, and if you get rejected by a corporation you can always sell its stock for revenge!

Doing your homework on corporate grantors can be more frustrating than researching federal or foundation sources. You will find much less information available on corporate grants awarded by companies that do not use a foundation to make their grants, and the information you do find will be much less reliable. The reason for the lack of sound data on corporate giving is that there are no laws allowing public review of corporate contributions programs. Companies must record their corporate charitable contributions on their Internal Revenue Service tax return, but no one, not even a stockholder, has the right to see the return.

Except for the portion of corporate grants that is awarded through corporate foundations, corporate data are not subject to validation, and hence the reporting is not always accurate. The data on corporate giving are derived from self-reported, voluntary responses to surveys and questionnaires. Even the corporate contributions data reported to *Giving USA* (published by the Giving USA Foundation) are based on a voluntary survey conducted by the Conference Board, a nonprofit organization with a reputation for keeping corporate responses confidential.

Irrespective of the difficulties in obtaining accurate corporate granting information, the corporate research strategies recommended in this chapter will at least provide you with the ability to gather the name, address, e-mail address, fax, and phone number of the corporate contact person: information you will find necessary to take the next step in your grant-winning strategy step—contacting a corporate grantor before submission.

Before you do so, it is important to decide whether you will incorporate researching corporate grantors in your action steps' chart. Figure 25.1 shows this step in the "ideal plan." However, you may decide to bypass the corporate marketplace as a result of the knowledge you gathered in chapters 24 and 25. But if this marketplace does hold some potential for you, be it funding or products, review your action steps' chart to determine where researching corporate grantors will fit and when you will have the time to do it.

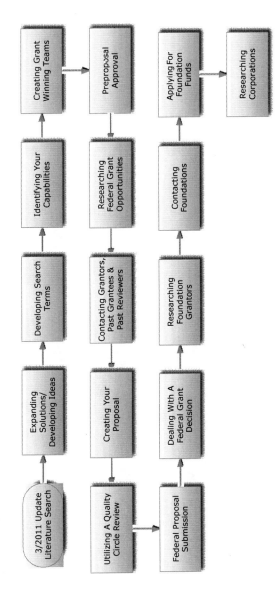

FIGURE 25.1
Action Steps' Chart: Researching Corporations

26

Contacting a Corporate Grantor before Submission

J UST AS WITH PRIVATE FOUNDATION GRANTSEEKERS, corporate grantseekers who discuss their projects with the appropriate corporate funding officials before submitting their proposals increase their success rates dramatically. A fivefold increase in success was found when preproposal contact was made with private foundation funding sources. Experience leads me to believe that the impact of preproposal contact on success rates is much higher in the corporate marketplace, and could approach a tenfold factor.

How to Contact Corporate Grantors

Often it is difficult for grantseekers to make preproposal contact with corporate grantors. This is because it takes more time to make profits than it does to grant the 1 percent of net earnings before taxes that most corporations award. In a sense, it costs the corporate grantor even more money to make grants when its time would be better spent on making more profits.

Corporate webbing and linkages become critical here (see chapter 7). It pays to figure out who may know whom, and who would be willing to make an appointment or open a door for you. If you do not have a linkage to any of your prospective corporate grantors, consider creating one by inviting selected corporate representatives to take part in your advisory group, or by hosting an open house or public forum.

Your initial point of contact may not always be the individual listed in your research as the corporate foundation contact or the chair of the corporate contributions committee. Your initial contact person could be a salesperson for the corporation, parents of your students who are employed by the corporation, clients of your organization who work for the company, and so on. Many corporations pay special attention to proposals that can be linked to employees that are volunteers of the prospective grantee's organization.

One big difference between private foundation grantors and corporate grantors is that the corporate grantor has an office or a facility. Even so, corporate grantors have a multitude of responsibilities and cannot spend unlimited amounts of time with grantseekers. Therefore, it is imperative that you follow the formal instructions your research uncovers. If you uncover a name, and an e-mail address or phone number, assume that you can contact the person listed. If your research states no contact except by letter or application, then follow those instructions. However, informal contact through an advisory committee member, advocate, or linkage is still advised. In these instances, the important thing is that *you* are not the one making the contact. If your advisory committee member, advocate, or linkage can orchestrate a conference call or preferably a face-to-face meeting, go with him or her. If you are instructed to request current guidelines or an application package, you can use the sample corporate inquiry letter/e-mail shown in exhibit 26.1. If the instructions call for a letter of inquiry or a letter proposal and do not allow for formal preproposal contact, go to chapter 27.

Contact by Telephone

If contact by telephone is allowed or encouraged, call to discuss how your project relates to the corporation's interest. Let the person to whom you are speaking know that you have done your homework. If it is a corporate foundation, use the information you obtained from its tax return (IRS form 990-PF) to show your knowledge of its past granting interests. If the corporate grantor seems interested in your project, do not be afraid to inquire about the possibility of a face-to-face meeting. If a visit is out of the question, then discuss the same issues over the phone as you would in person.

The Visit

While often the most anxiety producing, a face-to-face visit is usually the best way to discuss your project and to gauge the interest of the corporate grantor.

Who Should Go

It is advisable for you to take either an advocate, linkage, or an advisory committee member with you. A good listener who can summarize and reflect

EXHIBIT 26.1
Sample Inquiry Letter/E-mail to a Corporation

Name
Title
Address

Dear _____:

We at (nonprofit organization) are developing a project which deals with (problem) and provides benefit to [or in] (target population). Our research indicates that this area is an important concern of the (name of corporation or corporate foundation).

[Choose from the following paragraphs]

(Name and title) from our organization is planning a trip to (corporation's geographic location) and would appreciate being able to talk with you regarding an exciting project that we feel would be of mutual benefit. I will be contacting you soon to discuss this further.

[Or]

We would like to explain our innovative solution in a full proposal, and request that you send or e-mail us a request to apply or your application guidelines/form.

Thank you for your cooperation.

Name/Title
Organization
Address
E-mail

back what you believe is the grantor's position is a good choice. Successful corporate people are skilled at making sales calls, and they will expect you to be skilled when asking for their money. You do not want to appear as a fast-talking used-car salesperson, but your approach should be well rehearsed and professional, and your appearance should be conservative, reflecting that of the corporate official's as closely as possible. Remember, corporate people do dress for success.

Materials to Bring

Your proposal development workbook (Swiss cheese book) will be a great confidence builder since you will most likely be able to open it right to the areas of question. Also bring a short DVD that you can play on your laptop to document the need and the unique qualities you and your institution bring to the solution. Use your battery to power your short two- to three-minute presentation. If the corporate representative asks you to join his or her colleagues in a conference room, you could set up a PowerPoint presentation on the corporation's equipment. Make sure you are familiar with and ready to use the corporation's data projection system.

What to Discuss with a Corporate Grantor

Review the following topics of discussion and tailor them to your particular situation and prospective corporate funding source. Remember that the purpose of these discussions is to verify the information you gathered through your research and to gain more insight into how to produce a proposal that the prospective grantor will find impossible not to fund.

1. Discuss the need for your project/research and then introduce your solutions. Briefly explain the various approaches you are considering to solve the problem, and then ask if any one approach is preferred over the others. Asking for the corporation's input is often a good way to start.
2. Verify all information you have on the corporation's granting programs and patterns. Show the corporation's representatives that you have looked at their annual reports, or corporate foundation tax returns, by the comments you make and the questions you ask. For example, "I can see from my research that this area is important to your corporation because it represents 50 percent of all your granted projects. My research indicates that your board is very educated and sophisticated in this field. Will they be the group that reads and selects the proposals for approval?"

Corporate Grantor Report Form

Whether you, your advocate, linkage, advisory member, or staff person makes contact with the prospective grantor, make sure that *who* was contacted and *what* was discussed is documented. Complete a Corporate Grantor Report Form (exhibit 26.2) after each contact with a corporate funding source whether the contact was made in person, over the phone, or through an e-mail.

It is a good habit to place your intentions to contact corporate grantors on your action steps' chart (see figure 26.1). Adding this step to your chart will keep you out of trouble with your administration by serving as a visual reminder to obtain permission from your grants office to pursue these corporate opportunities prior to contacting them.

EXHIBIT 26.2
Corporate Grantor Report Form

Complete one of these forms after each contact with a corporate grantor.

Funding Source: _____

Funding Source Address: _____
_____

Funding Source Contact Person: _____

Telephone Number: _____   Fax: _____   E-mail: _____

Contacted On (Date): _____

Contacted By (Name): _____

Type of Contact: Phone _____   Visit _____   Other (Explain) _____

Objective of Contact: _____
_____
_____
_____

Results of Contact: _____
_____
_____
_____

Follow-up: _____
_____
_____
_____

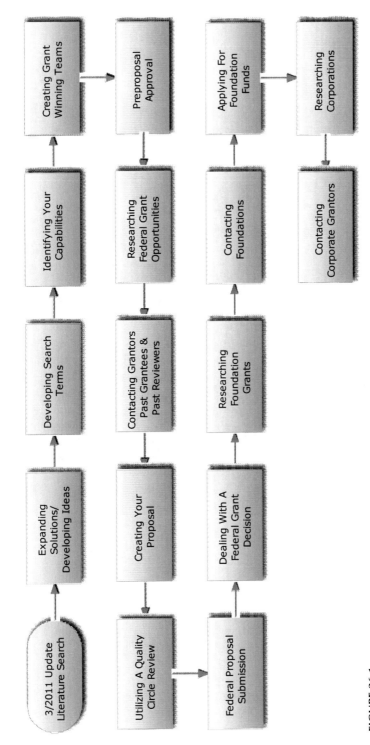

FIGURE 26.1
Action Steps' Chart: Contacting Corporate Grantors

27

Applying for Corporate Funds

MANY OF THE CORPORATE GRANTORS you will approach for funding have had experience developing applications for use with government grants and contract procurement programs as bidders and contractors. They strive to put together succinct and well-written proposals, sales and marketing materials, and presentations for their sales prospects. They value e-mail and correspondence that is effectively written. Of all the grantor types, they are probably the most critical and demanding audience you will encounter in your grants quest.

Construct your corporate proposal as outlined in this section, and have a quality circle or mock review of your proposal performed by corporate individuals from your advisory group. While you have chosen to make the nonprofit world your base of operation, you must recognize that your values glasses are different from those who have chosen the for-profit world as their primary frame of reference and that you must adjust your proposal writing style accordingly.

When I asked a corporate vice president what the biggest mistake was in proposals from the nonprofit world he said, "The vocabulary." When I asked him to clarify, he said that nonprofits should never use the "g" word. I asked him if he meant "g" for grants and he said, "No, 'g' for 'give.'" Proposal writers had repeatedly asked his company to *give* them funding. He suggested to me that they use the "i" word "invest" instead. Considering what you learned about corporate self-interest in chapter 24, this should make sense to you. To be successful in the corporate grants marketplace, you must be able to convince the prospective grantor that the company will get a *return on its investment* if it funds your project.

The fact that only a few of the larger corporations have staff members dedicated to contributions or community relations, and that most do not rely on outside readers or peer reviewers to evaluate submitted proposals, means your proposal will probably be read by individuals on the corporate foundation board, the corporate board, research and development types, salespeople, and/or marketing representatives. Corporate contributions' committees often comprise a mix of these types of individuals.

As with the private foundation marketplace, you will fail miserably if you take the one-size-fits-all approach and blanket the corporate community with the same proposal that starts with "We want _____. Please send money." To make matters worse, the corporations you approach with this method are likely to never forget the poorly developed, mass-produced proposal you submitted to them.

The successful corporate letter proposal follows the same basic order as the proposal to a private foundation. The main components are as follows:

- an introductory paragraph stating the reason for writing,
- a paragraph explaining why this grantor was selected,
- a needs paragraph,
- a solution paragraph,
- a uniqueness paragraph,
- a request for funds paragraph,
- a closing paragraph,
- signatures, and
- attachments, if allowed.

Some corporations specify a proposal format and rules on such things as number of pages on their websites. If they specify a short, one-page letter proposal or letter of intent but provide little in the form of guidance, use the proposal format suggested above. However, instead of addressing each component in a full paragraph, use just a sentence or two. The key is to identify the problem and how you will close the gap between what is and what should be.

Introductory Paragraph

If you have a linkage to the corporation, use it here. For example,

When this exciting project to increase the technology skills of educators was discussed with Karl Meister, the vice president of your corporate board, he suggested we ask the McGuiness Corporation to consider a role in increasing teacher competencies.

You could also mention a volunteer connection in your opening paragraph. This is a particularly good idea since many corporations will not invest in a local nonprofit organization unless their employees are voluntarily involved with it. Consider using your introductory paragraph to refer to the commitment of their employees to your cause. For instance,

Ellie Mung, your Region Four supervisor, and I have discussed Karson Computer's role in increasing the performance of our students through the use of applied technology. As chairperson of our school technology advisory committee, Ms. Mung has donated over one hundred hours of time and has been instrumental in making our computer laboratory a reality.

In the case of a research-related project, you might refer to an employee linkage who has served on your advisory committee, given a talk or lecture to your staff or students, served as a mentor, or allowed students to shadow workers to gain insight into the corporate marketplace.

Always check with your linkages before submitting your letter proposal, and provide them with a draft copy of the section that refers to them to be sure that they are agreeable. If you do not have a linkage to which you can refer in the opening paragraph, start your letter proposal by focusing on the grantor.

Why the Grantor Was Selected

This paragraph presents you with another opportunity to express your knowledge about the grantor. The purpose of this section of your letter proposal is to establish that the similarities between what the grantor values and what you and your organization value are why you selected this grantor. Align your organization with the values of the grantor by saying something such as the following:

As the McGuiness Corporation has become an international leader in innovative technology related to energy conservation, the Hudson Jain Laboratory has dedicated its research to the same field of study.

If it is a corporate foundation, you have access to its IRS return (990-PF) and should use it. For instance, if you know that in the past three years the corporate foundation has funded eight projects for over $1 million to assist nonprofits in conserving energy and lowering operating costs, mention it. Unfortunately, corporate contribution grants cannot be tracked. Therefore, you will have little, if any, research from which to work.

Needs Paragraph

This section of your corporate proposal must establish that you have a command of the current knowledge in your field. You must convince the reader/reviewer that you know what exists now in your field of expertise and that you know what needs to happen to close the gap between what is and what should be. The gap provides the reason why your proposal cannot be rejected. If the corporate grantor is truly interested in the area and in contributing toward solving the problem, then that corporate grantor must keep reading your proposal and ultimately fund your project.

The following example illustrates the proposal writer's expertise in the field and identifies the gap.

> The problem is simple, the solution is not. Current accepted theory used to explain the energy expended in the X reaction does not account for Y. The inability to predict Y costs our energy conservation effort billions of dollars in the United States alone.

Make sure that you do not mention your proposed solution or your organization in the needs section of your letter proposal except if you need to make reference to your own studies or findings. One way to ensure that you do not make this mistake is to include a transition sentence or two that enables you to move smoothly from the problem to your solution. For example, "What must be done to address and close this gap? We have developed an innovative solution that provides your corporation with an exciting opportunity."

Solution Paragraph

The purpose of this paragraph is to provide a short summary of the methodology that will be employed to solve the problem. Corporate executives are accustomed to using spreadsheets to analyze the steps and costs involved in planning and evaluating just about everything they do in the corporate world. Therefore, if space allows (you need to be able to submit at least three pages) it is a good idea to include a one-page project planner/spreadsheet (see chapter 13) as page two of your corporate proposal. Refer to this project planning aid as a one-page summary of your more detailed plan. Make mention that you have several more pages of project planners that detail the methods summarized on the page included in your letter proposal and that you would be happy to provide them upon request. Remember that corporate people are likely to ask for more detail, might visit you, and could ask you to come to them. While they may not designate a specific amount of time to grants, they do have an office and a travel budget.

Uniqueness Paragraph

The corporate grantor wants to be assured that you, your organization/institution, and your project are the right investment choice for it. Most nonprofits reflect on their organizations' missions and history when creating this section. While this may work with private foundations to demonstrate commitment to the field of interest, corporate grantors want facts, data, statistics, and examples of winning characteristics. They want to know that you have been a grant winner before. What really matters to them is the breakthroughs your institution, program, or lab have made in the field, and the competency and productivity of your staff. While you may have written the proposal, you will probably not be the individual to sign it. Therefore, it is okay to refer to yourself in this paragraph as the qualified leader to carry out the plan.

Think of this paragraph as part of a corporate marketing brochure. For example, what convinces you to buy a particular product from one company over another? It is probably that company's credibility, the proof that it stands behind its product, and its commitment to quality. These are the same attributes that corporate funding sources want to see in their grantees.

Request for Funds Paragraph

As in all proposals you must ask for the money. While you may think this is obvious, many corporations have reported that grantseekers sometimes refer to the total cost of the project without ever asking for the specific amount they want from them. If you are targeting a corporate foundation, you have access to its 990-PF IRS tax return and can use the data provided on that form to decide how much to request. However, it is difficult to know how much to request from a corporation that awards grants through a contributions program due to the lack of available public information. If you are unable to decipher an appropriate amount through preproposal contact, you will have to guess. As you learned in chapter 8, most grantseekers think that corporate grants account for $60 to $75 billion per year, when it actually is $14.1 billion. With this in mind, you might want to scale down your request. Anything over $100,000 is a very large corporate commitment.

If you are forced to divide your project into several fundable pieces, explain that in this paragraph. Also name-drop any of the grantors who have already granted you funds. You and your project are a junk bond until someone else with a good reputation buys in. Then you become a blue-chip stock.

Your project planner should help the corporate decision maker evaluate the appropriateness of your request. If you must present a budget, avoid dedicating a whole page to this purpose. Use a paragraph-form budget instead and refer to the column totals on your project planner.

Refer to the return for its investment by dividing the total cost by the number of people the project will serve. In a research proposal, compare the requested amount to the benefits that may occur as a result of answering the research question and closing the gap in the field or knowledge, and suggest what this may lead to in the future. Both of these approaches are quite successful with corporate grantors.

Corporate grantors want to know how you intend to continue a program or project that you will use their grant to initiate. How much will it take to continue this project, and how do you intend to procure that money? For example, the Boeing Company states on its corporate website that Boeing's philanthropic strategy is to contribute toward sustainable, measurable growth and self-sufficiency for the organizations with which it partners. This principle guided $57 million in charitable grant contributions in 2009.

Closing Paragraph

Do not start this paragraph off by stating that you would like to meet with the grantor; the grantor already knows you would. Instead, invite the grantor to meet with you and your key personnel and to visit your institution, organization, laboratory, and so on. Be sure to express your desire to provide any additional information and request that the prospective grantor contact you (or the individual responsible for the project) to provide that information or to answer any questions.

Signatures

Corporate people expect your proposal to be signed by an administrator or officer who holds rank and responsibility within your organization/institution. This is viewed by the corporate grantor as an institutional commitment and endorsement. It is best to have more than one signature. Therefore, if possible, include the signature from your consortia partner(s), which can be impressive to them.

Attachments, if Allowed

While most corporations do not *encourage* attachments, they may be allowed in proposals for research grants. In these instances, project planner spreadsheets detailing your protocol are recommended over text.

Corporate application instructions for other types of grants (nonresearch) will usually restrict the use of any attachments. For example, when applying for a $300,000 grant from the BellSouth Foundation, the application instructions received by my institution specifically stated that letter proposals were restricted to five double-spaced pages of 12 to 13 characters per inch and that no attachments were allowed. The guidelines also stated that the foundation would request further information from a select group of applicants from which one-half would be funded. We eventually received a letter stating that our proposal had made the first cut and that of the total two hundred applicants, we were one of the twenty under consideration. Along with that letter came a list of ten questions that the reviewers had regarding our proposal. We were required to answer these questions, limiting our responses to a total of three double-spaced pages. Our $300,000 successful grant consisted of eight double-spaced pages (four single-spaced pages).

Review the sample corporate proposal in exhibit 27.1. This sample includes the main components of a letter proposal outlined in this chapter. You are

EXHIBIT 27.1
Sample Letter Proposal to a Corporation

Nancy Owens, Executive Director
Nevada Power Foundation
1374 Chichester Highway
Spurks, NV 87999

Dear Ms. Owens:

Your corporation's support for the Nevada Student Success Fair and your $1 million contribution to the Power Our Students campaign speak louder than words of your concern and commitment to Nevada's students and their success. The board, staff, and volunteers at *Nevada Read by 3* share your values for education and tomorrow's workforce.

The latest surveys show Nevada leading the nation in unemployment (nearly 15 percent). In addition, our dropout rate before the current recession placed us in the lowest 20 percent of the United States. With our recent 25 percent cut in education, our dropout rate has gotten worse. In a recent *Las Vegas Sun* article Clark County reported the fifth worst graduation rate in the United States at 44.5 percent. Experts agree that for recovery to take place in our state we need to access affordable power (your job) and an educated, qualified workforce (our job).

EXHIBIT 27.1
(*Continued*)

An Alliance for Excellent Education study (funded by the MetLife Foundation) estimated that if Nevada's 15,998 dropouts for the class of 2007 graduated with their class in 2006–2007 their estimated additional lifetime income would have been $4,159,568,400.

Cutting the nation's dropout rate in half would yield $45 billion annually in new federal tax revenue (Columbia University Report). When you compare the cost of dropouts to that of the government bailout of banks, financial institutions, the auto industry, and AIG, you find that all of this is still less than the economic cost of just five years of dropouts in the United States.

How can we break this chain and support both economic and educational change that results in high school completion? The *Nevada Read by 3* program has an answer. We cannot impact all grades in all Nevada schools in three years. But we can implement a program that has proven effective in K–3.

Basically, the program

- provides teachers with the training and materials they need to help students in K–3 improve their reading scores, and
- only promotes those third-grade early learners who read at the appropriate level.

Many studies on dropouts cite inferior reading skills as one of the main causal factors. The program proposed by *Nevada Read by 3* will provide Nevada teachers at four pilot schools, two urban and two rural, with instruction, materials, mentors, and volunteers to get all of their students to the appropriate reading level. Students who take part in this program will have less disciplinary action, truancies, and problems with the law as they advance to grades 4–12.

We are uniquely suited to carry out this model project because we will be working under the guidance of a nationally recognized expert in the field, Dr. Tim Martin of the University of Nevada's College of Education. Dr. Martin will lead our team as the Nevada Power Foundation provides the initial catalyst to demonstrate the change we need. Your phase one funding of $100,000 will provide the start-up costs. In years two and three the participating schools will provide a match of 10 percent and 20 percent respectively. Our goal is to eventually have a self-sustaining program that is totally paid for by the schools.

Your name will appear on all materials and on the "Read by 3 Tool Box," as well as on software and all dissemination pamphlets. We have project cost analysis spreadsheets and full budget documentation available upon your request. We encourage you and your staff to contact Dr. Martin for any additional material and/or questions, or to arrange a site visit to our office. Dr. Martin can be reached at [telephone number] or [email address].

Sincerely,

Dr. Thomas Watkins, Executive Director
Nevada Read by 3

encouraged to develop your own style, but include these integral parts in any letter proposal you submit. Even when provided with an online application or specific guidelines like those in exhibit 27.2, try to incorporate the concepts suggested in this chapter into your proposal. For instance, in the needs section work in the fact that through your research you are aware of the company's strong commitment to resolving this problem. And, after the section outlining your solution, slip in a few sentences explaining to the prospective corporate funding source why you are a unique grantee and the best choice to implement the solution.

Just as with foundations, you may want to try this marketplace before you go after federal or state grant funding. If you are able to interest a corporation in supplying your program with equipment or software, you increase your fundability with these other funding sources. Once you have decided that preparing a corporate grant request is going into your plan, place "applying for corporate funds" on your action steps' chart (see figure 27.1). Where does this step fit in your overall plan?

EXHIBIT 27.2
J.P. Morgan Chase Philanthropic Grant Programs—Guidelines

How to Apply—U.S.

U.S. Domestic Grantees

To be considered for support, a potential grantee must first submit an online Letter of Inquiry. You will receive an automatic electronic notification after the Letter of Inquiry has been successfully submitted. If we are unable to consider your proposal for funding at this time, you will receive notification.

Questions on the letter of inquiry will include:

A brief description of your organization's
  —Mission
  —Program/project description
  —Program/project budget
  —Geography to be served
  —Your contact information

Documents to Provide

  —The organization's most recent audited financial statements.
  —A list of board members and their affiliations.

If the proposal is being considered and further qualifies, you will be contacted and asked to complete a full grant application.

Grant applications may be submitted throughout the year. A conversation with the appropriate Community Relations Officer prior to submitting a grant application is strongly encouraged. Please view list of contacts below. If you received funding in the previous year(s), you will be asked to submit an online report on use of funds prior to applying for new funding.

The grant application will be evaluated based on the following guidelines:

  —Alignment with our three focus areas of philanthropic giving
  —Demonstration of effective organizational, programmatic, and financial objective setting and management
  —Evidence of broad-based support, with an accounting of funds received from public and private sources
  —Description of target population to be served
  —Evidence that the service is a response to a valid need, is superior to other competing services, and/or encourages collaboration
  —Documentation of previous program success or substantial reasons to expect such success in the future.

List of Contact Information by State

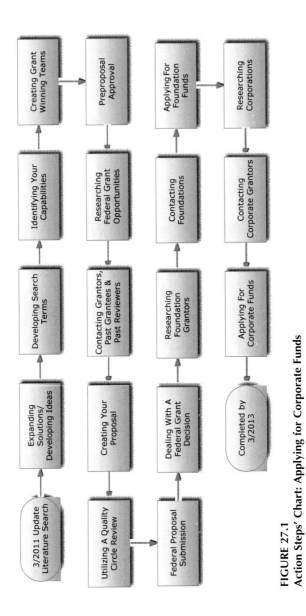

FIGURE 27.1
Action Steps' Chart: Applying for Corporate Funds

28

Proposal Submission,
the Decision, and Follow-Up

Corporate Grantors

B EFORE SUBMITTING YOUR PROPOSAL to a corporate grantor, put it through a quality circle (see chapters 14 and 23) that resembles the actual review process as closely as possible. The purpose of this exercise is to get an unbiased first impression of your proposal from individuals who view it from the perspective of enlightened, corporate self-interest.

Ask two or three of your colleagues and two of your advisory committee members from the corporate world, or a professor from your local college's business school, to participate. Encourage everyone to role-play being corporate executives. Unless you have information otherwise, inform all participants that the real reviewers will be corporate executives who will read your proposal in less than five minutes. They should also be made aware that the real reviewers (the corporate executives) will most likely not follow any specific scoring or rating system and will not provide any comments to the applicants. Therefore, you, the applicant, really need their feedback. Ask your quality circle participants to designate those areas of the proposal they think corporate executives would like with a plus sign (+) and those areas they think corporate executives would dislike with a minus (−) sign. Discuss suggestions for improving or highlighting the positive sections and for rewriting the negative sections.

It works well to conduct the quality circle in conjunction with an early breakfast or over lunch. The whole exercise should take less than one hour.

Submission

Many of the larger corporate grantors now allow online application and submittal. For the medium and smaller corporations you will likely be sending a print copy of your proposal to the contact person listed in your research. Even when you apply and submit online, print out your proposal to be certain that the font or any graphics are not altered. In addition, send a hardcopy of your proposal to the funding source just in case it does not receive the electronic version. Submit the proposal a few days before the deadline. When mailing your proposal, require a proof of receipt, and be sure to send it via a carrier that can guarantee delivery like the United States Postal Service, United Parcel Service, or FedEx. As with foundation grant submittals, you could offer to forward a copy of your proposal for each corporate board member.

Also, send copies of your final proposal to your corporate linkages so that they know you finally submitted your proposal and are aware of exactly what you requested. Thank them for the assistance they provided up to this point and for the assistance they may provide in the future to help get your submitted proposal funded.

The Decision

Corporate grantors may communicate only to those to whom they will award a grant. They may not take the time and effort to notify those they reject. In any case, your research will provide you with the dates that the corporate board meets, and from these dates you can approximate when you should hear from the grantor.

Rejected

If you do not hear from the grantor by six months after the deadline date, your proposal was probably rejected. If you do not receive a rejection letter, you may also receive little to nothing in the way of constructive criticism, redirection of your efforts, or reapplication rules. Some corporate grantors do not allow you to resubmit immediately. For example, I was once told by a corporate foundation that I could not resubmit for three years. Other grantors may advise you never to resubmit due to new restrictions or changes in their priorities and philosophy. Learn what you can from the grantor, your advocates, and your linkages and reapply when it is allowable and advisable.

Even if rejected, send a thank-you letter that acknowledges the time the funding source invested in the selection process, and express your gratitude for its foresight in dedicating profits to impacting these problems and areas of interest. Credit them for their commitment and do not be a sore loser.

Awarded

If your proposal is funded, send a thank-you letter as outlined above, but include an invitation to visit your institution/organization to see the important work you are conducting and the unique qualities you mentioned in your proposal. You should also request any comments the grantor may have that would help you improve on a future proposal to it or another corporation. However, do not expect a response.

Follow-Up

Whether you are successful or not in your corporate grants quest, try to maintain professional contact. Like you, corporate decision makers are trying to keep up on the advances in your mutual field of interest. Send them an interesting article that your research uncovers, or even an article of yours that is scheduled for publication. Let them know you are alive between the deadline dates. Seek them out at conferences and meetings, and ask them questions about their next grant opportunities.

Persistence and the maintaining of a professional interest in their area of concern will pay off. You will improve your relationship with them and have chances to learn of their upcoming grant priorities. Remember that being persistent is different from being a pest! Keep your relationship focused on the need for your projects and research and their opportunities for involvement.

The best approach to grantseeking is to develop a long-term and mutually beneficial relationship between you, your organization, and the grantor. This relationship should be based on honesty and a sincere concern for the grantor's needs. Saying thank you is a crucial element in building such a relationship.

29

Putting It All Together to Work for You

ACH OF YOU GRANTSEEKERS IS UNIQUE in your organization and in your desire to attract grant funding. Because of this, it is a challenge to create one book that will work for all of you. However, I am confident that you *all* will be rewarded if you practice the strategies outlined in this book. Once when I had a proposal rejected, the grantor confided in me that the board used my proposal before their next meeting to show the members what a well-constructed proposal looked like. He also told me that the board had changed its priorities at that meeting and that there was no way I could have known this in advance.

The proactive grant strategies presented in this book need to be consciously and consistently applied to your grants effort in order to be effective and efficient. Follow the steps outlined in each chapter and review the figures found at the end of the chapters that diagram the step-by-step process and illustrate the sequence and progression of the steps. Skip any of the steps and your probability of success will be reduced. My grant fellows consistently achieve a 70 percent success rate by sticking to this method.

A major challenge for you is how to integrate grantseeking into your already busy professional life. Like it or not, the realities of life impact your grantseeking. Not only do you have to find the time to accomplish the steps to grants success, but you must also deal with the demands of your job. Some of you have administrative and/or program responsibilities. Others are busy teaching, preparing labs, counseling students, and so on. And what about the personal life you are trying to carry on in between all of this? No wonder self-help books on time management are so popular.

The good news is that the time management techniques outlined in chapter 3 can be applied to *all* areas of your life, and not just to your grantseeking activities. I suggest you apply the time management and organizational techniques you have learned to at least your professional life so that you can integrate your grantseeking into your job-related, real-world scenario. Put those job tasks that are directly related to your grantseeking into your monthly plan/timeline along with your proactive grants steps. For example, you may be working on a publication that you will need to use as a citation in your problem/needs section of your search of relevant literature. This work can be done simultaneously with your other grantseeking steps during the same month, and you do not necessarily have to finish the publication before you accomplish a step in your proactive grants system. It may not be a publication. It could be a survey that you want to administer, meeting with your advisory group, speaking at a conference, and so on.

One way of keeping track of your grantseeking-related professional tasks and incorporating them with the proactive grants steps outlined in this book is to visualize them on an action steps' chart (see chapter 3). Figure 29.1 shows the tasks in the boxes that are occurring simultaneously. Those that are prerequisites or must be completed before others are placed in such a manner that the proper sequencing is readily seen.

There is no wrong way to construct or utilize a monthly action steps' chart. The process should evolve and be tailored in a way that works best for you. One of my grant fellows made her monthly action steps' chart into her screensaver. This way, she is reminded each day of the steps she has planned to achieve grants and professional success. It has been my experience that irrespective of the adaptation of the conceptual framework you apply, you are bound to receive extraordinary benefits by charting the proactive steps to your success.

Take a few minutes to plot out your five-year plan as discussed in chapters 1 and 3. Place grantseeking steps, publications, grants deadlines, conferences, trips to see program officers, and so forth on your proactive grants chart. Success doesn't just occur from random acts. It results from working your plan, and to do that you must first have a plan.

In addition to saying "When you come to a fork in the road, take it," Yogi Berra also said, "If you don't know where you are going, you might wind up someplace else." Build your road map for success so you know when you are there and how you got there.

The ability to develop grant funding for projects, programs, and research has been critical to my reaching my personal and professional goals. Sharing my formula for success in this book is a great honor and privilege. Plan well and do well, and thank you for purchasing this book.

FIGURE 29.1
Action Steps' Chart: Sample Plan for Putting It All Together

List of Resources

Y OU MAY WISH TO LOOK AT COPIES of these recommended grant tools before you purchase them. Many of the resources listed include locations where you can find the materials and get assistance from helpful staff. Many institutions have developed joint or cooperative grants libraries to reduce costs and encourage consortium projects.

The list of resources is divided into the following sections:

- Government Grant Research Aids
- Foundation Grant Research Aids
- Corporate Grant Research Aids
- Government, Foundation, and Corporate Grant Resources
- Electronic Resources

Government Grant Research Aids

Tips

1. There are nearly 1,250 federal depository libraries throughout the United States and its territories. All the government publications listed below are available in print copy at these libraries. To locate a federal depository library near you, visit www.gpoaccess.gov/libraries.html.
2. Many federal agencies have newsletters or agency publications. You can ask to be placed on their mailing lists to receive these publications. Some are available online.

3. Contact federal programs to get the most up-to-date information.
4. All of the government grant publications listed here are also available through your congressperson's office.

Government Publications

Catalog of Federal Domestic Assistance (CFDA)

The *Catalog* is the government's listing of federal programs, with details on eligibility, application procedures, and deadlines, including the location of state plans. It is published at the beginning of each fiscal year, with supplementary updates during the year. Indexes are by agency program, function, popular name, applicant eligibility, and subject. Access is free online at www.cfda.gov. A hardcopy is also at federal depository libraries.

Code of Federal Regulations (CFR)

This is the codification of the general and permanent rules published in the *Federal Register* by the executive departments and agencies of the federal government. Access is free online at www.gpoaccess.gov/cfr/.

Congressional Record

The *Congressional Record* covers proceedings and debates of the United States Congress. Access is free online at www.gpoaccess.gov/crecord/index.html. A hardcopy is also available at federal depository libraries, or for purchase at the Government Printing Office's (GPO) online bookstore at bookstore.gpo.gov.

U.S. Government Printing Office
Mail Stop: IDCC
732 N. Capitol St., NW
Washington, DC 20401
Toll-free: (866) 512-1800
DC area: (202) 512-1800

FedBizOpps (Federal Business Opportunities)

FedBizOpps is a database of federal government contracting opportunities including notices of proposed government procurement actions, contract awards, sales of government property, and other procurement information. It's available free online at www.fbo.gov.

Federal Register

Published five times a week (Monday through Friday), the *Federal Register* supplies up-to-date information on federal assistance and supplements the *Catalog of Federal Domestic Assistance (CFDA)*. The *Federal Register* includes public regulations and legal notices issued by all federal agencies and presidential proclamations. Of particular importance are the proposed rules, final rules, and program deadlines. An index is published monthly. It is available for free at www.gpoaccess.gov/fr/index.html. A hardcopy is also at federal depository libraries.

Grants.gov

This is the central storehouse for information on over one thousand federal grant programs and access to approximately $500 billion in annual awards. Access is free online at www.grants.gov.

United States Government Manual

This is the official handbook of the federal government and provides comprehensive information on the agencies of the legislative, judicial, and executive branches. It is available online for free at www.gpoaccess.gov/gmanual/index.html. A print copy can be purchased from the U.S. Government Online Bookstore at bookstore.gpo.gov. It can also be located in federal depository libraries.

Other Popular Government Websites

Department of Education, www.ed.gov
Department of Housing and Urban Development, www.hud.gov
National Endowment for the Humanities, www.neh.gov
National Institutes of Health, www.nih.gov
National Science Foundation, www.nsf.gov

Commercially Produced Publications

Federal and Foundation Assistance Monitor

This web-based news service features a comprehensive review of federal funding announcements, private grants, and legislative actions.

Price: Twelve months online $399.00; twelve months print and online $449.00

Order from: CD Publications at (800) 666-6380 or online at www.cd publications.com

Federal Staff Directory

The *Directory* includes names, addresses, and phone numbers of federal government agencies and key personnel.
Price: $348 print version; also available in online version, request price at directorysales@cqpress.com
Order from: www.cqpress.com or CQ Press
2300 N Street, NW
Suite 800
Washington, DC 20037
Toll-free: (866) 427-7737
DC area: (202) 729-1900

Federal Yellow Book

This directory of federal departments and agencies is updated quarterly.
Price: $525.00
Order from:
Leadership Directories, Inc.
104 Fifth Avenue, 3rd Floor
New York, NY 10011
Phone: (212) 627-4140
Fax: (212) 645-0932
Or order online at www.leadershipdirectories.com

The Grant Application Writer's Workbook: National Institutes of Health, 2010

This is a guide on how to succeed with new changes at NIH.
Price: $75.00
Order online from:
Grant Writers' Seminars & Workshops LLC
www.grantcentral.com/workbooks.html

The Grant Application Writer's Workbook: National Science Foundation FastLane

This workbook deals with how to prepare for FastLane submission of grant proposals.

Price: $75.00
Order online from:
Grant Writers' Seminars & Workshops LLC
www.grantcentral.com/workbooks.html

The Grant Application Writer's Workbook: Successful Proposals to Any Agency

This workbook provides information on preparing successful application submittals to agencies other than NIH or NSF.
Price: $70.00
Order online from:
Grant Writers' Seminars & Workshops LLC
www.grantcentral.com/workbooks.html

Guide to Federal Funding for Governments and Nonprofits

This two-volume manual offers access to funding details on more than 750 federal aid programs. A subscription to the guide includes *Grantswire*—a weekly e-mail service and tool to help grantseekers monitor application deadlines and grant-related regulatory happenings.
Price: $399.00
Order from:
Thompson Publishing Group
Subscription Service Center
P.O. Box 26185
Tampa, FL 33623-6185
Phone: (800) 677-3789
Or order online at www.thompson.com

Washington Information Directory, 2010/2011

This directory is divided into three categories: agencies of the executive branch, Congress, and private or nongovernmental organizations. Each entry includes the name, address, telephone number, and director of the organization, along with a short description of its work.
Price: $150.00 print edition; also available in online version, request price at directorysales@cqpress
Order from:
CQ Press
2300 N Street, NW

Suite 800
Washington, DC 20037
Toll-free: (866) 427-7737
DC area: (202) 729-1900

Foundation Grant Research Aids

Many of the following research aids can be found through the Foundation Center Cooperating Collections Network. If you wish to purchase any of the following Foundation Center publications, order online at www.foundation center.org/marketplace or contact
The Foundation Center
Customer Service
79 Fifth Avenue
New York, NY 10003-3076
Phone: (800) 424-9836
Fax: (212) 807-3691

The Foundation Directory, April 2010, 2,866 pages

The most important single reference work available on grant-making foundations in the United States, this directory includes information on the ten thousand largest foundations and over sixty thousand sample grants. Each entry includes a description of giving interests, along with address, telephone numbers, current financial data, names of donors, contact person, and IRS identification number. Several indexes are included to help you locate your best leads.
Price: $215.00
Order from: The Foundation Center

The Foundation Directory, Part 2, April 2010, 2,159 pages

This directory provides information on ten thousand midsize foundations and more than fifty thousand sample grants.
Price: $185.00
Order from: The Foundation Center

The Foundation Directory Supplement, September 2010, 1,250 pages

The *Supplement* updates the *Directory* so that users will have the latest addresses, contacts, policy statements, application guidelines, and financial data.

Price: $125.00
Order from: The Foundation Center

Foundation Giving Trends: Update on Funding Priorities, February 2010, 104 pages

This publication describes recent grant-making patterns of more than one thousand large U.S. foundations.
Price: $45.00
Order from: The Foundation Center

Foundation Grants to Individuals, eighteenth edition, 1,427 pages

This directory provides a comprehensive listing of over 8,300 independent and corporate foundations that provide financial assistance to individuals.
Price: $75.00
Order from: The Foundation Center

Foundation Growth and Giving Estimates: Current Outlook, April 2010, 18 pages

This publication estimates 2009 giving, provides 2008 actual giving and assets, includes the top 100 foundations list, and presents the 2010 outlook.
Price: $20.00
Order from: The Foundation Center

Foundation Yearbook: Facts and Figures on Private and Community Foundations, July 2010, 80 pages

This publication provides the growth in number, giving amounts, and assets of all active U.S. foundations—1975 to 2008.
Price: $45.00
Order from: The Foundation Center

Social Justice Grantmaking II, August 2009, 120 pages

This publication includes an analysis of social justice giving by foundations and examines the evolving nature of social justice funding strategies through interviews with leading grant makers.
Price: $40.00
Order from: The Foundation Center

Private Foundation IRS Tax Returns

The Internal Revenue Service requires private foundations to file income tax returns each year. Form 990-PF provides fiscal details on receipts and expenditures, compensation of officers, capital gains or losses, and other financial matters. These may be viewed online for free at

- foundationcenter.org/findfunders/990finder/, and
- www.guidestar.org.

Directories of State and Local Grant Makers

Visit the Foundation Center Cooperating Collection closest to you to determine what directories are available for your state and surrounding region. You can also go to foundationcenter.org/getstarted/topical/sl_dir.html to obtain a bibliography of state and local foundation directories.

Other Popular Foundation-Related Websites

Council on Foundations, www.cof.org
Philanthropy News Network Online, www.pnnonline.org
Foundation Center's homepage, www.fdncenter.org

Corporate Grant Research Aids

Corporations interested in corporate giving often establish foundations to handle their contributions. Once foundations are established, their Internal Revenue Service returns become public information, and data are compiled into the directories previously mentioned under Foundation Grant Research Aids.

Corporate contributions that do not go through a foundation are not public information, and research sources consist of

- information volunteered by the corporation,
- product information, and
- profitability information.

2009 Corporate Contributions Report

The results of this annual survey include a detailed analysis of beneficiaries of corporate support but do not list individual firms and specific recipients.

Price: Free for members; $495.00 for nonmembers

Order online from: www.conference-board.org/publications/publication detail.cfm?publicationid=1723

The Conference Board

845 Third Avenue

New York, NY 10022

Phone: (212) 339-0345, customer service

Fax: (212) 836-9740

Corporate Giving Directory

This directory provides detailed entries on one thousand of the largest corporate foundations and corporate giving programs in the United States.

Price: $562.50 for first-time standing orders

Order online from: infotoday.stores.yahoo.net/corgivdir202.html

Information Today

143 Old Marlton Pike

Medford, NJ 08055-9750

(609) 654-6266, customer service

Dun & Bradstreet's (D&B) Million Dollar Database

This is a subscription-based database available on the Internet. It provides basic data on U.S. companies, such as addresses, ticket symbols, key officers, number of employees, and sales. It also provides brief, searchable executive biographies and titles, listings of international office of U.S. companies, and the ability to download to spreadsheet or print out lists of companies. Also available online from Dun & Bradstreet is the *D&B North American Million Dollar Database* that provides information on U.S. and Canadian public and private businesses, and the *D&B International Million Dollar Database* that provides information on international companies.

Call company for pricing.

D&B Corporation

103 JFK Parkway

Short Hills, NJ 07078

(800) 234-3867, customer service

The National Directory of Corporate Giving, fifteenth edition, August 2009, 1,640 pages

Information on over 2,800 company-sponsored foundations, plus an additional 1,200 corporate giving programs, is provided in this directory.

Price: $195.00
Order from:
The Foundation Center
79 Fifth Avenue
New York, NY 10003-3076
Phone: (800) 424-9836
Fax: (212) 807-3691
www.foundationcenter.org/marketplace

North American Industry Classification System Manual, 2007

Developed for use in the classification of establishments by type of activity in which they are engaged.

Price: print version $59.00; CD-ROM version with search and retrieval software $79.00

Order online from www.ntis.gov/products/naics.aspx
National Technical Information Service (NTIS)
5301 Shawnee Rd.
Alexandria, VA 22312
Phone: (800) 553-6847 or (703) 605-6000
Fax: (703) 605-6900

Standard & Poor's Register—Corporate (File 527)

This database is available online through Dialog. The corporate database provides information on over one hundred thousand public and private corporations worldwide, including current address, financial and marketing information, and a listing of officers and directors with positions and departments.

Price: Call for pricing
Order from:
Dialog Corporation
2250 Perimeter Park Dr.
Suite 300
Morrisville, NC 27560
Phone: (800) 334-2564
Fax: (919) 804-6410
www.dialog.com

Standard & Poor's Register of Corporations, Directors, and Executives, three volumes

This is the print counterpart to the online biographical and corporate files.
Price: Call for pricing

Order from:
Standard & Poor's Corporation
55 Water St.
New York, NY 10041
Phone: (800) 523-4534

Who's Who in America 2011, sixty-fifth edition

This publication is known for its life and career data on noteworthy individuals. The 2011 edition chronicles American leadership with information on approximately ninety-six thousand individuals. It is available in hardcopy and on the Internet.

Price: $710.00 for print version, first-time orders; call for online pricing
Order from:
Marquis Who's Who
P.O. Box 10
New Providence, NJ 07974-1218
Phone: (800) 473-7020
Fax: (908) 673-1189
www.marquiswhoswho.com/booksellers/publications

Other Corporate-Related Websites

Business Journals' Book of Lists, www.bizjournals.com
Corporate Information, corporateinformation.com
Hoovers, www.hoovers.com
Prospect Research Online, www.iwave.com/
Securities and Exchange Commission (SEC), www.sec.gov

Government, Foundation, and Corporate Grant Resources

The following grant guides can be purchased from CD Publications. They are $69.00 each. Order by phone at (800) 666-6380 (reference priority code B430) or online at www.cdpublications.com/b430.

Directory of Funding Sources for Disability Services

A compendium containing detailed listings for more than seventy grant-making organizations specializing in disabilities programs.

Directory of Grants for Children & Youth Services, second edition

Contains more than 120 private grants exclusively for programs serving youth and children.

Directory of Grants for Native American Tribes and Organizations

Online, downloadable, and printable grants directory containing eighty funding opportunities.

Directory of Private Grants for Seniors Programs

Contains grant opportunities for a wide range of programs, including nutrition, caregiving, employment, homecare, elder abuse, and more.

Directory of Social Service Grants, second edition

Contains more than 180 private grants for social service programs with a nationwide giving emphasis.

Grantseeker's Guide to Substance Abuse Funding

Outlines the major federal funding programs and includes details on private funders that support substance abuse programs.

Guide to Private & Federal Funding for K–12 Education Programs

Contains grants exclusively for K–12 needs, including funding for other fields with education components.

The Housing & Community Development Grantseekers Guide

Features details on over 130 federal and private funding opportunities.

Private Grants for Community Health Programs

Contains more than two hundred foundation grants for a wide range of needed local services, including migrant health, education/prevention, and wellness.

The following three annual directories can be purchased from GrantSelect, Schoolhouse Partners. Order by phone, by downloading a printable order form, or from Schoolhouse Partners' online bookstore at shop.school housepartners.net.
GrantSelect
Schoolhouse Partners
P.O. Box 2059
Nashville, IN 47448
Phone: (812) 988-6400
Fax: (812) 988-6479
grantselect.com/pubs/

Directory of Biomedical and Health Care Grants 2009, twenty-first edition

This directory provides information on biomedical and health-care-related programs sponsored by the federal government, corporations, professional associations, special interest groups, and state and local governments.
Price: $109.95

Directory of Grants in the Humanities 2009, twentieth edition

Current data on funds available to individual artists and art organizations from corporations, foundations, and professional associations as well as from the National Education Association, National Endowment for the Humanities, and state and local arts and humanities councils.
Price: $109.95

Directory of Research Grants 2010, two volumes

Information on government, corporate, organizational, and private funding sources supporting research programs and projects. The directory lists grants from all sectors and fields of interest.
Price: $149.95

Giving USA 2010

Annual report of philanthropy for the year 2009.
Price: $75.00

Order online, by phone, or by fax from:
The Giving Institute
4700 W. Lake Ave.
Glenview, IL 60025
Phone: (847) 375-4709
Fax: (888) 374-7258
www.givinginstitute.org/

The PRI Directory, **October 2009, 430 pages**

This directory deals with the funding of nonprofits via program-related investments and loans by foundations. Often used to support community revitalization, low-income housing, microenterprise development, historic preservation, and human services, this directory lists leading funders, recipients, project descriptions, and includes tips on how to secure and manage a PRI. Published in partnership with PRI Makers Network.
Price: $95.00
Order from:
The Foundation Center
79 Fifth Ave.
New York, NY 10003-3076
Phone: (800) 424-9836
Fax: (212) 807-3691
www.foundationcenter.org/marketplace

Electronic Resources

There is a wealth of information available through free and subscription online databases. Check with your librarian and your grants office to locate those electronic resources to which you may already have access.

BIG Online America

This is a membership-based key word and field searchable database with detailed information and profiles on twenty-five thousand American and Canadian foundations, corporate donors, matching gifts programs, in-kind donations, and government grant makers.

For information call BIG Online at (888) 638-2763 or e-mail info@big database.com.

The Celebrity Foundation Directory, **November 2009, 476 pages**

This digital publication includes descriptions of thousands of foundations started by VIPs in business, entertainment, politics, and sports. Contact information is provided, as well as purpose, fields of interest, donors, financial data, staffing, and application procedures.

Price: $59.95
Order from:
The Foundation Center
79 Fifth Avenue
New York, NY 10003-3076
Phone: (800) 424-9836
Fax: (212) 807-3691
www.foundationcenter.org/marketplace

Community of Science (COS) Funding Opportunities

COS Funding Opportunities is a comprehensive database of funding information available on the web and contains more than twenty-five thousand records.

Price: *COS Funding Opportunities* is included with fee-based membership in the Community of Scholars. Other small businesses and institutions may purchase access to *COS Funding Opportunities* for a fixed annual subscription fee. Subscription pricing is determined by the amount of external research funding your institution manages.

Visit www.cos.com for further information.

Corporate Giving Online

Corporate Giving Online contains more than 3,500 company profiles; over 40,000 grant makers, including foundations and corporate giving programs; and descriptions of approximately 350,000 recently awarded grants. It provides information on giving priorities, purpose and activities, fields of interest, types of support, and financials.

Price: $59.95 per month; $595.00 annually
Subscribe online at cgonline.foundationcenter.org or order from:
The Foundation Center
79 Fifth Ave.
New York, NY 10003-3076
Phone: (800) 424-9836
Fax: (212) 807-3691

Foundation Directory Online Subscription Plans

The Foundation Center has several different online subscription plans, including *The Foundation Directory Online Professional, The Foundation Directory Online Platinum, The Foundation Directory Online Premium, The Foundation Directory Online Plus,* and *The Foundation Online Directory Basic.*

The basic subscription allows you to search the nation's largest ten thousand foundations and provides detailed grant maker profiles including trustees, officers, donors, and recent IRS form 990s for $19.95 per month or $195.00 per year.

Contact the Foundation Center at (800) 424-9836 for information and pricing for the other plans.

Foundation Grants to Individuals Online

This database includes descriptions of more than 8,500 foundations and public charity programs that fund individuals for scholarships and fellowships; writer residencies; composing; film; visual and performing arts; academic research and professional support; and emergency medical and financial needs.

Price: one month, $19.95; three months, $36.95; one year, $99.95
Order from:
The Foundation Center
79 Fifth Ave.
New York, NY 10003-3076
Phone: (800)424-9836
Fax: (212)807-3691
foundationcenter.org/marketplace

Grant Guides

There are a total of twenty-five digital *Grant Guides* available in a variety of subjects including AIDS/HIV research and patient care; arts, culture, and the humanities; cancer research and patient care; capacity building, management, and technical assistance; children and youth; community and economic development; disaster relief and recovery: U.S. and international; elementary and secondary education; employment; environmental protection and animal welfare; foreign and international programs; higher education; hospitals and health organizations; housing; information technology; libraries and information services; medical research; mental health, addictions, and crisis services; minorities; people with disabilities; public health; religion, religious welfare, and religious education; services for the homeless; the aging; and women and girls.

Price: $39.95

Order from:
The Foundation Center
79 Fifth Ave.
New York, NY 10036-3076
Phone: (800) 424-9838
Fax: (212) 807-3691
www.foundationcenter.org/marketplace

GrantSelect

This online database provides information on more than 13,000 funding opportunities from over 5,800 sponsors. Subscriptions to the database allow unlimited access to all of the targeted segments including arts and humanities; biomedical and health care; children and youth; community and economic development; education; environment/energy/agriculture/animal; faith-based grants; international programs; minority populations; operating grants; research; and scholarships and fellowships.

For pricing information, visit grantselect.com.

Subscribe online, or off-line by printing out and faxing or mailing the completed subscription form to:

Attn: Accounts
Schoolhouse Partners
P.O. Box 2059
Nashville, IN 47488-2059
Phone: (812) 988-6400
Fax: (812) 988-6479

Illinois Researcher Information Service (IRIS)

The IRIS Database of funding opportunities contains records on over nine thousand federal and private funding opportunities in the sciences, social sciences, arts, and humanities. It is updated daily.

Price: IRIS is a fee-based service. It is available to colleges and universities for an annual subscription fee. For more information on the subscription policy or an IRIS trial period, contact:

Illinois Researcher Information Service (IRIS)
University of Illinois at Urbana-Champaign
433 Grainger Engineering Library Information Center
1301 W. Springfield Ave.
Urbana, IL 61801
Phone: (217) 333-9893
Fax: (217) 333-7011
www.library.illinois.edu/iris/

The Sponsored Programs Information Network (SPIN)

SPIN is a database of federal and private funding sources. The price depends on the institution's level of research and development expenditures.

For pricing, more information, or to order, contact:

InfoEd International, Inc.
1873 Western Ave.
Suite 201
Albany, NY 12203
Phone: (800) 727-6427
Fax: (518) 464-0695
www1.infoed.org/

Other Electronic Grant Resources

The Chronicle of Philanthropy's Guide to Grants,
www.philanthropy.com/grants

David G. Bauer Associates, Inc.
Ordering Information

ORDER THE FOLLOWING GRANTSEEKING and fund-raising materials directly from David G. Bauer Associates, Inc. Prices do not include shipping charges and are subject to change without notice. To order call (775) 781-0552, Monday–Friday, 9–5 Pacific Standard Time.

Grantseeking and Fund-raising Materials

Creating Foundations for American Schools (techniques for creating and using school foundations—$49.95).

How to Evaluate and Improve Your Grants Effort, second edition (provides information on the roles and responsibilities of an effective grants office; particularly useful for those in the process of setting up a new grants office or evaluating an existing one—$59.95).

Successful Grants Program Management (practical tool for the superintendent or central office administrator to assist in developing a district-wide grants support system—$40.00).

Technology Funding for Schools (techniques schools can use for obtaining funding for their technology-related goals—$45.00).

The Fund Raising Primer (provides basic information on various fund-raising strategies—$24.95).

The Principal's Guide to Winning Grants (strategies principals can apply to support grantseeking at their schools—$42.00).

The Teacher's Guide to Winning Grants (a systematic guide to grantseeking skills that work for classroom leaders—$38.00).

In-House Seminars and Consulting

David G. Bauer offers seminars to institutions and organizations to increase faculty, staff, administration, and board members' skills and interest in the following areas: federal grantseeking, foundation and corporate grantseeking, using quality circles to improve proposals, team building, fund-raising, evaluating a grants or fund-raising system, and motivation/productivity. David G. Bauer also provides a unique faculty development program aimed at increasing the grants success rates of faculty at colleges and universities throughout the United States. For more information on these services visit www.dgbauer .com or call (775) 781-0552, Monday–Friday, 9–5 Pacific Standard Time.

Index

About the Author

David G. Bauer has been a successful grantseeker for forty years. His experience in applying winning grants strategies has provided for a successful career as a K–12 educator, college professor, director of development and grants management, and consultant to major nonprofit organizations. Over his career he has trained more than forty thousand individuals seeking grants from a variety of target populations and for many causes. This breadth of experience has enabled him to develop materials that are clear, simple, and easy to apply. He has authored ten books on winning grants and administering grants programs, some having appeared in several editions. He has also developed several videotape series and two software programs in the field.

As president of David G. Bauer Associates, Inc., Bauer is continually developing new techniques, products, and programs to increase grants success. One such program is his highly successful research fellows program that he has conducted at several universities, including the University of Alabama, Wake Forest University, Marquette University, and Western Michigan University. Faculty members in these programs spend a year in intensive grants training and Bauer coaching based on Bauer's tried and proven techniques. A significant increase in grants success has been contributed to these programs that are based on the techniques presented in *The "How To" Grants Manual*.